Defining Moment
at
Wirtzfeld

Defining Moment at Wirtzfeld

The Story of the Military Police Platoon, 2nd Infantry Division, in World War II

By James D. Edwards

BROWN
BOOKS
PUBLISHING

© 2013 James D. Edwards

Defining Moment at Wirtzfeld

Brown Books Publishing Group
16250 Knoll Trail Drive, Suite 205
Dallas, Texas 75248
www.BrownBooks.com
(972) 381-0009

A New Era in Publishing™

ISBN 978-1-61254-089-4
Library of Congress Control Number: 2012953122

Printed in the United States
10 9 8 7 6 5 4 3 2 1

For more information or to contact the author, please go to:
www.DefiningMomentAtWirtzfeld.com

In honor of all those who served and for the heroes who gave their all.
Your sacrifice is not in vain.

And to my beautiful wife, Marsha, who understood my passionate desire to write this book. Without your love, patience, and support over the last five years, the story of the MP Platoon would still be just a dream. I love you.

Let the word go forth from this time and place, to friend and foe alike, that the torch has been passed to a new generation of Americans. . . .

Let every nation know, whether it wishes us well or ill, that we shall pay any price, bear any burden, meet any hardship, support any friend, oppose any foe, in order to assure the survival and the success of liberty. . . .

Now the trumpet summons us again—not as a call to bear arms, though arms we need; not as a call to battle, though embattled we are—but a call to bear the burden of a long twilight struggle . . . a struggle against the common enemies of man: tyranny, poverty, disease, and war itself. . . .

In the long history of the world, only a few generations have been granted the role of defending freedom in its hour of maximum danger. I do not shrink from this responsibility—I welcome it. . . . The energy, the faith, the devotion which we bring to this endeavor will light our country and all who serve it—and the glow from that fire can truly light the world.

And so, my fellow Americans: ask not what your country can do for you—ask what you can do for your country.

My fellow citizens of the world: ask not what America will do for you, but what together we can do for the freedom of man. . . .

With a good conscience our only sure reward, with history the final judge of our deeds, let us go forth to lead the land we love, asking His blessing and His help, but knowing that here on earth God's work must truly be our own.

—John F. Kennedy
Presidential inaugural address, January 20, 1961

Table of Contents

Acknowledgments

I wish to thank my publisher, Milli Brown of Brown Books Publishing Group, and her staff for their hard work and dedication to making this book a reality. Without your help and guidance, another part of America's history would simply be lost to time and forgotten.

James Randolph Cantrell: To have J. R. Cantrell come into my life and for me to personally get to know my father's friend so many years after Dad passed away is a blessing in itself. Ultimately, J. R. is one of the catalysts from whom I gained the inspiration to write this book. His memories and the personal testimonies he so graciously shared with me helped form a vital part of the MP's story. My friend J. R. will be greatly missed; thankfully my fond memories of him and his legacy will be preserved in this story of the MP Platoon for many years. To the Cantrell family, thank you for sharing J. R. with me.

George F. Swearingen: Like Mr. Cantrell, George was the other miracle veteran WWII survivor who simply appeared in my life one day. If J. R. Cantrell represented the cake in this book recipe, George provided the frosting that focused on his personal life and the dangers and tragedies that all MPs faced each day. His timely appearance was more than just a coincidence, it was God sent. As he did with my father before me, George became my friend too, and in the last years of his life he took some of the precious time he had left to help me make this book a reality.

Faye Young, the daughter of George Swearingen, and the Swearingen family: Thank you for your kindness and for placing your trust in me that this book will be a reflection of George's character and his strong desire to help others.

Max North: The son of Major William North. Thank you for providing the detailed materials and the multitude of other items your father kept and protected for the last sixty-seven years.

Through your generosity, our fathers' stories can now be revealed posthumously through their eyes.

Mark Hillis: The son of James Earl Hillis. Thank you for sharing your father's photos and other documents. The stories you provided about your father are priceless.

Paul M. Porter: The son of Sergeant Paul B. Porter. Thank you for providing your father's documents and photos.

Glynn Raby, Richard Schwab, and James Branch: Real 2nd Infantry Division combat veterans whom I am honored to know and who provided personal stories of their own. Your unselfish contributions to this book reflect the kind of character that is present in your generation. I am humbled by your generosity.

Tyler Alberts, Combat Reels of Fort Worth, Texas: Thank you for providing the raw combat footage of the 2nd Infantry Division in Europe during D-Day. Due to your efforts in bringing to life the men who fought in World War II, I have a short video clip of my father standing on his ship just off of Omaha Beach on June 9, 1944.

National Archives and Records Administration and the National Personnel Records Center: Thank you to all of the archivists who spent many hours assisting me in searching through After Action Reports and Morning Reports of the 2nd Infantry Division.

Friends of US 2nd Infantry Division WWII: To all of my friends, the most humbling words I can think to express would not far exceed the simple expression "Thank you."

Jonathan Gawne: Because you had the foresight to publish your book, *Finding Your Father's War*, you helped me find my father's war.

Introduction

Soon after I set out on a mission to discover what my father did for five years of his life beginning in 1940, I realized that the information I uncovered in my research was more than a chronicle of Dad's experiences in the war. This book is a bridge not only between a father and his sons but also between two generations. For me, the writing of this book was a very personal and emotional journey into the past. For the brave young men of the Military Police Platoon, their journey began at different times and from separate locations all across America in the early 1940s. Some came from homes in big cities and others from small towns or farms. Due to the Great Depression, the majority of these young men came from very poor homes. A smaller number were from more prominent families. Many enlisted right after the Japanese bombed Pearl Harbor, and many more were drafted when the United States was forced to declare war on Japan and Germany in 1941. Regardless of their social status, they all came together for a common cause, driven by honor, commitment, and patriotic duty.

This story of the Military Police Platoon of the 2nd Infantry Division provides a close-up view of World War II seen through the lens of my father's camera, complete with personal photographs, newspaper clippings, personal testimonies, military documents, and family letters. The majority of the personal photographs are from Dad's collection; other photos used for illustrative purposes were acquired from the National Archives and Records Administration (NARA) in College Park, Maryland. The Morning Reports and After Action Reports were obtained from the National Personnel Records Center in St. Louis, Missouri, and from the NARA. Still other documents were provided by a friend I have never met, Michael Hitt, of Roswell, Georgia. The Swearingen, North, Cantrell, Porter, and

Hillis families provided many personal photographs, as well as detailed information, saving me hundreds of hours in additional research. Many of the documents and photographs appearing in this book have rarely been seen outside of a military museum, and some of these represent the last of such surviving records.

Although it was an exhausting journey to resurrect the lives of the MPs, it was also very rewarding and well worth the effort to honor the Military Police Platoon, my father, and his friends. While this book offers a glimpse into the history of the platoon and the duties and personal activities of the men, it is by no means a detailed representation of battles or campaigns. However, through considerable research and personal interviews with the men mentioned in this book, the battles in which the MP Platoon participated and the details I have described are accurate. The names, locations, and dates on each photo are correct based on the details my father provided after he returned home. To my knowledge, this part of the MP Platoon's history has never been written about until now.

Although it appeared I had sufficient material as I began the writing process, I had to conquer a number of other obstacles that consequently cast doubt on the completion of this book from the very beginning. My own personality had to be overcome as my propensity is to begin a project and fail to complete it. Personal schedules, family matters, job responsibilities, finances, and a lack of proper writing skills all played a role in delaying this book's progress. However, as I refocused my goal to honor the MPs, the unbelievable occurred.

The story grew clearer with the discovery of each photo and fact until it materialized into the MP Platoon's poignant struggle for survival. In the pages of this book are dozens of coincidences that would be impossible to make up. Some of these coincidences are obvious; others will not be until you have read this book more than once. I did not intentionally add any of them; they simply happened.

As I progressed through the storyline, I became intensely aware that my own existence was determined by so many moments over which I had no control. If my dad had not survived the war and returned home from Europe in 1945, it certainly would have affected my entire family. We all know there are a lot of "what ifs" in this life, but it was not until I looked back at the battles these men fought that I truly appreciated the ultimate sacrifice so many paid.

As I focused on those who fought in the greatest war in history, I recognized that my parents' generation was appropriately named. Who else but the "Greatest Generation" would be so completely capable of fighting such a war? The sixteen million men and women who served in our nation's military branches then endured deplorable conditions on a daily basis. This book isn't just about my dad's military service but about the circumstances of World War II that the Greatest Generation survived, which has led to the lofty respect and admiration we have for them.

Certainly this appreciation for them shouldn't come as a surprise to those of us who are baby boomers and remember this generation as our parents. After all, we are the recipients of their value system and are charged with the responsibility of passing this torch on to our families. Didn't they teach us family honor, integrity, strength of character, hard work, self-discipline, and determination? Haven't these values made our generation more responsible, appreciative, and accountable? Doesn't it make perfect sense that our nation was, then, "one nation under God"? What does the passing of the Greatest Generation mean for America's future?

According to the US Veterans Administration, America is losing more than a thousand World War II veterans each day. By 2028, they are all expected to be deceased, and with their passing, all that they knew will be gone as well. When I look back over the years and view history from my present perspective, I can plainly see that God in his ultimate wisdom gave us the

Greatest Generation as a reference point against which to model the morals and values of future American generations. I for one am not ready to give this generation up. To those who read this book: If you encounter a kindly, white-haired man or woman, take the time to greet them with a smile, a handshake, or just a warm hello. Chances are they sacrificed much before you were born. You can still make a difference in their lives.

—James Daniel Edwards
Son of Private First Class James Douglas Edwards,
Military Police Platoon,
2nd Infantry Division, 1940–1945

1

The Journey Begins

I am the third son of James Douglas Edwards and Aleta A. McWilliams Edwards. Born in 1959, I am just barely within the generation considered post-World War II baby boomers. As a six-year-old boy I was very curious about things that were off-limits to my prying hands and inquisitive nature, and there was always something to explore. My heart's desire was usually an undiscovered gadget in my parents' bedroom closet or chest of drawers. During my moments of exploration there were times when my entire body disappeared into the abyss of my father's closet in my effort to discover the unknown. These activities usually resulted in my being thrown out of such areas. Although the road to satisfying my curiosity was difficult—on occasion I met with a harsh tone from my father, and sometimes with his black leather belt—I continued to pursue my curiosity.

The fact is that one of us eventually had to give up or give in, and occasionally my father was the one who relented. At one point, I was allowed a glimpse of a brown paper grocery sack while rummaging through his sock drawer. To a young boy, treasure is anything that he doesn't have access to on a regular basis. The shiny new objects contained in the sack were radically different from my own usual toys.

But my analysis of this discovery was inevitably interrupted by my dad, who, as many fathers do, simply said, "Get out of there!" My attempts to negotiate for more time only made things worse, and at Dad's insistence I finally gave up. Defeated, I put the sack back in the drawer and moved on to something less entertaining, never completely forgetting about this mystery.

While I was never able to fully examine all of the items in the sack, I do remember catching a glimpse of the contents of a small cigar box containing various metal shapes and colored ribbons. At the time, I had no idea they were army medals, unit awards, and an assortment of other uniform attachments that Dad had worn on his army service coat. I do recall that I was excited by the unfamiliar objects, mesmerized somewhat by items unlike anything I had ever seen before.

Later, on more than one occasion, I asked my father, "What were the things in the sack?" His answer was usually something to distract my attention elsewhere. Though I would like to believe that he told me they were items he had kept from when he was in the army, I simply don't remember if he ever did. As is the case with many veterans, Dad never spoke about the war enough to reveal his role in it as the source of my newly discovered bounty. Sadly, with my father's death in 1979 it seemed the detailed answers to my questions concerning the contents of the brown grocery sack and the cigar box would remain a secret forever.

It wasn't until my mother passed away in May 2004 that I came upon the cigar box once again. It was among the personal items she left to me upon her passing. Mom must have known that—even though many years had passed since her little boy had first gazed into that cigar box—my curiosity about its contents would not have diminished. After thirty-nine years, what were the chances that my treasure would have remained intact?

As my heart pounded with excitement, I slowly opened the lid of the cigar box, anticipating that my treasure would still be there, waiting for me to rediscover it after so many years. As I lifted the lid, my anticipation turned to disappointment. In 1965, the box had been filled to the rim with many items. This time when I peered inside, I was shocked to see that it contained only a remnant of the valuable contents it once sheltered.

The medals were missing, detached from their ribbons, and certain other items I could only remember as trinkets (as they seemed to a six-year-old boy) were missing as well. A few military documents remained, along with some patches and other items. Although they were interesting to look at, none of these items appeared of value to me. I was not able to determine their significance as I had no experience in military memorabilia. After a few minutes of examining each of the dozen or so items, feeling more disappointed and defeated than I had felt in 1965, I closed the little cigar box lid for what I believed would be the last time and put away the box.

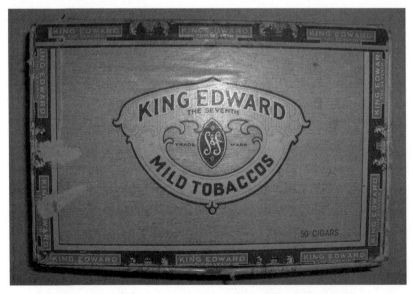

The original cigar box containing my father's military paraphernalia.

Three years would pass during which the cigar box remained untouched, but—as it did many years ago—eventually curiosity got the better of me. I simply refused to give up until I had verified the origin of the contents of that box. Armed with a childlike faith and a renewed desire to learn more about Dad's lifelong secret, I set out on a journey for information. I had a theory to test: could my father have been a veteran of the US military?

As I began my search for information, I remembered that, in addition to Dad's things, my mother had kept a newspaper clipping of Dad's obituary. As I read the clipping, I discovered that it listed him as a member of the 115th Military Police unit during World War II. After searching the Internet to locate more information on the 115th MPs, I learned that the information in the obituary was incorrect. No such unit existed in World War II in any branch of the service.

Confused by all the wrong information I had to begin with, I followed many paths that led nowhere in my quest to determine what the surviving items in the cigar box represented and how I might use them to identify my father's correct military unit. I soon located a patch that had a figure of an American Indian wearing a feather bonnet set against a black background. I compared the patch that had belonged to my father with current military symbols. The Indianhead patch revealed that Dad had served with the 2nd Infantry Division during World War II, a unit that had a long and distinguished history in battle.

Uncovering the significance of the Indianhead patch was a key development in my research. Equally important was a lone photo I found of my father sitting in a chair wearing an incomplete uniform. This led me on a search for other family memorabilia that might solve the mystery. As I gained more clues, each discovery usually led to another question. Within a few months, I received phone calls from two of my brothers. They had discovered a number of letters and photographs in various places, including in our mother's cedar chest. All of these new items added valuable information to the incomplete account of our father's military service. They revealed that he was stationed in the United States, Ireland, and various countries in continental Europe during World War II. I soon learned from these documents that he had been a member of the Military Police Platoon that was attached to the 2nd Infantry Division.

Our father sent many letters home to our mother, and they were often accompanied by photographs and undeveloped film. As I examined the letters and the pictures, it soon became evident to me that God had a purpose for their survival—to preserve the story of those gallant men who appeared in them. Although most of the photos were in very good shape and had maintained their clarity well for their age, many were devoid of details such as dates, locations, or even a name for the faces staring back. The letters were fewer in quantity than the photos, but most did carry dates and general locations, such as the country in which they were taken. There were few specific details, as such information would have been removed by the army censors.

These documents allowed me to trace Dad's movements with the 2nd Infantry Division's Military Police Platoon throughout Europe. In one final discovery in 2010, my brother Mike located a medium-sized tin box containing dozens of photographs and several more military documents that were practically untouched by time. I now had more than 250 photographs representing pieces of Dad's time in the military. The best news of all was that these photos had notes on them, specifying the dates they were taken, their locations, and the names of those who appeared in the pictures. I concluded that Dad must have added the details to each of the photos after he returned home. Otherwise the army censors would have removed the information prior to mailing them back to the United States.

Over the course of the last five years, I have spent hundreds of hours piecing together facts about my dad's war experience. Only some of the information I sought was available in books.

Army records were an excellent source of information, but the most valuable source to me at the time was the surviving veterans themselves. On January 9, 2007, I joined an online group known as "Friends of US 2nd Infantry Division WWII." This group, of which I am still an active member, was created in 1999. Many of its original members were World War II veterans. Using today's modern technology, these men have done their best to educate those of us who knew very little about our fathers' war.

Remarkably, almost immediately after my first post I had several responses from extremely knowledgeable members. They offered suggestions for how I might find the information I was seeking about my dad. At some point in our exchange, members suggested that I contact the National Personnel Records Center located in St. Louis, Missouri, for Dad's discharge records. Additionally, they suggested that I contact the National Archives and Records Administration in College Park, Maryland, as well.

Making use of these new resources, I submitted a request for documents on my father. To my pleasant surprise, within a few weeks I received a photocopy of my father's honorable discharge. Enclosed with the discharge was a letter of explanation telling me of his award entitlements and the expected time in which the medals would arrive in the mail. A few months later, I opened my mailbox to discover a large brown envelope inside. Wasting no time to politely open the envelope, I tore the flap and removed the contents. Moved almost to tears, I felt my efforts to restore my father's life become real when I held the medals for the first time. Although not the originals, they were similar to the ones I had caught a glimpse of in the cigar box more than forty-five years before.

During my time as a member of the online group, I have been fortunate enough to benefit from the expert advice of many veterans, a handful of whom were in the 2nd Infantry Division themselves. Our World War II veterans are extraordinary survivors of the greatest war in our nation's history. These men are real combat soldiers, given a second chance to live after questioning their own survival every day as so many of their friends perished. These are men who remained tight-lipped most of their lives about what they had done and what they had witnessed. Their silence is not only the mark of a true combat soldier but also a credit to the humility possessed by the Greatest Generation.

In the early stages of my research, I corresponded by e-mail with a member of the group, Michael Hitt, of Roswell, Georgia. Michael provided me with a great deal of information about the Military Police Platoon of the 2nd Infantry Division during World War II. Responding to one of my posts about the MPs, Michael contacted me by phone and revealed that he had located a living MP who had served in my dad's unit. This was outstanding news, but I was puzzled because I had not been able to locate any living members of the MP Platoon myself.

In the course of that phone conversation, I retrieved one of the few surviving pieces of memorabilia that was still in the cigar box Dad had kept all those years. Thinking that I had hit a goldmine, I located the address book that my dad had kept from June 18, 1945. This small brown book contained the names of all of the members of the MP Platoon Dad served with—or so I thought. Searching for the name Michael had relayed to me, I carefully turned each page and studied all seventy-three names. But the name I hoped to discover, "J. R. Cantrell," did not appear anywhere in the address book, nor could I find it on any of my father's documents that had survived the sixty-seven years since the war.

Although confused, I took the opportunity to telephone the number Michael had provided and made contact with Mr. Cantrell a short time later. As Mr. Cantrell spoke, it was soon clear that he remembered Dad very well. A short time later, I made a trip to visit Mr. Cantrell at his Texas home. It goes without saying that I was very excited when I finally met him, especially because I had given up hope of finding any of Dad's friends still alive after all of these years.

Roughly around the same time that Michael discovered Mr. Cantrell, he also located another surviving member of the same unit, George F. Swearingen of Jacksonville, Florida. The fact that Mr. Swearingen was still alive was amazing in itself, but what made that an even greater improbability was that he was ninety-four at the time. Anyone who has set out to reconstruct a soldier's service in World War II, whether they are a relative or an expert researcher, will agree that finding one surviving veteran who knew your soldier is a miracle. Finding two, after so many years, is virtually impossible.

Jumping at the opportunity to speak with another of my father's friends, I contacted Mr. Swearingen by telephone. George answered my call and I promptly introduced myself, but soon realized that his hearing loss was significant and he was almost unable to hear me speak. Shortly after my initial attempt to contact George, I began receiving letters in the mail from him. Each letter was typed on an old manual typewriter, carefully and thoughtfully prepared.

I was so humbled that this grand old gentleman would take the time and effort to share his thoughts with me along with his memories of my father and a war they fought together many years ago. Even at his advanced age, George is the picture of health and a unique story of survival. He takes no medications, has no illnesses, gets plenty of rest, and—until 2009—lived by himself and prepared his own meals daily.

Although George suffers from hearing loss and his eyesight has failed him to the point that he can no longer see well enough to type, he does not allow his age to limit him. Always finding ways to overcome and adapt, George has not failed to keep in touch with me. For four years in a row George invited me to attend his birthday celebrations in Jacksonville. It was not until September 2010, on his ninety-eighth birthday, that I was fortunate enough to be able to travel to Florida.

As I entered the room, I had no problem recognizing George. Although many years older than he was in the photographs I had seen from 1944, he still retained the same general appearance. He wore a white shirt with the 2nd Infantry Division Indianhead patch on one sleeve and his Silver Star pinned above his left pocket. George greeted me as if he had known me all his life, a testimony to the character of his generation. George has already started planning his one hundredth birthday. When I asked about his ninety-ninth, he simply looked up at me and asked if I could make it to "the big one." I said, "You know I will, George."

As the son of a World War II veteran, I cannot stress enough the importance of preserving the memory of these men who so gallantly defended the United States of America and liberated a continent. Men like Corporal J. R. Cantrell, Pfc. George Swearingen, my father, Pfc. James D. Edwards, and the entire MP Platoon of the 2nd Infantry Division deserve to be honored and remembered.

More than four hundred thousand American soldiers died in all theaters of World War II, and many thousands more lived shortened lives, suffering from their wounds or dying after returning home. It is an extraordinary miracle that any of our fathers survived. While these may appear as just statistics and numbers pressed between the pages of this book, consider the following for a moment. Most of our World War II veterans were young men barely old enough to shave. Many of them never had the chance to marry, become fathers or grandfathers, or grow old. Some left a spouse and children at home and never came back to their families. Many others never returned to their parents' home to live out their dreams.

Girls who were engaged to a soldier before the war and lost him in battle took off their engagement rings and eventually married someone else. The wives of fallen soldiers remarried, and children born of a deceased father became someone else in this life, never knowing what might have been. We will never know the full consequences of what those losses meant or grasp the great loss that many families felt when they received the news that their son or daughter would not be coming home. As Americans, we owe our veteran World War II survivors a debt of gratitude that can never be repaid.

In the end, many lives were changed, but our world is a better place because of the sacrifices of these long-lost strangers. For those who perished and never had a chance to enjoy life as we have, we owe them our very lives for giving theirs so that we may live in freedom. Should we not fight to preserve the blessings of liberty for these United States of America? They did.

This book is intended to honor all veterans for their sacrifices on the battlefields of the European and Pacific theaters during World War II. It further honors military police everywhere who have served America in the honorable tradition of military service, exemplifying high levels of esprit de corps. It brings recognition to one of the oldest units in America's military history. More specifically, this book recognizes and pays tribute to a small group of men: the MP Platoon of the 2nd Infantry Division who fought in Europe in World War II. From "D-Day Plus 1" (the day after the initial wave of troops came ashore) at Omaha Beach, through the defeat of Hitler and Nazi Germany, to their final destination of Pilsen, Czechoslovakia, on May 7, 1945, and the conclusion of the war, this small group of men performed above and beyond their call of duty, earning the Meritorious Unit Service plaque for their contributions to the war effort. This MP unit had a large role in supporting and participating in combat operations and in the eventual defeat of a determined enemy.

On May 31, 1944, General George S. Patton put into perspective the value of each soldier's contribution to the overall war effort when he gave his famous speech to the 3rd Army. Following is a portion of that speech.

All of the real heroes are not storybook combat fighters, either. Every single man in this Army plays a vital role. Don't ever let up. Don't ever think that your job is unimportant. Every man has a job to do and he must do it. Every man is a vital link in the great chain.

What if every truck driver suddenly decided that he didn't like the whine of those shells overhead, turned yellow, and jumped headlong into a ditch? The cowardly bastard could say, "Hell, they won't miss me, just one man in thousands." But what if every man thought that way? Where in the hell would we be now? What would our country, our loved ones, our homes, even the world, be like?

No, Americans don't think like that. Every man does his job. Every man serves the whole. Every department, every unit, is important in the vast scheme of this war. The ordnance men are needed to supply the guns and machinery of war to keep us rolling. The quartermaster is needed to bring up food and clothes, because where we are going there isn't a hell of a lot to steal. Every last man on KP has a job to do, even the one who heats our water to keep us from getting the "G. I. Shits."

Private First Class James D. Edwards, Company I, 9th Infantry Regiment, 2nd Infantry Division, July 25, 1941.

2

From the Farm to the Fort

1930s–1942

My father, James Douglas Edwards, a young man from Richland, Texas, grew up living with his grandparents, G. L. and Sallie Edwards, in a small town in Navarro County. In the late 1930s, America was still reeling from the Great Depression and jobs were scarce. It had been more than twenty years since Armistice Day and the end of World War I. America, eager to climb out of the economic devastation that had been caused by the stock market crash of 1929, had already begun producing abundant new resources. The country's raw material was its population of young men and women who would later be known as the Greatest Generation. These young people were destined to change the world, and their early lives prepared them for their fate. Many of them had grown up in various states of deprivation, and they were ready to face the tough realities of the war that loomed ever closer.

Not immune to the difficulties present in rural Texas in the early thirties, the Edwards family—like so many others— struggled to acquire even the basic necessities of food and clothing. In 1933, the state of Texas passed a law requiring all students attending public schools to wear shoes to class every day. My father's grandparents were unable to purchase shoes to keep him in compliance with the new state requirement. Young James wrote to his mother in Tennessee asking for a dollar to buy a pair of shoes. Within a few weeks a reply came in the mail, and family history tells of the harsh response he received from his mother that sealed his educational fate: "Get a job!"

Left with little choice, James dropped out of school after completing only the seventh grade. He was forced to find odd jobs around town, which was nearly impossible for a young boy. On April 6, 1939, a few months after celebrating his seventeenth birthday, he enlisted in the Civilian Conservation Corps. The CCC was designed to provide relief for young men who had a very hard time finding work during the Great Depression. It was probably in the CCC that my father finally earned enough money to buy his first pair of new shoes.

In the previous month, on March 16, 1939, Germany started to show its true intentions to the world, overwhelming Czechoslovakia by military force and seizing its government. By September of the same year, with the invasion of Poland, Hitler had begun his takeover of Europe. On September 3, 1939, Britain, France, Australia, and New Zealand declared war on Germany. The war waged on in Europe as Germany continued the assault against neighboring countries, but the United States had not yet felt the sting of Hitler's war machine and in turn enjoyed relative peace.

Having declared the nation's neutrality, America felt secure for a time, separated from the wars that were being waged around the world by the vast Atlantic and Pacific oceans. Not fearing immediate attacks by Germany or Japan, America's young men and women eagerly enlisted in the US military by the tens of thousands. Many of them believed that joining the ranks would provide them with an opportunity to make a better living and help their families recover from the poverty that had kept its grip on the nation's economy for more than ten years. But America would soon depend on these men and women for another purpose.

This photo of Nazi soldiers marching in formation, taken in 1933 as Hitler and the Nazi party rose to power, was used in propaganda throughout the war.

Like so many of the young men of this era, James Edwards was eager to serve his country and become a vital part of something greater than himself. At the age of eighteen, James was honorably discharged from the Civilian Conservation Corps. He left the CCC on July 2, 1940, and enlisted in the US Army the very next day at a recruiting station in Dallas, Texas.

Soon after enlisting, Edwards traveled by train to Fort Sam Houston in San Antonio, Texas, to begin twelve weeks of new recruit training. Like all new recruits, he would have received medical evaluations for physical and mental health and acuity tests for vision and color blindness. As is still a necessity today, new recruits also received a battery of inoculations for diseases that the medical knowledge of the time could prevent.

CIVILIAN CONSERVATION CORPS

Company _____ Camp _____ Post Office ~~Waxahachie, Texas~~
TO: (State Director of CCC Selection)or
    (~~~~~~~~~~~~~~~~~~~~~~~~~~~~~~)

                                              ~~July 2~~   1940

Littlefield Bldg.
(Street Address)   ,   Austin, Texas
                                          (City and State)
    In compliance with War Department Regulations, CCC, you are informed of
the discharge of the following named CCC Enrollees:

Name and serial number
              ~~(Last)~~   '~~James~~   ,   ~~D~~   , ~~CC9-979773~~
Junior __x__ Veteran ____ (First)   (Middle)   (Serial Number)
                   (Check one) White __x__ ,Colored____ Other ____

~~Home address at time of discharge~~ ~~Gen. Del., Richland, Texas~~

Future address(If different from home address)____ Same

County and State from which selected ~~Navarro~~   ~~Texas~~
                                     (County)   (State)
Address of local selecting agency... ~~Corsicana, Texas~~

Monthly Allotment (or deposit). . . $ 22.00

Date of last enrollment. . . . . . ~~April 6,1939~~

Name of allottee(or indicate deposit
        in lieu of allotment)__ ~~Mrs. Sallie Edwards (None)~~

Address of allottee. . . . . ~~Gen. Del., Richland, Texas~~

Date of discharge . . . . ~~July 2,1940~~

Type of discharge awarded . . . . . ~~Honorable~~

Reason for discharge (Incl.notations)
If discharged to respond to urgent
call or return to school,give reasons
for call or name and address of school__ ~~To enlist in the US Army.~~

If discharged to accept employment
give name and address of employer ...

Total service, including all enroll-
ments, since July 1,1937.   14   24
                                   (Months)   (Days)

Age at date of discharge.   18   7
                                   (Years)   (Months)

                                        Very truly yours,

DISTRIBUTION
State Selecting A
individual Serv   ROBERT W. EVANS, CCC Co.Commdr. Commdg.

*The original honorable discharge James Edwards received upon leaving the
Civilian Conservation Corps on July 2, 1940.*

Edwards at boot camp with a friend, Private Carr.

During the first several weeks of boot camp, Dad's unit traveled west to Sabinal, Texas, in order to receive training in infantry tactics and fast-water river crossing techniques. As they took breaks from training, the recruits were able to enjoy the scenery of Texas's Hill Country and relax by the Sabinal River.

Private Edwards by the Sabinal River, which flows at a rapid pace in the background.

Rifle inspection at Camp Bullis, Texas. Private Edwards (far left) wears sunglasses and shoulders a Browning automatic rifle with bipod. The 9th Infantry crest is visible on his garrison cover.

Upon completion of boot camp, Private Edwards returned to Fort Sam Houston, the home of the 2nd Infantry Division. There he was assigned as a rifleman to the 9th Infantry Regiment, also known as "Manchu," one of the oldest and most distinguished military units in the history of the United States Army, its unit history dating back to 1798.

Edwards (second from the right) upon completion of boot camp, standing with three other recent graduates in front of the Company I barracks at Fort Sam Houston.

The parade grounds at the center of Fort Sam Houston where the 2nd Infantry Division held graduation for the new recruits in early October 1940. Family and friends are gathered around to congratulate the new graduates.

Cover of the Christmas program for the festivities held at Fort Sam Houston over Christmas, 1940.

Company "I"

FORT SAM

ROSTER

SECOND LIEUTENANTS

H. S. GRIFFITH, Jr., Commanding
W. H. CARMICHEAL, Mess Officer
R. M. SCIORTINO, Supply Officer
ROBERT V. EVANS
R. L. FLEETWOOD
ROBERT J. WHEMPNER

FIRST SERGEANT	STAFF SERGEANT
Riley, Perry N.	Calaway, Jim E.

SERGEANTS

Callaway, W. E.	Funkenbush, J. E.	McFalls, George R.
Everett, Fred .G	Leverette, Ben O.	Russell, Edgar L.
Franks, Kenneth C.	Linsey, James H.	Scott, Charles W.
	Metcalfe, Johnnie J.	

CORPORALS

Bilbro, Cornelius M.	Jorden, Armon	Seale, Milton W.
Boyd, Samuel P.	Kochen, John	Skidmore, Cooper
Flowers, Doice	Leal, Joe A.	Walters, Audrey R.
Hadaway, John W.	Lepori, Rollie E.	Wright, Willie
Hearn, Sam H.	Nowlin, Stanley E.	Wydock, Bernard J.
Hunt, Willie B.	Nichols, Milford W., Jr.	

nth Infantry

STON, TEXAS

PRIVATES FIRST CLASS

Abbott, Stanton L.
Baird, Floyd
Bartley, Archie L.
Bilnoski, Coy
Breithaupt, Fred, Jr.
Brickey, Wyman E.
Brooks, Hubert N.
Burba, Baird B.
Burns, Wilie E.
Calfee, Donald W.
Carroll, Douglas H.
Cloud, Fred C.
Cockrell, Arthur D.
Coln, Melvin E.

Davis, Cecil W.
Delaney, Sam W.
English, Roger F.
Ford, Robert L., Jr.
George, Gerald D.
Hernandez, Paul A.
Holland, Billy J.
Holloway, V. H.
Ingle, Dawn V.
Johnston, John E.
Jones, Orland C.
Lunsford, McAdoo
Lowe, Jack
Martin, Orvis R.

Massey, William W.
McDaniel, Carroll
Montgomery, Nathan
Moore, Woodrow W.
Norris, Johnnie
Owens, Otis W.
Pennington, William J.
Sewell, Perry H.
Shipp, Clements A.
Shoemaker, B. F.
Skidmore, Otis
Sleminski, Louis B.
Walker, Audrey L.
Williams, John

PRIVATES

Abbott, Bill L.
Barela, Gabriel H.
Barnett Bennie T.
Brett, Robert B.
Cagle, Wanowen E.
Carr Acie C.
Carter, W. C.
Cragg, William P.
Crider, Bryan J., Jr.
Davis, Eugene D.
Edwards, James D.
Foster, K.
Foster, L.
French, Claud H.
Hamilton, Dalton D.
Hamilton, Paul A.

Hensley, Austin B.
Howe, Ardean J.
Johnson Dave A.
Keith, Jack
Kennemer, C. M.
Kutin, Joseph E., Jr.
Loyd, Lewis T.
Luke Paul B.
McDaniel, James D.
McDonald, Freeman W.
Melvin, Louis
Melton, Edward C.
Millsap, Roy J.
Osburn, Joseph W.
Perry, Jonathan E.

Phillips, Edgar M.
Phillips, Jessie J.
Pierce, Omar J.
Rodriquez, Joe O.
Schewed, Alvin E.
Scott, Norman J., Jr.
Shelton, Rufus B.
Tarin, Lucas R.
Thompson, Theron C.
Vasquez, Miguel V.
Vaughn, J. D.
Vostatek, Joe
Watson, John O., Jr.
Wood, Charles B.
York, Woodrow W.

With Company I, 9th Infantry, Edwards ultimately received intense combat training and in the long process became a highly skilled soldier. Although he was still very thin and young—not yet nineteen years old—training would soon be accelerated by the army in order to prepare him and the 9th Infantry for overseas deployment and the commitment of the 2nd Infantry Division troops to battle. Forced by necessity to prepare America for war, the Selective Service Act was signed into law by Franklin D. Roosevelt on September 14, 1940. Although the numbers vary slightly from different sources, it is estimated that sixteen million men registered for the draft from 1940 to 1946.

By December 1940 Private Edwards had matured and begun to excel at his duties. While at Fort Sam Houston, he developed lasting relationships, befriending the men who would be his new family for the next few years. As was traditional at Fort Sam Houston, the yearly Christmas party was held for the officers and men of the Ninth Infantry. The entire Christmas program for Company I, Ninth Infantry—recently discovered by my oldest brother in the personal items left to us by our mother upon her passing—is a treasured heirloom in our family.

───────────────

As James Edwards settled into army life at Fort Sam Houston, he was still unaware of another new recruit with whom he would later form an unbreakable bond of friendship. James Randolph Cantrell, who also answered the call of duty without hesitation, enlisted in the army on October 5, 1940, just two weeks after his twentieth birthday.

Military records indicate that James Cantrell enlisted at a recruiting station in Fort Worth, Texas. Soon after his enlistment, J. R. Cantrell boarded a train destined for San Antonio and Fort Sam Houston where he began his twelve weeks of basic training. During those weeks, he trained and became proficient in the use of military tactics and weapons employed by the infantry. All enlisted men joining the army at this time were considered infantrymen first and foremost, and trained as such.

It wasn't until after basic training was completed that these recruits were given the opportunity to choose their Military Occupational Specialty, or MOS. The MOS for a Basic Rifleman was 521. MOS 677 referred to the Military Police Corps, to which both James Edwards and J. R. Cantrell would eventually be assigned. The military police are the law enforcement branch of the army. Their official duties during World War II included enforcing military laws, controlling traffic, guarding roads and equipment, and processing prisoners of war.

It is important to note that many enlisted men, regardless of their job classification, would be called upon to fight when wartime casualties became high and no replacements were available. The necessity of arming rear echelon troops would become readily apparent to the 2nd Infantry Division as they advanced across Europe, most notably during the Battle of the Bulge.

Meanwhile the war waged on in Europe. The Luftwaffe had begun its blitzkrieg assault on Britain. The neutrality of the United States grew ever more tenuous as Germany, Italy, and Japan signed the Tripartite Pact on September 27, 1940, making their partnership official. Nazi Germany's war machine worked its way west, country after country surrendering to the massive invasion forces of the German military. In every case, the German army was so overwhelmingly powerful that the defensive forces of the countries lying in her path relied heavily on diplomacy for their survival rather than on their meager defenses, which were quickly crushed by the Wehrmacht, as Nazi Germany's armed forces were known.

Although the United States had maintained her distance from the war at this point, the inevitable appeared to be on the horizon. In June 1941, President Roosevelt ordered that all of the assets of Germany, Italy, and Japan held in the United States be frozen and announced an oil embargo against those aggressor states. Roosevelt also severed diplomatic ties with Japan and recalled the US ambassador from that country.

By May 1941, Greece, Yugoslavia, Romania, Hungary, France, Norway, Belgium, Luxembourg, the Netherlands, Denmark, and Finland had all fallen to the German war machine. Italy, Germany's new ally, invaded its neighbors to the south with Hitler's blessing, moving its forces into North Africa. Japan, the other member of the triple alliance known as the Axis, had begun its conquests of China and the Southwest Pacific islands.

During the summer of 1941, the 2nd Infantry Division, along with eighteen other army divisions and fifty thousand army vehicles from around the United States, participated in war games. The mock battles, later known as the Louisiana Maneuvers, had one purpose: to simulate a war environment, preparing America's soldiers for the war that had already consumed Europe and now threatened to spread around the world. George F. Swearingen, who was with the 23rd Infantry prior to his transfer to the MP Platoon of the 2nd Infantry Division, participated in these war games. In a conversation I had with Swearingen, he shared with me that the men had to endure the intense humidity and heat of Louisiana during the maneuvers, but what stood out most of all in his memory was how the chiggers and mosquitoes accounted for a significant amount of discomfort.

By late summer of 1941, the Louisiana Maneuvers were over and the 2nd Infantry Division returned to Fort Sam Houston. The war games were deemed a success by Army Chief of Staff General George C. Marshall, who had added several names to his list of new army officers who could battle against the best military leaders Germany had to offer. Brilliant military minds such as Bradley, Stillwell, Robertson, Clark, Patton, and Eisenhower became the backbone of US Army leadership.

After the men of the 2nd Division returned to Texas, Edwards, still with the 9th Infantry Regiment, had the chance to visit San Antonio and attend a rodeo there in the summer of 1942. By this time, he had achieved the rank of corporal in the army. Edwards, Cantrell, and Swearingen would all spend the next few months continuing their training at Fort Sam Houston.

Edwards poses in uniform in Brackenridge Park in San Antonio, Texas. I developed this photo recently from a negative I found in an envelope from 1942.

Edwards at the San Antonio rodeo, summer 1942.

Although no records are available to help determine the date on which J. R. Cantrell completed basic training, it is clear that he had done so by the time the following photo was taken in December 1941.

By October 16, 1941, the Division had received orders to prepare for a permanent change of station. On October 27, they received the announcement that Lieutenant Colonel Jesse P. Green had been designated as the Provost Marshal of the 2nd Infantry Division. This meant that Lieutenant Colonel Green would command a platoon of military police as a subordinate and

A. G. FILE
Fort Sam Houston, Texas.
OCT 27 1941

HEADQUARTERS 2D INFANTRY DIVISION

GENERAL ORDERS
NO - 38

Fort Sam Houston, Texas,
October   27, 1941.

SECTION I - ANNOUNCEMENT OF ASSISTANT TO THE DIVISION COMMANDER
SECTION II ANNOUNCEMENT OF PROVOST MARSHAL

SECTION I

Colonel WALTER M. ROBERTSON, (O-3378), 9th Infantry, in addition to his other duties, is announced as Assistant to the Division Commander, vice Colonel PAUL C. PASCHAL, (O-3714), 38th Infantry, relieved.

SECTION II

Lt.Col. JESSE P. GREEN, (O-5626), Infantry, having reported for duty, in compliance with paragraph 6, Special Orders No. 196, Headquarters 2d Infantry Division, c.s., is announced as Provost Marshal, 2d Infantry Division. (AG 210.3-Div.Staff).

By order of Colonel PROCTOR:

JAMES C. SHORT,
Lt. Col., G. S. C.,
Acting Chief of Staff.

OFFICIAL:

L. C. BOINEAU,
Lt. Col., Adjutant General's Department,
Adjutant General.

The official General Order, dated October 27, 1941, announcing the appointment of Lieutenant Colonel Jesse Green as Provost Marshal and officially forming the MP Platoon of the 2nd Infantry Division.

permanent unit of the 2nd Infantry Division. Essentially this was the day that the MP Platoon of the 2nd Infantry Division was born. At this time, the army would have started to transfer men from other divisions into this newly formed military police unit. James Edwards, George Swearingen, J. R. Cantrell, and many others would eventually find themselves among these transfers.

Private First Class James R. Cantrell, wearing a military police uniform, stands outside the Fort Sam Houston library, December 1941.

J. R. Cantrell, now a proud member of the Military Police Corps, is shown here wearing his MP badge, MP brassard, and his sidearm, which was probably a model 1911 .45-caliber automatic pistol. If you look closely, you can see that Cantrell has his police whistle secured by a chain near his left arm and is wearing the black necktie that would later be replaced by a khaki-colored version in February 1942.

The uniform style shown in the photo is reminiscent of World War I–era uniforms, and was upgraded to a more modern look shortly after this picture was taken. During World War II, many new uniforms were introduced to the army and were quickly adapted to meet the demands of different warfare environments. Both Edwards and Cantrell would spend the first two years and four months of their army service at Fort Sam Houston, where they would train for war and live in close proximity to each other. Although they still had not formally met, the destiny they would later share was already unfolding and would soon bring them together in a faraway land.

This group photo—known as a "yard" photo due to its length of three feet—was sent to me by Al Castillo, a fellow member of the online group Friends of US 2nd Infantry Division WWII and whose father was also in the 9th Infantry. Corporal James D. Edwards is seated on the first row, far right, just above the photographer's signature.

George Swearingen while he was still with the 23rd Infantry Regiment, Fort Sam Houston, summer 1942.

The group photo above of Company I, 9th Infantry Regiment, was taken on Saturday, December 6, 1941. Although many of the men are smiling in this photo, by the same time the following day their mood would change dramatically. Having been repeatedly assured of Japan's commitment to a mutually peaceful relationship, the United States was unprepared for the unprovoked surprise attack launched by the Japanese Imperial Navy upon the US Pacific Fleet at Pearl Harbor, Hawaii, on Sunday, December 7, 1941. The following day, in one of the most dramatic speeches given by any US president in history, Franklin D. Roosevelt announced to the world that the United States had formally declared war on Japan. This historical announcement quickened the pace of the nation's preparation for war.

From the late summer of 1941 until August 1942, the 2nd Infantry Division conducted further maneuvers at Fort Sam Houston, including training in airborne deployment. In a final farewell to Fort Sam Houston, on Wednesday, November 11, 1942, the 2nd Infantry Division marched in the San Antonio Armistice Day parade, recalling the victorious close of World War I. This

The 2nd Infantry Division marches in the Armistice Day parade.

event was documented by the 2nd Infantry Division newspaper, the *Spearhead*, a copy of which James Edwards saved. Amazingly this newspaper survived nearly seventy years in various boxes and other places of storage. It has now been preserved for the future enjoyment of other generations of the Edwards family.

Family history is unclear as to when James Edwards first met the woman who would later be his wife. Nonetheless, it is clear from the dates recorded on several photos of them that my father had met Aleta McWilliams by November 13, 1942.

James Edwards and Aleta McWilliams at Fort Sam Houston, November 13, 1942.

Mom and Dad
Fort Sam Houston, Texas
November 13, 1942

James Edwards and Aleta McWilliams outside Fort Sam Houston,
November 13, 1942.

On the reverse side of the second photograph, Dad wrote *We tried to get married and couldn't.* Most likely this was due to my mother being too young. Dad's uniform reflects that he is still an infantry soldier with the 9th Infantry Regiment. He would continue to serve in that capacity for several more months.

On the 2nd Infantry Division's last day at Fort Sam Houston—November 26, 1942—hundreds of soldiers marched across Arthur MacArthur Field in front of their commander, Lieutenant General Walter Krueger, for a farewell review. On November 27, the entire Division, approximately fifteen thousand men, boarded trains for a three-day trip to Camp McCoy near Sparta, Wisconsin. It was at Camp McCoy that the 2nd Infantry Division would undergo intense training in winter warfare, designed to help prepare them for the harsh winters on the battlefields of Europe.

3

From Infantry
to Military Police

November 1942–September 1943

The 2nd Infantry Division arrived at Camp McCoy on Monday, November 30, 1942. As the men collected their gear and stepped off the train, any thoughts they may have had about big city lights or good times in the local towns vanished when they surveyed the landscape for the first time. Located halfway between the small towns of Sparta and Tomah in this secluded Midwestern state, Camp McCoy was, both geographically and culturally, far removed from what many of the men were accustomed to.

Limited as it may have been, Camp McCoy served several purposes prior to World War II. At different points in time, the camp served as an ordnance depot for the army, a summer artillery training facility, and, after the National Defense Act of 1920 was passed, a citizens military training camp. The camp also served as a supply base for the Civilian Conservation Corps as part of the New Deal program during the Great Depression. At a cost of three billion dollars, CCC camps like the one at Camp McCoy educated a total of three million youths in conservation and health programs. The jobs that the CCC gave the youth of our nation paid them thirty dollars a month and provided them with uniforms, lodging, and food.

For the remainder of the 1930s, the camp was maintained by the War Department, but in 1939 all activities at the camp were suspended and the camp was placed on standby. By August 1940, as the United States grew increasingly concerned about possible involvement in World War II, Camp McCoy was chosen as the site for the Second Army maneuvers. These maneuvers involved sixty-five thousand troops from seven states—the largest troop concentration this part of the United States had seen since World War I.

A soldier equipped with army-issue snow skis.

The isolation of this camp made it the perfect location from which to conduct combat training in an environment free from the distractions of a metropolitan area. Once settled in, the 2nd Infantry Division began a four-month regimen that served to simulate battle conditions and introduce the Division to survival techniques useful in extremely cold weather conditions. Utilizing new equipment, many members of the infantry trained in the use of snow skis and snowshoes.

The typical contents of a soldier's backpack, including a number of items designed to protect them from the cold winters in Wisconsin, Michigan, and ultimately on a winter battleground yet to be imagined by the men of the 2nd Infantry Division. (From the North photo collection.)

The complete contents of the cold weather kit shown above included several pairs of glove liners, gloves, thermal underwear, wool caps, wool socks, shoe insulators, a thermos, a winter sleeping bag, a small tent, tent stakes, a canteen, a shovel, an ax, and a number of other useful gadgets for living in the frozen countryside. The entire contents, when stuffed into the pack and attached to the frame, weighed approximately one hundred pounds. This of course did not include a soldier's helmet, weapon, and ammunition, which could have easily weighed another fifty pounds.

An artist's rendition of the Military Police Headquarters at Camp McCoy, Wisconsin. This drawing obviously depicts a warmer time of the year than that which was experienced by the men of the 2nd Infantry Division in late 1942 and early 1943.

During this period, Camp McCoy served as a winter training camp for army troops preparing for deployment overseas. However, I uncovered very few facts about the Division's activities at the camp in my research. Thus the personal photos of Private First Class William Davidson and Private First Class James Earl Hillis documenting this period of the Division's training are an invaluable part of this collection. Apart from a few documents from the National Archives and my father's Ranger Battle Training program, I was able to locate very little specific information concerning the Division while it was stationed there from November 1942 to September 1943.

My investigation into the activities of the 2nd Infantry Division at Camp McCoy did, however, produce further information about my father's experiences there. A few years ago, I made a request for Dad's autopsy report. In that report, I found that the doctor had listed a four-inch oblique scar on his right thigh. I was intrigued by this discovery, as it evoked an old

Private First Class William Davidson. Judging from the previous illustration of the Military Police Headquarters, he is standing in front of the building at the right, as evidenced by the ladders running up the side of the building.

Private First Class James Earl Hillis, 1942.

memory. According to family folklore, Dad's leg had been injured during a skiing accident, but we never knew exactly what the real story behind this injury was. Having uncovered the photos of soldiers training with skis, I guessed that Dad ran into trouble in just such a training exercise. In the ensuing fall, evidently his ski pole broke in half and impaled his right thigh above the knee. The accident was severe enough that it left a four-inch gash on his leg and accounted for the thirty-one days lost under Article of War 107, as noted on his honorable discharge.

By February 28, 1943, the MP Platoon had moved to the CCC Camp located at James Lake in Upper Michigan, where they joined the rest of the 2nd Infantry Division for winter maneuvers. According to my friend George Swearingen, the temperature during these exercises fell as low as forty-five degrees below zero during many of the fifteen days and nights the troops spent in the field.

Soldiers participating in the winter maneuvers early in 1943.

In the photo on the previous page, neither man is armed with a weapon, both are clean shaven, and both are wearing winter clothing, which was generally unavailable to the men on the front lines in Europe due to equipment shortages. The two men are constructing what is known as a "lean-to," a sloping structure made of available materials such as tree limbs or wooden boards, designed to offer some protection from the elements.

At the conclusion of the winter maneuvers, the 2nd Infantry Division returned to Camp McCoy by 0130 hours on March 16, 1943, and began another phase of intense training that included battle indoctrination. As the men of the Division continued to hone their skills for war, announcements of division command personnel, unit designations, and assignments were being finalized in preparation for overseas deployment.

James Earl Hillis, La Crosse, Wisconsin, April 1943.

In the previous photo, MP James Earl Hillis stands in full uniform next to a bridge near La Crosse, Wisconsin, which passes over a section of the Mississippi River known as the West Channel. La Crosse is located approximately ten miles west of Camp McCoy. This photo was taken in early April as the snow began to melt and the men of the 2nd Infantry Division were able to leave Camp McCoy on pass.

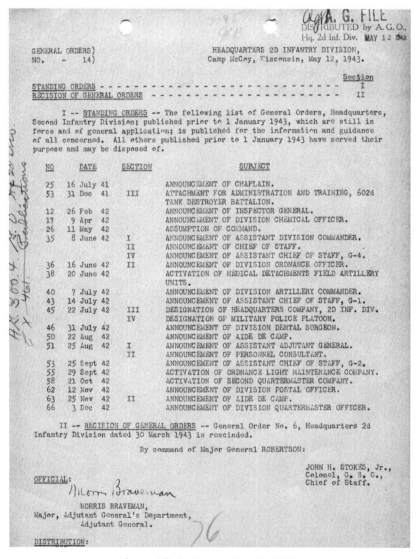

General Order No. 14, May 12, 1943.

On the previous page, General Order No. 14, dated May 12, 1943, provides a list of assignments to the 2nd Infantry Division with corresponding dates. According to the same General Order, the MP Platoon of the 2nd Infantry Division was officially designated as a Military Police Platoon on July 22, 1942.

Per General Order No. 19 (below), Captain William F. North was announced as Provost Marshal of the MP Platoon of the 2nd Infantry Division on June 21, 1943, while at Camp McCoy, relieving Lieutenant Colonel Jesse P. Green who had been the Provost Marshal since October 27, 1941 (see page 26). At the same time William North was promoted to Provost Marshal, he also received an increase in rank to major.

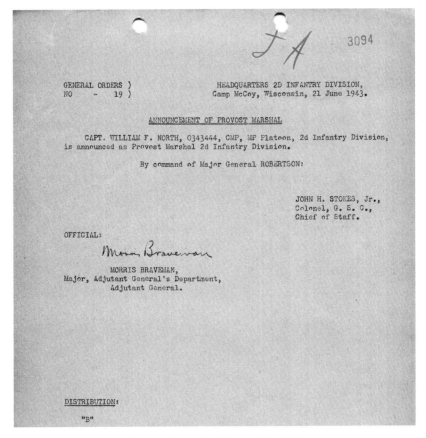

General Order No. 19, June 21, 1943.

After returning to Camp McCoy, the majority of the Division returned to their typical training routines with the exception of a small number of soldiers who were selected to undergo specialized training in the newly established Ranger Battle Training Course, which trained them to perform difficult, specialized missions in combat. Each man trained half the day with the Ranger class, learning skills such as night patrolling, terrain appreciation, hand-to-hand combat, and the use of special equipment. James Edwards was one of three men from the 2nd Infantry Division

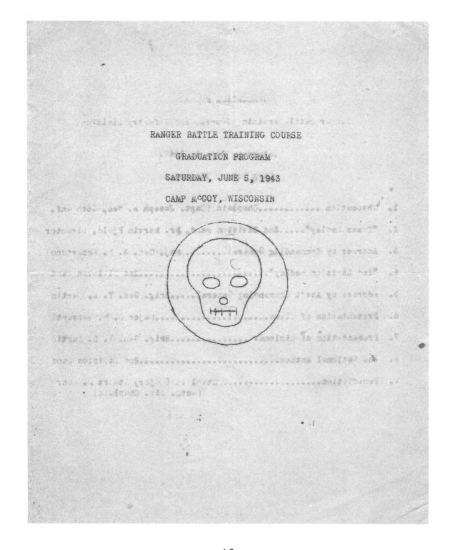

(more specifically, the 9th Infantry, Company "I") selected for Ranger Battle Training. Following is the program for the graduation ceremonies held at Camp McCoy upon completion of the training, as well as the certificate announcing Edwards's successful completion of the course. The program, which provides a more detailed account of the Ranger Battle Training, was in my mother's possession on the day of graduation, June 5, 1943. Aleta had traveled to Wisconsin from Texas and was present at James Edwards's graduation from Ranger Battle Training.

GRADUATION PROGRAM

Ranger Battle Training Course, 2nd Infantry Division

Saturday, June 5, 1943.

Camp McCoy, Wisconsin

1. Invocation ....Chaplain (Capt. Joseph A. Nee, 38th Inf.

2. "Texas Medley".....2nd Division Band, Mr. Marvin Fjeld, Director

3. Address by Commanding General........Maj. Gen. W. M. Robertson

4. "2nd Division Medley"..........................2nd Division Band

5. Address by Ass't Commanding General.....Brig. Gen. T. L. Martin

6. Presentation of Class....................Major O. M. Barsanti

7. Presentation of Diplomas...............Brig. Gen. T. L. Martin

8. The National Anthem........................2nd Division Band

9. Benediction................. Chaplain (Major) Stuart M. Rohre
                                (Actg. Div. Chaplain)

Ranger Battle Training was instituted in the Second Division to train a limited number of selected individuals in subjects that would enable them to perform difficult, specialized missions in combat. Each man trained one-half day with the Ranger class and the other half with his parent organization.

Intensive training in Ranger patrolling with emphasis on night patrols has been given during the course which also included map reading, terrain appreciation, compass, hand to hand combat, bayonet and grenade combat, use of toggle rope, explosives and demolitions, sketching, messages and reports, use of portable radio, and camouflage. A stiff physical conditioning program was maintained to keep these men hardened for this type of work.

PERSONNEL

Commandant of Ranger Battle School   Brig. Gen. T. L. Martin

Director   Major O. M. Barsanti, 38th Infantry

1st Lt. Louis D. Wittkower, Jr.	38th Inf.
1st Lt. Boyd E. Arringdale	38th Inf.
1st Lt. Halland W. Hankle	38th Inf.
1st Lt. William E. Kopplin	2nd Engr.
1st Lt. Herbert C. Byrd	23rd Inf.
2nd Lt. Larry C. Lomax	9th Inf.
2nd Lt. Alston G. Penfold	9th Inf.
2nd Lt. Vere E. McClement	23rd Inf.
2nd Lt. Claude L. Toll	23rd Inf.
2nd Lt. Anton J. Graham	9th Inf.

Ranger Battle Training Course graduation program.

A reproduction of the Ranger Battle Training Course certification that was presented to James D. Edwards on June 5, 1943.

A black wool patch with a figure of a white skull stitched on it—the insignia of the Rangers—was among the items I found in my father's old cigar box. It is likely that he was presented with this patch and his certificate by Brigadier General T. L. Brown. He proudly sported his skull patch even after he was transferred to the MP Platoon from the 9th Infantry on July 5, 1943.

The Rangers skull patch worn by James D. Edwards on the lower left sleeve of his service coat throughout the war.

On June 20, 1943, a fistfight broke out between black and white teens on Belle Island in the city of Detroit, Michigan. Tensions were high in this city, which had grown by more than 350,000 people since the United States entered the war in December 1941. Newly arrived workers who had come to this large metropolitan area seeking employment in the booming defense industry had to contend with a number of problems including a shortage of housing and racial unrest.

Rumors and false claims continued to fuel the riots. As the fighting escalated, the governor of Michigan sought help from the federal government. President Roosevelt ordered Major General Walter M. Robertson, the commanding general of the 2nd Infantry Division, to send troops to quell the violence. Troops commanded by Major Ralph Steele quickly boarded trains for the overnight trip to Detroit. James D. Edwards was one of the 851 enlisted men sent to stop the violence that week.

Once the troops arrived, they began to reestablish order, arresting the perpetrators responsible for the violence and enforcing a curfew that limited the number of people on the streets after specific hours. After three days of violence, the 2nd Infantry Division troops restored order and brought the rioting under control. The following day, the men of the Division returned to Camp McCoy, where they soon received new orders.

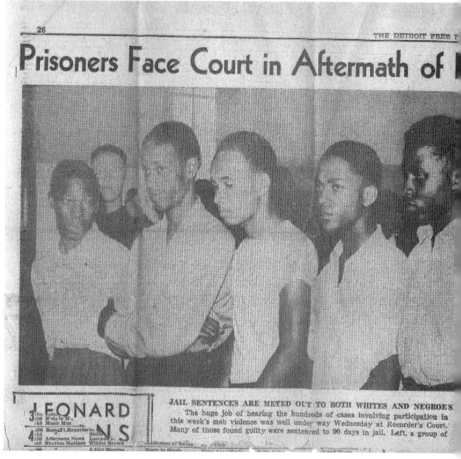

A newspaper article from the Detroit Free Press *dated June 24, 1943. This is the original newspaper clipping that my father kept as a record of the historical events he was a part of while in Detroit, Michigan.*

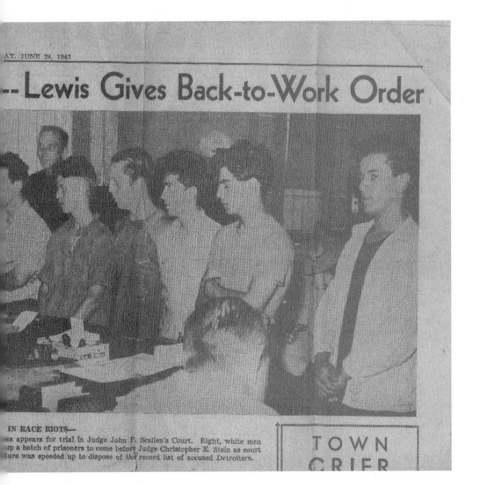

AY. JUNE 24, 1943

--Lewis Gives Back-to-Work Order

IN RACE RIOTS—
es appears for trial in Judge John P. Scallen's Court. Right, white men
ıp a batch of prisoners to come before Judge Christopher E. Stein as court
ure was speeded up to dispose of the record list of accused Detroiters.

TOWN
CRIER

In July 1943, James Edwards was transferred from the 9th Infantry to the MP Platoon of the 2nd Infantry Division. James Edwards was among the last to join the MP Platoon, leaving the 9th Infantry as a corporal and transferring to his new unit as a private first class because the MP Platoon already had a surfeit of corporals. At this point, the majority of the 2nd Infantry Division had completed their training, and a fifteen-day furlough was granted to every man in the Division, spread out over four groups at different times. From April to August, each soldier was given an opportunity to visit their families and loved ones. Dad was in the last group to receive his furlough, and he traveled back to Texas in August 1943. It was on this furlough that he and Aleta were finally married.

James Edwards and his soon-to-be wife in Cleburne, Texas, August 1, 1943—the day before they were married.

War ration books issued to James Edwards and Aleta McWilliams shortly before their marriage.

Lieutenant Colonel Matt Konop was announced as the 2nd Infantry Division Headquarters Commandant on August 12, 1943.

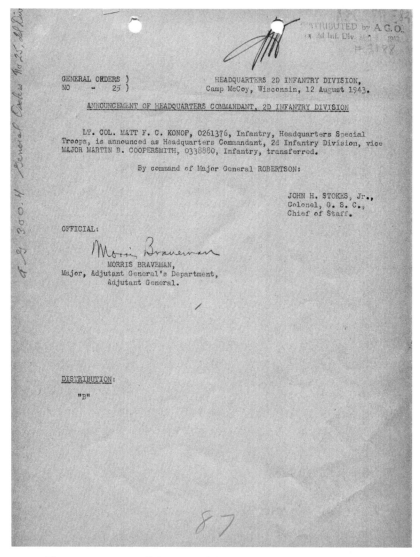

GENERAL ORDERS)
NO - 25)

HEADQUARTERS 2D INFANTRY DIVISION,
Camp McCoy, Wisconsin, 12 August 1943.

ANNOUNCEMENT OF HEADQUARTERS COMMANDANT, 2D INFANTRY DIVISION

LT. COL. MATT F. C. KONOP, 0261376, Infantry, Headquarters Special Troops, is announced as Headquarters Commandant, 2d Infantry Division, vice MAJOR MARTIN B. COOPERSMITH, 0338880, Infantry, transferred.

By command of Major General ROBERTSON:

JOHN H. STOKES, Jr.,
Colonel, G. S. C.,
Chief of Staff.

OFFICIAL:

MORRIS BRAVEMAN,
Major, Adjutant General's Department,
Adjutant General.

DISTRIBUTION:

"B"

The announcement of Lieutenant Colonel Matt Konop as Headquarters Commandant of the 2nd Infantry Division, August 12, 1943.

Having finally completed the necessary training to prepare them for war, the 2nd Infantry Division received orders on September 28, 1943, to move to staging areas in New York for eventual overseas deployment. The following day, September 29, most of the men were granted a short pass in order to visit the nearby towns of Sparta or Tomah for the last time.

The original enlisted man's pass issued to my father in September 1943.

Camp Shanks, New York

At 0245 hours on October 2, 1943, the 2nd Infantry Division boarded troop trains and departed Camp McCoy for the East Coast. The Division arrived at Camp Shanks, New York, at 2200 hours on October 3, 1943. Upon their arrival, the men of the 2nd Infantry Division were housed in temporary barracks measuring twenty feet by one hundred feet and furnished with two rows of bunks. Three coal-burning potbellied stoves located in the middle of the barracks provided heat. Here the Division awaited the next phase of their journey.

Camp Shanks as it appeared in the winter of 1943.

Camp Shanks and Fort Hamilton in New York and Camp Kilmer in New Jersey were the three staging areas on the East Coast for troops headed to Europe. Combined, the three camps were the largest staging areas in the world for troop deployments. The purpose of these camps was to ensure that every soldier leaving the United States was fully equipped prior to crossing the Atlantic. Due to a lack of large depot areas in England, the troops awaiting transport underwent a final field inspection to identify any equipment in need of repair or replacement. Basically, the task of seeing that every soldier had what he needed was accomplished at this final point.

By October 1943, the number of troops deploying to England had peaked, and Camp Shanks had reached its limit. In November, final inspections at the camp ceased in favor of improved logistics in England. At this phase of the war, the administration determined that troop replacements and equipment could be handled more efficiently after the bulk of the ground forces had arrived overseas.

During their stay at Camp Shanks, the men received a three-day pass for R&R to visit New York City. For most of the

2nd Infantry Division and other units awaiting deployment, it would be a final opportunity for the men to visit a big city for the first time; for others it would be their last.

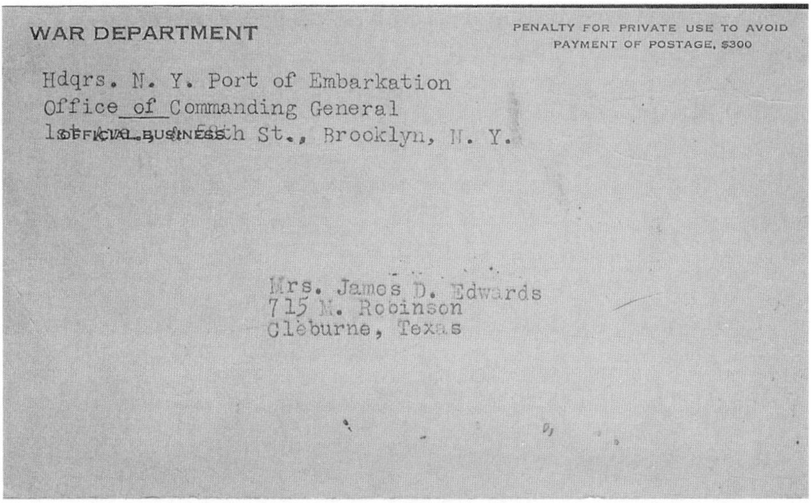

WAR DEPARTMENT

PENALTY FOR PRIVATE USE TO AVOID
PAYMENT OF POSTAGE, $300

Hdqrs. N. Y. Port of Embarkation
Office of Commanding General
1 OFFICIAL BUSINESS th St., Brooklyn, N. Y.

Mrs. James D. Edwards
715 N. Robinson
Cleburne, Texas

(Front) The postal forwarding card James Edwards sent to his wife just prior to leaving New York City.

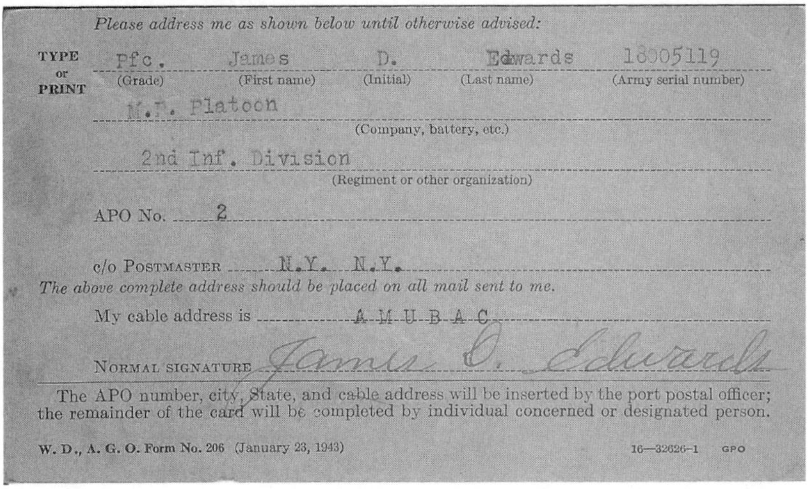

Please address me as shown below until otherwise advised:

TYPE
or
PRINT

Pfc.   James   D.   Edwards   18005119
(Grade)   (First name)   (Initial)   (Last name)   (Army serial number)

M.P. Platoon
(Company, battery, etc.)

2nd Inf. Division
(Regiment or other organization)

APO No. 2

c/o POSTMASTER N.Y. N.Y.
The above complete address should be placed on all mail sent to me.

My cable address is A M U B A C

NORMAL SIGNATURE James D. Edwards

The APO number, city, state, and cable address will be inserted by the port postal officer; the remainder of the card will be completed by individual concerned or designated person.

W. D., A. G. O. Form No. 206 (January 23, 1943)   16—32626-1   GPO

(Back) The postal forwarding card James Edwards sent to his wife just prior to leaving New York City.

Finally, at 0130 on October 7, the Division received its departure orders and immediately boarded ships to embark from New York. According to the MP Morning Reports, the MP Platoon and other Division units departed New York Harbor on October 8, 1943, among a convoy of many ships. My father sailed aboard the *Susan B. Anthony* with other members of the 2nd Infantry Division and the MP Platoon.

The Susan B. Anthony; *this ship and others like it would transport thousands of American troops across the Atlantic Ocean to Europe in the coming months.*

4

Northern Ireland
and Wales

October 1943–June 1944

Under the protection of battleships, destroyers, and a fighter escort, the convoy proceeded out of New York Harbor with orders to maintain blackout conditions during the voyage across the North Atlantic to Northern Ireland. During their ocean crossing, the convoy implemented a zigzag procedure to prevent German U-boats from getting a clean shot at them with a torpedo.

In a personal letter George F. Swearingen wrote to me, he recalled that the trip from New York Harbor was routed along the eastern seaboard of the United States. From there they traveled northeast toward Greenland, then southeast to Northern Ireland. The men had a view of land for most of the trip. After a twelve-day voyage, the 2nd Infantry Division's convoy arrived at the port city of Belfast, Northern Ireland, on October 20, 1943.

Upon disembarking their ships, the Division boarded railcars and trucks for a short trip to County Armagh, where they were housed in a variety of different locations and buildings. Many of the men were housed in Nissen huts left over from World

War I. These buildings were semicircular corrugated steel shapes intended to provide protection from shrapnel and bomb blasts.

Although garrison life at Fort Sam Houston and Camp McCoy had not been particularly comfortable compared to today's standards, they were preferable to the conditions the men found in Ireland. Many were shocked when introduced to beds constructed of wood planks and straw-stuffed mattresses and covered by British wartime blankets, which were scratchy and uncomfortable. Even the sanitation arrangements for British civilians were primitive compared to American standards at that time. The mail service suffered too, with letters from home often delayed or gone off course as they made their way to the men posted in Armagh, as evidenced below by the letter Major North's wife sent him during this period.

The envelope above is addressed to Major North from Marilee North, his wife. The return address on the back shows it was sent from Arkansas.

This letter is a good example of the many pieces of mail that were sent to the troops in Europe and displays the necessary information a letter needed to make its way to its rightful owner. Every letter was examined by army censors for information that the Germans could have used to their benefit should the document fall into their hands. Often a censor would cut out tiny pieces of the letter, sometimes leaving the recipient guessing as to what the writer had tried to say. The letter above arrived in Belfast, Northern Ireland, on November 3, 1944—many months after the Division had moved on. The 2nd Infantry Division had arrived in Northern Ireland in October 1943 and would depart from there in April 1944.

During the Division's stay in Armagh, the men adjusted quickly to the customs of the Irish people, and many of them made friends easily with their Irish neighbors. Although training continued daily, the men were allowed to tour the Irish countryside, visit pubs, and attend social gatherings. On many occasions, the men were invited to share meals with Irish families in their homes. Many soldiers were issued passes and roamed Belfast and other Irish towns. Though the infantry and other units were able to relax and enjoy their time off, one unit—the Military Police Corps—was constantly charged with the responsibility of maintaining order between the troops and the civilian population.

It was in County Armagh that one of the original 2nd Infantry Division MPs, Corporal J. R. Cantrell, spent his days and nights on foot patrol watching for the disorderly conduct of soldiers in the streets and pubs of these normally quiet little towns. Typically the military police would patrol in pairs in order to deal with less cooperative subjects or in the event that force needed to be applied to control a bad situation. On several foot patrol assignments, J. R. Cantrell was paired with Private First

Class James D. Edwards, known to his army buddies as "Eddie." Evidently it was necessary for the other MPs to give James Edwards a nickname since there were a number of other men in the platoon with the first name James. I surmise that my father received this nickname because he was the newest member of the MPs.

During one of my conversations with J. R. Cantrell, he indicated to me that he and my father, although members of the same platoon, were not acquainted with each other until they reached Northern Ireland. Although they had been living alongside each other for more than three years, it had taken two changes in station, a voyage across the Atlantic, and a shared patrol route in a small Irish town halfway around the world for them to meet for the first time. Although they had been within walking distance of each other at both Fort Sam Houston and Camp McCoy—and they enlisted in the army within three months of each other—it was not until they were several thousand miles from home that they finally became friends.

In the days, weeks, and months to follow, Cantrell and Edwards spent their days and nights getting to know each other better and formed a bond as only soldiers in wartime can. Their devotion to duty and their courage, which each would display during the Division's battles with the German Army, would reveal the similarities of character that drew the men together.

These new, inseparable friends each posed for unique photos, which have survived sixty-eight years in various locations since they were taken on November 11, 1943, in Armagh. In a recent discovery, I located a photo of my father nearly identical to a photo of Cantrell that he provided to me. In my father's photo, he is pictured with my mother, whom he had married just three months earlier. J. R.'s first daughter, Carolyn, had been born in May 1943 and appears in his photo with him.

Private First Class James D. Edwards (thinking of Mrs. Edwards), Armagh, Northern Ireland, November 11, 1943. Note the skull patch, which he received after completing Ranger training, visible on his left sleeve.

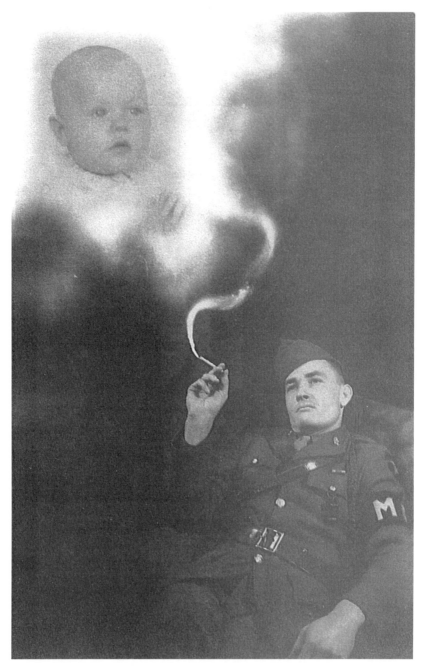

Corporal James R. Cantrell (thinking of his daughter), Armagh, Northern Ireland, November 11, 1943.

During the six months that the 2nd Infantry Division was in Northern Ireland, they continued their training and preparation for war. By April 1944, the Division was fully equipped and ready to receive its next orders. On April 1, General Patton addressed the 2nd Infantry Division troops assembled on the Mall of Armagh, sharing with the soldiers what they had yet to face. James D. Edwards would later serve under General Patton's command in Germany as a member of the occupation forces.

General George Patton conducts a final inspection of the 2nd Infantry Division troops in Armagh, Northern Ireland. The 2nd Infantry Division Indianhead shoulder patch is clearly visible on the men in the photo.

In the photo above, Major General Walter M. Robertson looks on while Colonel John H. Stokes, Assistant Division Commander, stands at attention just in front of Patton. In the background and to Colonel Stokes's right, the double stars on the helmet of Major General Robertson can be seen. Just two months later, on the eve of D-Day, General Patton would deliver his famous "Give 'Em Hell" speech.

Men of the 2nd Infantry Division in Armagh, Northern Ireland.
(From the personal collection of James Edwards.)

The photo above appears to have been taken in a rural setting, perhaps while the MPs were training. Most of the men in these photos are wearing the daily field uniform. An MP in the third row holds a small black and white puppy. This is likely the first appearance of the remarkable dog known as "Lady," who would accompany James Edwards and the MPs of the 2nd Infantry Division for the remainder of their time in Europe.

The next two images contain Morning Reports from the MP Platoon while they were in Ireland, which I photocopied from the microfilm records that have been preserved at the National Personnel Records Center in St. Louis. To honor all of the men who served with the MP Platoon, I felt it appropriate to include a couple of those Morning Reports in this book for anyone searching for some record of their family member who served in this MP Platoon during World War II.

Left Form

COMPANY MORNING REPORT ENDING 2400 4 January 194 4

STATION APO #2, Armagh County Armagh, Ireland
ORGANIZATION MP. Plat, 2nd Inf. Div. CMP

SERIAL NUMBER	NAME	GRADE	CODE
18005765	Sinkule, Jerry A.	Sgt.	
	Fr duty to D/S Lisburn, Ireland		
34306207	Plyler, Bruce L.	Pfc.	
6830977	Ghormley, Hubert J.	Pvt.	
30060907	McNamara, John	Pvt.	
	The above 3 EM fr duty to D/S Keady, Ireland.		
16003845	Roberts, John C.	Cpl.	
33030724	Sealera, James D.	Pfc.	
39011001	Silveria, Joe T.	Pfc.	
	The above 3 EM fr D/S Keady, Ireland to duty.		
16021452	Cantrall, James R.	Cpl.	
35108765	Dalton, Vincent W.	Pvt.	
35154243	Kent, Norman D.	Pfc.	
34121131	Lawrence, Luther A.	Pvt.	
34371166	Cothron, Randall W.	Pvt.	
18004719	Edwards, James D.	Pfc.	
18012124	Lawless, Earnest G.	Pvt.	
18001066	Conaway, Orville H.	Pvt.	
	The above 8 EM fr D/S Newry, Ireland to duty.		

PAGE 1 OF 2 PAGES

Right Form

COMPANY MORNING REPORT ENDING 2400 4 January 194 4

STATION APO #2, Armagh County Armagh, Ireland
ORGANIZATION MP. Plat, 2nd Inf. Div. CMP

SERIAL NUMBER	NAME	GRADE	CODE
36121764	Ciesmicki, John W.	Sgt.	
34370891	Wilson, Willie R.	Pfc.	
6967321	Lester, Dalton J.	Pvt.	
19075175	Sheehan, John H.	Pvt.	
14150089	Davidson, William L.	Pfc.	
34808089	Anderson, Eugene M	Pvt.	
37615903	Gittemeier, Linus J.	Pvt.	
33651319	Gibson, Moscoe C.	Pvt.	
33680033	Cook, Francis	Pvt.	
	The above 8 EM fr duty to D/S Newry, Ireland		

OFFICER STRENGTH	FLD O & CAPT		1ST LT		2D LT		WO		FLT O	
	PRES	ABS'T	PRES	ABS'T	PRES	ABS'T	PRES	ABS'T	PRES	ABS'T
ASGD	1		1	1						
TOTAL	1		1	1						

ENLISTED MEN	PRESENT FOR DUTY	PRESENT NOT FOR DY	ABSENT	PRESENT AND ABSENT
ASGD	45	3	25	73
OTHER ORGS	31			31
TOTAL	76	3		104

RATIONS: Not Used

PAGE 2 OF 2 PAGES

SIGNATURE Henry S Kurowski, 2nd Lt CMP

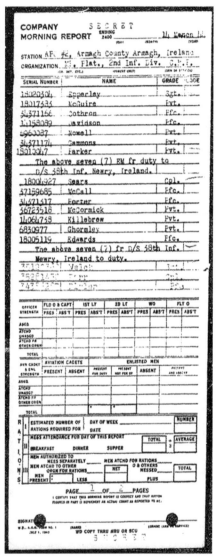

The Morning Report on the previous pages reflects the departure and return of small groups of MPs to and from the nearby towns of Newry and Keady while the Division was in Ireland. A noncommissioned officer appears to have accompanied each group on every occasion. James Edwards was on detached service to the 38th Infantry on March 14, 1944, with a group of six others.

On April 18, 1944, the MP Platoon departed Northern Ireland with other 2nd Infantry Division units aboard the United States Army Transport (USAT) *James A. Parker*. They traveled from Belfast across the Irish Sea, docking in Newport, Wales, later that day.

The USAT James A. Parker *during World War II.*

From there, units in the Division were relocated to various other areas in the south of Wales. The MP Platoon traveled west to Tenby in Pembrokeshire, where they were billeted in an assortment of quarters ranging from deserted houses to public buildings.

A group photo of the 2nd Infantry Division staff, commanded by Major General Walter M. Robertson. The reverse side of the photo identifies each officer by name and rank. The exact location where this photograph was taken is unknown; however, given the date, it is clear the photo was taken while the Division was in Tenby, Wales.

In early May 1944, Major William North assigned Private First Class George F. Swearingen the task of traveling by jeep from Division Headquarters to Carmarthen, Wales, to pick up a new officer recently assigned to the MP Platoon from the 9th Infantry Regiment. Upon his arrival at headquarters, 2nd Lieutenant I. C. "Chet" Meeth joined the MP Platoon as one of three 2nd lieutenants.

All this time, top secret plans were being made by the Allies for the invasion of the Nazi-dominated European continent. Only those officers in the highest levels of the command knew the approximate date and time the order would be given for the troops to board ships for the crossing of the English Channel and eventual landing on the beaches of Normandy, France. High security was enforced and every enlisted man was required to produce proper identification when challenged by military police. Due to the danger of enemy espionage, top secrecy was vital to the success of the invasion, and the highest levels of security protocols were implemented and adhered to. On May 22, 1944, Major William North was issued a permanent pass by headquarters, which allowed him free movement in and around the marshaling and embarkation areas.

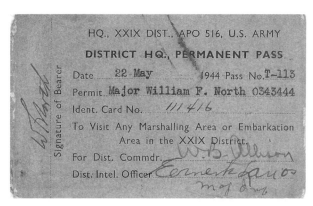

Major North's permanent pass, issued on May 22, 1944.

Three weeks prior to the invasion, the MP Platoon required every man, including officers, who would operate a military vehicle to demonstrate driving proficiency. Private First Class James D. Edwards completed that proficiency test and was authorized to operate the 1/4-ton army jeep and trucks up to 3/4-ton capacity.

The driver's license issued to James Edwards, authenticated by 2nd Lieutenant I. C. Meeth on May 15, 1944.

On the same date, Provost Marshal Major William North demonstrated his proficiency and was authorized to operate the 1/4-ton jeep, 3/4-ton truck, and motorcycle. Major North's son, Max North, was kind enough to provide me with his father's World War II documents and photos in order to help tell the story of the MP Platoon.

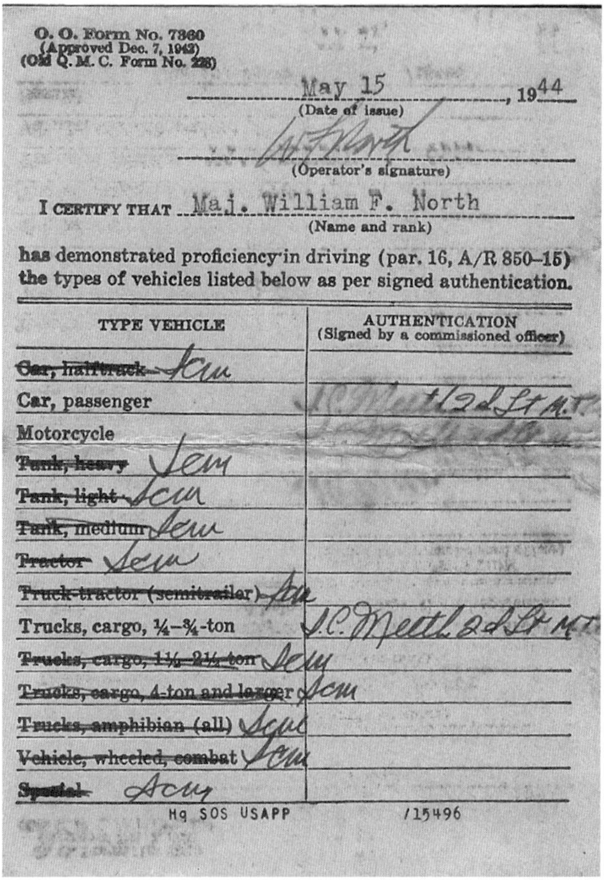

O. O. Form No. 7360
(Approved Dec. 7, 1942)
(Old Q. M. C. Form No. 228)

May 15, 1944
(Date of issue)

(Operator's signature)

I CERTIFY THAT Maj. William F. North
(Name and rank)

has demonstrated proficiency in driving (par. 16, A/R 850–15) the types of vehicles listed below as per signed authentication.

TYPE VEHICLE	AUTHENTICATION (Signed by a commissioned officer)
~~Car, halftrack~~ Scm	
Car, passenger	J.C. Meeth 2d Lt M.T.
Motorcycle	
~~Tank, heavy~~ Scm	
~~Tank, light~~ Scm	
~~Tank, medium~~ Scm	
~~Tractor~~ Scm	
~~Truck-tractor (semitrailer)~~ Scm	
Trucks, cargo, ¼–¾-ton	J.C. Meeth 2d Lt M.T.
~~Trucks, cargo, 1½–2½-ton~~ Scm	
~~Trucks, cargo, 4-ton and larger~~	Scm
~~Trucks, amphibian (all)~~ Scm	
~~Vehicle, wheeled, combat~~ Scm	
~~Special~~ Scm	

Hq SOS USAPP /15496

The driver's license issued to Major William North on May 15, 1944.

Motorcycles were an important component of the MP Platoon, as these agile, lightweight vehicles were an efficient means of transportation in tight spots where trucks or jeeps could not pass. A number of men in the MP Platoon were issued motorcycles licenses, including Joe Beckwith and Bruce Plyler, who appear next to their motorcycles in the following picture.

Joe Beckwith and Bruce Plyler pose together with MP motorcycles. It is likely that the MP Platoon—and the motorcycles—were part of a parade that marked the 2nd Infantry Division's arrival in Pembrokeshire, Wales.

Beckwith and Plyler are shown wearing their fall uniforms. The garrison caps the men are wearing would have had green and gold piping on them to identify them as military police. Plyler has the 2nd Infantry Division patch on his left shoulder; it appears that Beckwith's uniform shirt is devoid of a division patch. The words *Military Police* are plainly visible on the windshields of the motorcycles. A siren is located just above each headlight, and an ammunition box is mounted to the left side of each bike at the front wheel. Although difficult to see in the photo, each motorcycle would have been identified by number on the edge of the front wheel fender. The motorcycles all resemble Harley-Davidson brand bikes.

2nd Lieutenant I. C. Meeth sits atop one of the MP motorcycles in Wales.

Although 2nd Lieutenant Meeth had joined the MP Platoon in early May, his transfer was not officially recorded on the MP Platoon Morning Reports until June 7—the day after the Allied invasion of France began.

Such small errors continue to be a source of frustration for people trying to reconstruct the footsteps of friends or family members who served in World War II. The Morning Report asserts that Meeth's transfer occurred on May 28, 1944. However, his signature is clearly visible on the driver's licenses that he signed for Major North and James Edwards on May 15. Inaccuracies in records, while not common, did occur—especially when units were engaged in combat with the enemy and record keeping became a secondary concern.

75

A Morning Report from June 1, 1944, identifies the coastal city of Bournemouth, England, as the point from which the 2nd Infantry Division would depart for France. Operation Overlord—the code name for the Allied invasion of German-occupied Europe—would begin on June 6, 1944. Thousands of troops, many of them American, were about to face the unimaginable. War was upon them at last.

5

Operation Overlord and the Normandy Campaign

June–August 1944

We are determined that before the sun sets on this terrible struggle, our flag will be recognized throughout the world as a symbol of freedom on one hand and of overwhelming force on the other.

—General George C. Marshall

You are about to embark upon the great crusade toward which we have striven these many months. The eyes of the world are upon you. . . . I have full confidence in your courage, devotion to duty, and skill in battle.

—General Dwight D. Eisenhower
D-Day, June 6, 1944

Transports of every kind await their orders. They will soon be filled with men for the D-Day invasion.

Upon receiving their orders for Operation Overlord, select units of the 2nd Infantry Division's Combat Engineer Battalion and the infantry assault teams departed from Cardiff, Wales. They sailed around Land's End, crossed the eighty-mile section of the English Channel, and came ashore in Normandy, France, with elements of the 1st and 29th Divisions on D-Day, June 6, 1944. In the early morning hours of this day, more than two thousand American soldiers were killed assaulting the beachhead, many of them before they could leave their landing craft. The blood of dead American soldiers turned the water red for more than a day; their bodies and destroyed equipment littered the beaches for several more days. Brave men waded ashore under heavy fire from German machine guns, which were protected by concrete pillboxes high atop the hills beyond the beach.

D-Day invasion troops make their way toward the beach.

An American soldier killed in action on Omaha Beach. The crossed rifles in the sand are a comrade's tribute to this soldier who sprang ashore from a landing barge and died at the barricades on June 6, 1944.

In the bitter fighting and chaos that followed, those who had not lost their lives as soon as they stepped from their landing craft were forced to cross hundreds of yards of soft sand to seek protection from the German guns. The odds were against them: each man had a backpack weighing close to one hundred pounds, and they were under constant heavy machine gun, artillery, and mortar fire. In many cases, men who were forced—or chose—to abandon their landing craft early to avoid heavy fire drowned in water just a few feet deep because they were unable to swim with their heavy packs.

Troops give first aid to survivors of a sunken landing craft on D-Day.

The job of the advanced landing forces was to neutralize the German defenses in order to allow the remainder of the invasion force to disembark under minimal hostile fire. Unfortunately, the initial assault force met with considerable resistance. They were unable to eliminate all of the German defenses embedded in the rocky bluffs on the first day of fighting. By June 7, the majority of the 2nd Infantry Division's three regiments—the 9th, 23rd, and 38th—began landing at Omaha Beach under slightly different conditions from what the initial wave of soldiers had seen the day before. The tide was higher, which allowed the landing craft to get closer to the bluffs, leaving the disembarking troops less distance to travel. Still, as the second and third waves of men came ashore, many of the soldiers found themselves under moderate fire from the pillboxes still unbreached in the cliffs high above the beach. A soldier who relaxed a little too soon after leaving the protection of his landing craft discovered he might be the recipient of more machine gun rounds or a sniper's bullet.

In my research, I was able to determine that the MP Platoon departed from the port of Bournemouth in southern England on three different ships and on three separate dates. In my conversations with J. R. Cantrell, he shared with me that he and several other MPs—including Major North and George Swearingen—landed on Omaha Beach on D-Day Plus One (June 7, the day after the initial invasion on June 6) in the vicinity of Easy Red sector. These men hastily jumped from the protection of their landing craft, M-1 carbines in hand, and made a dash for cover under enemy fire.

Once on shore, the MPs under the immediate command of Major North undertook the duties for which they had been trained. The MP Platoon had the responsibility of clearing the beaches of equipment, directing traffic, setting up checkpoints, helping lost soldiers reunite with their units, and in some cases assaulting pillboxes to flush out remaining German infantry. The duties of the MPs were enormous. Eventually, over the course of the war, the responsibility for the security of the 2nd Infantry Division's 70,307 captured German POWs would fall upon this unit.

Although many of the 2nd Infantry Division MPs arrived in Normandy on D-Day Plus One, other MPs from the Division,

Lieutenant Meeth among them, would remain in Bournemouth until the final units departed on June 19, 1944. Private First Class James D. Edwards, however, was among the second wave of MPs that landed on Omaha Beach on June 9, 1944.

By this time, the beachhead was almost completely cleared of enemy activity except for the occasional sniper, who in many cases would take shots at the Division Command Post, hoping to inflict death upon a high-ranking officer. The MP Platoon was charged with securing the area around the command posts for the protection of the Allied generals and their command staffs, and in some cases the MPs had to seek out the German defenders and deliver deadly return fire against those forces. Late in the morning of June 9, the second wave of the MP Platoon arrived just off the coast of Normandy on a stretch of Omaha Beach code named the Easy Red sector.

James Edwards on the deck of his ship arriving at Omaha Beach in the same sector where the first wave of soldiers came ashore.

The image on the previous page is a still frame from the raw combat footage that has been reproduced by Combat Reels of Fort Worth, Texas. In the photo, my father, MP Private First Class James Edwards, stands in the center of the photo among other soldiers and looks directly at the cameraman, Sergeant Cook of the 165th Signal Corps. Only a father's son could be certain as to the identity of this soldier. Dad's mannerisms, grin, personality traits, and physical appearance are all present in this man, which convinced me that the otherwise anonymous MP in this image is James Edwards. The wristwatch he is wearing was a gift from my mother on their wedding day, and is exactly like the one that appears in the photo of my father on page 292.

This photo is believed to depict Company I, 23rd Infantry Regiment, 2nd Infantry Division as they march inland from the landing zone on Omaha Beach.

The same photo appeared in the Stars and Stripes *newspaper, which was found in the personal document collection of Major William North. This particular* Stars and Stripes *article is sixty-eight years old.*

Although the 2nd Infantry Division had made limited gains in breaking through the German lines at this point, two very important objectives had been achieved. The first was the initial securing of the beachhead. The second was gaining a foothold deep enough into enemy territory to ensure that troops and equipment could move forward off the beach.

On June 12, the Division moved to an area near the Cerisy Forest, where they encountered the German troops of the 3rd Parachute Division. As they moved into the Saint-Georges-d'Elle sector, the Division faced other German strong points, which were well-equipped with German soldiers determined to deny the 2nd Infantry Division further progress in the area. For the next month, the town of Saint-Georges-d'Elle would change hands several times before the Division could fully secure it and remove the remaining German defenders.

A building in Trevieres, France, badly damaged by the battles fought in the area in June 1944.

As the fighting continued inland toward Saint-Lô, the bulk of the MP advance units prepared to move off the beach to an area closer to the fighting. Ultimately, this would allow them to secure the roads in the Division's sector and handle prisoners. According to the Morning Reports, the remainder of the MPs departed from Bournemouth, England, on June 19 aboard the Liberty Ship USS *John A. Campbell*.

This ship is an example of the class of vessel routinely used to transport troops across the ocean.

Private First Class Rocco Festa on board the USS John A. Campbell, *June 19, 1944.*

This popular World War II photo shows an MP studying a French to English translation guide. The original Signal Corps photographer listed the date as June 15, 1944, and correctly identified the MP as Private First Class Rocco Festa from Brooklyn, New York. However, based on the Morning Report detailing the movements of the 2nd Infantry Division MP Platoon, the actual date this photo was taken would have been June 19, 1944, after the last group of MPs boarded ships and started across the English Channel.

In the photo, Festa is armed with an M-1 carbine, but MP Morning Reports dated June 18, 1944, reveal that this rifle was actually replaced by the M-1911 pistol, which became the basic weapon of the MP Platoon, on the same day this photo was taken. In my father's personal address book, where he kept a record of his platoon members, Rocco Festa's name and home address appear near the back.

Because a change of station was imminent for the MP Platoon, the USS *John A. Campbell* remained just offshore as their temporary headquarters until June 29, when the entire unit completed their movement inland to the vicinity of Cerisy-la-Forêt. The final units of the platoon disembarked from the USS *John A. Campbell* at 0930 that morning and traveled by truck into France. They arrived just two miles south of the Cerisy Forest, near the town of Berigny, at 1600 hours, where the 2nd Infantry Division continued to push through the stubborn German defenses. Here the MPs were now able to operate as a complete unit, utilizing the entire platoon in a single, coordinated effort to support the infantry's advances.

James Edwards with Lady before she had her pups, Cerisy-la-Forêt, France, June 1944.

In the photo above, Lady, a very expectant mother-to-be, sits for her master. In a letter my father wrote to my mother in October 1944, he stated that his dog had *two new pups*. Although this photo was censored by the army so that the face of the soldier sitting in the jeep is unrecognizable, the man in this picture is without a doubt Private First Class James D. Edwards. As was the custom at the time, many soldiers had inscribed their equipment with the name of a loved one. Just above the left rear wheel, Dad had the name "Leta" painted on his jeep—in honor of his wife, Aleta. The exact date of this photo was not documented, but it was probably taken in the hedgerow country of France while the MP Platoon was bivouacked just south of the Cerisy Forest.

The following letter was sent to me by Faye Young, daughter of MP George Swearingen. She recalls a story her father told her and details an event that took place near a forest in France—very likely while the MP Platoon was stationed near Cerisy-la-Forêt.

Hello,

I will apologize for being so slow to send this to you. I hope you understand that I have tried, but God said, "Not yet." I have finally found a peace in my heart that allowed me to be more with the program.

It may seem strange, and such a small thing, but I find such comfort in knowing that Dad can see again. So very often he would say, "I wish I could see so that I could write my stories and work on my books." Being nearly deaf and in a wheelchair were not important to him. God's love has allowed all his hopes and dreams to be his now. Small steps.

One of my favorite stories is one of the little cat. God does watch out for us in unusual ways. Dad always loved children, so I know that he was comfortable in leaving the little cat when the time came to move on. Here is the story I will share with you:

"While I was in the army we were getting ready to go into France. One day a small golden cat came along and hopped into the jeep that I was driving. I put him out as I got ready to leave, but he just climbed back in. When I decided that he wasn't going to leave, I fed him and made him a small bed under the driver's seat of the jeep. He would sleep there at night and stay close by during the day.

"He traveled many miles with me and Lt. Meath [sic]. When we got in the jeep to go somewhere, I would hit the horn once and the little cat would come running.

"One night Lt. Meath and I were asleep in the jeep at the edge of some woods. The little cat heard something and suddenly jumped up into my lap. This woke me up. After a minute or so, I could hear footsteps coming toward us. I shouted and asked who was there and all I heard was someone running away. After a few minutes, the cat crawled back under the seat and went back to sleep.

"The next morning I went into the woods where the sounds had come from. I found a sword and a knife that someone had dropped. These were not items from someone in the US Army. This little cat had saved our lives. We had not heard any noise, but he did and woke me to alert us. We would not have been aware of any trouble if it hadn't been for that little cat.

"When it was time for us to leave France, we stopped in a small town to get a few supplies. There were several children playing on the side of the road, waiting for their parents to come from the store. The little cat jumped out of the jeep and went over to them.

"When it was time for us to leave, I hit the horn one time. The little cat just turned around and looked at us. When I called to him to come so we could go, he just sat there. As I started the jeep, the little cat looked at me one more time, then turned and went to the children. I guess he had done what he was supposed to do for us and had now found a new home.

"I will never forget that little cat."

As remembered by Faye Young, daughter of George F. Swearingen. I hope this will be useful to you.

Thanks,

Faye

For nearly a month, the 2nd Infantry Division fought through hedgerow after hedgerow, slowly evicting the Germans who had embedded themselves in the thick brush and earthen barriers. Finally, on July 11, having eliminated that resistance, the Division launched another major offensive with the objective of taking Hill 192. By nightfall on July 11, the 2nd Infantry Division had finally seized the hill, which was the highest point of observation in the region.

A friend of mine, Dick Schwab, was a young infantry scout with the 38th Infantry Regiment who fought in the push to uproot the Germans from Hill 192, which was located about halfway between the towns of Saint-Georges-d'Elle and Saint-Lô. Dick was kind enough to provide me with his account of the attack on Hill 192, which began on July 11, 1944, with a tremendous Allied artillery bombardment and culminated with a final assault on the hill that drove the Germans from their positions. Although Mr.

Schwab was not an MP, he and the other men of the 2nd Infantry Division who wore the Indianhead patch throughout the war shared a common bond that would forever link them to this time and place.

24 January, 2012

As a replacement in Company I, 38th Infantry, 2nd Division, I knew no one and knew nothing. Combat is difficult under the best of conditions, but arriving as a replacement is especially difficult.

My brief story pertains to the use of artillery as an integral part of the offensive weapons of attack. The location was Hill 192, so named for its elevation above sea level. This hill provided whoever held it with the primary observation all the way to the coast.

The date was July 11, 1944. At 0500 hours we were ordered to pull back in preparation for another attempt to take the hill. We would pull back five hundred yards, take defensive positions, and wait for the artillery to soften up the Germans prior to our attack.

At precisely 0600 hours, an artillery attack began on the enemy that lasted for one hour. Still being relatively new to combat, I was stunned by the intensity of the attack. Virtually everything that the US Army and Navy had in its arsenal was thrown at the enemy immediately in front of us. Everything was used—from 81-millimeter mortars to 155-millimeter division and corps artillery to the guns from ships still off Omaha Beach. P-51 and P-47 fighter bombers also participated. For the last thirty minutes of this attack, the artillery used proximity fuses to allow the tanks to roam underneath this wall of fire to use their machine guns and cannons. All of this happening five hundred yards in front of us.

In my lifetime, previously and subsequently, I have never witnessed such an assault. All of my foxhole buddies, including myself, expected a cakewalk when the barrage was lifted. Disillusionment #1 in my young life; how any living thing survived such an attack, I have no idea. But when we crossed over our previous positions as we started the attack to take this vital hill, we were met by a lot of angry

Germans with a lot of weapons.

Ultimately, by the end of the day we prevailed, but at a terrible cost.

This single event helped me to form my opinion of artillery as a tool in warfare. You can't do without it, but it's only a tool and not necessarily the "do-all" weapon of warfare. The infantry unit is still the ultimate winner of battles, and the longer you survive combat, the more you realize that an infantry division is a self-contained fighting unit, from the lowly dogface to the service units, from the artillery to the commanding officers.

The moral of this story: Artillery in our hands is an infantryman's best friend—incoming artillery from the enemy is your worst nightmare.

Dick Schwab

Company I, 38th Infantry Regiment, June 13, 1944 to October 13, 1945

Dick Schwab, Company I, 38th Infantry Regiment, near Saint–Georges-d'Elle, July 1944.

During operations to seize Hill 192, a handful of German paratroopers from the 9th German Paratrooper Regiment survived the fierce fighting and were captured by the 2nd Infantry Division on the last day of battle. There were more than three thousand soldiers in this German regiment, but only 124 men from this particular unit survived the battle. The rest fought to the death in their attempt to defend this highest point of observation in the Saint-Lô sector in Normandy.

Nazi Comedown

Three German paratroopers (left), captured in the St. Lo sector in Normandy, start a jeep right to a prisoners' camp behind the line guarded by an American soldier (right). *Associated Press Wirephoto*

A newspaper article that was preserved by the North family. Major North is seen behind the wheel of his jeep during the mop-up phase after Hill 192 fell to the Allies on July 11, 1944.

After the 2nd Infantry Division's victory at Hill 192, the MPs had full responsibility of all 521 German prisoners of war who were captured during that battle. Ironically, my mother celebrated her seventeenth birthday while her new husband celebrated this small victory with the Division. Major North received the Bronze Star Medal for meritorious service against the enemy during the period from June 9, 1944, to July 9, 1944.

R E-S-T-R-I-C-T-E-D

G.O. No. 65   Page 2   22 July 1944

In accordance with AR 600-45 and Circular 66, Headquarters First United States Army, dated 18 May 1944, the Bronze Star Medal is awarded to Lieutenant Colonel KENNETH E. BELIEU, 0360591, 2d Signal Company, who has distinguished himself by exceptionally meritorious achievements in performance of outstanding service against the enemy in Normandy from 7 June 1944 to 9 July 1944. Entered Military Service from Oregon.

In accordance with AR 600-45 and Circular 66, Headquarters First United States Army, dated 18 May 1944, the Bronze Star Medal is awarded to Lieutenant Colonel CECIL F. JORNS, 0291498, 2d Medical Battalion, who has distinguished himself by exceptionally meritorious achievements in performance of outstanding service against the enemy in Normandy from 7 June 1944 to 9 July 1944. Entered Military Service from Texas.

In accordance with AR 600-45 and Circular 66, Headquarters First United States Army, dated 18 May 1944, the Bronze Star Medal is awarded to Major WILLIAM F. NORTH, 0343444, Military Police Platoon, 2d Infantry Division, who has distinguished himself by exceptionally meritorious achievements in performance of outstanding service against the enemy in Normandy from 7 June 1944 to 9 July 1944. Entered Military Service from Arkansas.

By command of Major General ROBERTSON:

JOHN H. STOKES, JR.,
Colonel, G. S. C.,
Chief of Staff.

OFFICIAL:

Morris Braveman

MORRIS BRAVEMAN,
Lt. Col., Adjutant General's Department,
Adjutant General.

DISTRIBUTION:

"D" Special

R E-S-T-R-I-C-T-E-D

General Order from July 22, 1944, announcing that Major North will receive the Bronze Star Medal for "outstanding service against the enemy in Normandy."

General Robertson pins the Bronze Star Medal on Major North, July 1944. This photo is an original that was in Major North's collection. It also appears in the 2nd Infantry Division history book.

In addition to Major North, six other MPs were awarded the Bronze Star in July as the Division moved inland from Omaha Beach. Sergeant John W. Ciesnicki Jr., Corporal John P. Sears, Private First Class Frances E. Traynor, Private Luther A. Lawrence, Corporal Heinz W. Thiel, and Private First Class George R. Kingery were all honored in similar ceremonies.

As combat operations continued during the summer of 1944, the MP Platoon stayed busy, securing a vast number of captured German soldiers. Following the fall of Brest, they had netted more than thirty-one thousand POWs (this number is founded on the 2nd Infantry Division MP Platoon Morning Reports from the months of June through September, 1944). According to a letter I received from George Swearingen, the MP Platoon set up camp near Cerisy-la-Forêt, in an area with a farmhouse, barns, and small buildings, and remained there from June 29 to July 30. The building that appears in the following set of photos suggests they were taken in the location that George Swearingen referred to.

James Edwards with Lady and her pups, Cerisy-la-Forêt, June 1944.

2nd Infantry Division MPs Herring and Sinkule in Cerisy-la-Forêt, July 1944.

*From left, MPs Bennett, Plyler, McGuire, Swearingen, and Helfer, Cerisy-la-Forêt,
July 1944.*

MPs McMahan and Hillis, Cerisy-la-Forêt, July 1944.

A group shot of 2nd Infantry Division MPs, Cerisy-la-Forêt, July 1944.
Front row, left to right: Hillis (with two puppies), Davidson, Edwards (with Lady),
Swearingen.
Back row, left to right: Herring, Ross, McMahan, unidentified MP.

The image on the previous page was found in my father's personal things along with dozens of other photos and documents. The center of attention in this photo is Lady and her newborn pups. On the back of this photo, all of the MPs are identified except the one directly behind George Swearingen. While all of these men are facing the camera, the new mother is more interested in the well-being of her litter.

From June 20 through July 10, during a lull in action, the MP Platoon took advantage of their spare time to improve their prisoner of war enclosures (PWEs) and collection methods for German prisoners. They refined their methods of quickly relieving the infantry units of prisoners they had captured, which in turn allowed the infantry to return to their units in a timely manner. Communication between the Provost Marshal and the MPs in the field was improved by the installation of sound-powered radios in the MP's jeeps, as well as at major road checkpoints throughout the Division area. Sergeant Jerry A. Sinkule, who was in charge of the MP motor pool, coordinated with the quartermaster to supply trucks for transporting large numbers of prisoners when necessary. Major North also worked closely with the 2nd Infantry Division's engineers in an effort to create and maintain suitable prisoner of war enclosures.

On July 30, the MP Platoon moved within a half mile north of the town of Saint-Jean-des-Baisants via motorized convoy and established its command post there. As the 2nd Infantry Division secured towns one by one, the MP Platoon provided the usual traffic control, maintained security in the rear areas, handled prisoners, and conducted building searches to clear out remaining Germans who were in hiding.

The following letter was sent to me by Mark Hillis, the son of MP James Earl Hillis.

James,

Dad only told me a few stories [about the war]. *Some I overheard when he was talking to another vet. He didn't like talking about it. He only watched one or two World War II movies with me. One was* A Bridge Too Far. *I remember him commenting that the British were always stopping to drink tea when they needed to be fighting. Dad didn't have a very good opinion of the British. He was very independent and didn't like being bossed around, so he didn't think much of the military. That was why he always worked for himself. While training in the United States, they were conducting war games with some live-fire exercises. Dad dove into a foxhole and landed on a porcupine. He said that was very painful, and I think that was in Wisconsin.*

He said that he landed on Omaha Beach while driving a jeep and pulling a wagon loaded with ammo. When he drove off the landing craft ramp, he was chest deep in water. He drove onto the beach, stopped to remove the waterproofing on the engine, then drove off the beach. He either drove into or near a wooded area after getting off the beach, when a German MG [machine gun] *opened up on him and disabled his jeep. I asked him what he did then since his jeep was put out of action. He said he walked.*

Also, Dad insisted that he landed on June 6, contrary to the official division record of June 7. Dad was always an honest, practical man, and was the leader of his family even though his parents were still alive and he was not the eldest sibling. I never doubted what he told me. Once he and another soldier (a sergeant?) went out after dark in a jeep to reconnoiter ahead of their position, and they were supposed to be back before daylight because of enemy fighter planes, but they got stuck in a minefield. It was daylight before they got out of it. He said that he was driving the jeep in no-man's-land between lines. I think this was in France when the Germans were retreating and the US forces were trying to keep up.

Anyway, they were racing down a road when they spotted a German plane overhead. It started to dive. Dad locked up the brakes and his partner jumped out before the jeep came to a stop. The other MP ran into some trees for cover. By the time the jeep stopped, it was too late for Dad to run for cover. He said that he dove under the jeep as the German fighter strafed the jeep with Dad under it. He said a bullet went through the driver's seat, the gas tank, and hit in the ground next to him. The gas from the tank poured on him. He said that was when he decided that he was in the wrong place, and he then ran for the same trees his partner ran into while the German plane was making its turn. As the German plane made another pass, it shot up Dad's jeep. Since the jeep was out of commission, they walked back to their lines. Dad was apparently unlucky with jeeps when Germans and machine guns were around.

He went through Paris. Was wounded in the leg by a bullet and received the Purple Heart. I don't remember if he told me where he was at that time. He told me that he was on Elsenborn Ridge when the Germans began the Ardennes Offensive. He said there were tanks coming at them with German infantry behind them. "What did you do?" I said. He said they hunkered down in their foxholes while the tanks passed over them, then popped up and shot the infantry behind them. "What about the tanks behind your lines?" He said they let the guys with the bazookas worry about them.

He had a first cousin, Red Safely, with the 101st, who lost both legs at Bastogne. He survived even though he only had stumps for legs, and you would never call him disabled. They were truly the "Greatest Generation." They were the last of the old-time Americans that built this country.

When they got to Czechoslovakia, he said everyone including the Germans pretty much knew the war in Europe was over. Dad said they were on one ridge and the Germans were on another ridge. They were close enough to see each other clearly but no one was shooting. They just watched each other walk around.

After the German surrender, he said they didn't wait too long before they started shipping back to the United States. He said they were in Texas on trains when word reached them that the Japs were *going to surrender. He said no one ever officially told them that they were headed for Japan, but they knew they were. I thank God for the atomic bomb. Dad (and a great many others) may have not made it through the invasion of Japan. He was discharged in Texas, I think. That's all that I can remember currently. I wish that I could give better details, but Dad has been gone almost twenty-four years. If I can think of anything else, I will let you know. Keep me posted on your book.*

Your most humble and obedient servant,
Mark Hillis

James Earl Hillis, Cerisy-la-Forêt, July 27, 1944.

Hillis with German POWs, Normandy, 1944.

The 2nd Infantry Division MP Platoon had seen its share of casualties by this time. Private First Class James Pearson and Sergeant John Rentko were cited in General Order No. 92 for wounds sustained for the period June 9 through July 31, 1944. Furthermore, Lieutenant I. C. Meeth and Sergeant Jerry A. Sinkule were cited in General Order No. 95 for wounds they sustained in battle during the push through the Lower Normandy region. All four men were awarded the Purple Heart for their actions.

RESTRICTED

G.O. No. 92   Page 7   8 August 1944

   FLORES, MANUEL J.   39104046   Tec 5   20 June 1944 to 20 July 1944
   FRALIX, CHARLES B.   18013974   Tec 5   10 June 1944 to 5 August 1944
   FRANKLIN, R. C.   38073282   Tec 5   11 June 1944 to 26 July 1944
   FREY, ROBERT G.   33625060   Pfc   10 June 1944 to 5 August 1944
   GAUTHIER, LEON A.   31257143   Pfc   10 June 1944 to 26 July 1944
   GRAY, JOHN L.   01100123   1st Lt   21 June 1944 to 5 August 1944
   HANSEN, ORVILLE V.   37074063   Pfc   10 June 1944 to 26 July 1944
   HARVEY, NORMAN A.   36061723   Tec 5   11 June 1944 to 26 July 1944
   HARRISON, RICHARD D.   39036747   Pfc   17 July 1944 to 26 July 1944
   JONES, CARLTON C.   33190771   Pfc   10 June 1944 to 5 August 1944
   LEONARD, EDWARD J.   39611688   Pfc   10 June 1944 to 26 July 1944
   McINTOSH, STANLEY F.   39126399   Pfc   18 July 1944 to 21 July 1944
   McPHEE, ARCHIE L.   36180728   Pfc   10 June 1944 to 26 July 1944
   RICKERD, MARSHAL L., JR.   39340130   Pvt   7 June 1944 to 6 August 1944
   WHITTEN, JAMES W.   34657309   Pvt   1 July 1944 to 5 August 1944

2D MEDICAL BATTALION
The citations are as follows:

   GRIFFIN, WILLIAM R.   01689670   Capt   30 July 1944 to 6 August 1944
   HUBBELL, ORVILLE   39454870   Cpl   5 July 1944 to 6 August 1944
   MARLEY, HAROLD V.   01693803   Capt   1 August 1944 to 7 August 1944
   MAUERT, LLOYD A.   6951065   Sgt   10 June 1944 to 7 August 1944
   PILTER, WILLIE E.   18009509   Tec 4   5 July 1944 to 5 August 1944
   RYKACZEWSKI, FRANK C.   32215426   Tec 4   29 July 1944 to 5 August 1944
   SPRING, DAVID   01689819   Capt   1 August 1944 to 7 August 1944
   VAUGHN, JAMES E.   18005813   S Sgt   10 June 1944 to 7 August 1944
   WEAVER, JAMES G.   6366979   T Sgt   30 July 1944 to 6 August 1944
   ZAORSKI, THADDEUS J.   38366652   Pfc   29 July 1944 to 3 August 1944

HEADQUARTERS SPECIAL TROOPS, 2D INFANTRY DIVISION
The citation is as follows:

   BALDWIN, JOHN L.   35455382   T Sgt   22 June 1944 to 31 July 1944

2D RECONNAISSANCE TROOP
The citations are as follows:

   BLAIR, ERNEST S.   18011692   Sgt   9 June 1944 to 3 August 1944
   POOSHEE, SAMUEL J.   01030239   1st Lt   9 June 1944 to 3 August 1944
   HEFLEY, GENERAL P.   01030373   1st Lt   9 June 1944 to 3 August 1944
   MOORE, DAVID B.   18038486   Tec 4   9 June 1944 to 3 August 1944

MILITARY POLICE PLATOON, 2D INFANTRY DIVISION
The citations are as follows:

   PEARSON, JAMES B.   34370523   Pfc   9 June 1944 to 31 July 1944
   RENTKO, JOHN J.   35012755   S Sgt   9 June 1944 to 31 July 1944

2D SIGNAL COMPANY
The citations are as follows:

   BAIRD, CARROL A.   6289043   Sgt   8 June 1944 to 5 August 1944
   CARLSON, ROBERT J.   01633106   1st Lt   8 June 1944 to 5 August 1944

(Over)
RESTRICTED

General Order citing Private First Class James Pearson and Sergeant John Rentko as wounded in battle.

R E S T R I C T E D

G.O. No. 95   Page 14   15 August 1944

HINOJOSA, JUAN H., JR.	0370944	Capt	9 June 1944 to 5 August 1944
IESSICK, LAWRENCE	G950533	Tec 5	7 August 1944
NELSON, EVERETT J.	0363115	Capt	9 June 1944 to 5 August 1944
TOFT, RICHARD C.	33334592	Pfc	15 July 1944 to 10 August 1944

2D RECONNAISSANCE TROOP
The citations are as follows:

HEEG, EDGAR	35030496	Sgt	9 June 1944 to 13 August 1944
JOSEY, R. A.	18030305	Sgt	9 June 1944 to 13 August 1944
O'NEAL, STEVE	12042197	Tec 4	9 June 1944 to 13 August 1944

702D ORDNANCE LIGHT MAINTENANCE COMPANY
The citations are as follows:

DUNN, CARL D.	35208689	Tec 4	22 June 1944 to 23 July 1944
HOFFMANN, GEORGE D.	01552296	1st Lt	12 June 1944 to 12 August 1944
SCHOEN, JOHN	38421592	Pvt	22 June 1944 to 23 July 1944
VAHRENKAMP, HERBERT T.	18013036	T Sgt	22 June 1944 to 23 July 1944

2D SIGNAL COMPANY

The citations are as follows:

HARRIS, ROY B.	18029763	M Sgt	10 June 1944 to 10 August 1944
PROFFITT, STANLEY	6988356	Sgt	1 July 1944 to 10 August 1944
SLOAN, KENNETH J.	39167344	Tec 5	10 June 1944 to 10 August 1944
ZEVELOFF, HAROLD	32021738	T Sgt	10 June 1944 to 10 August 1944

MILITARY POLICE PLATOON 2D INFANTRY DIVISION
The citations are as follows:

MEETH, IRA C.	01293085	2d Lt	28 June 1944 to 6 August 1944
SINKULE, JERRY A.	18005765	Sgt	28 June 1944 to 6 August 1944

612TH TANK DESTROYER BATTALION
The citations are as follows:

BACHORSKI, GEORGE R.	16169691	Pvt	21 July 1944
BARNOSKI, JOHN	33356266	Pfc	11 July 1944
BATTLES, WOFFORD J.	38324735	Sgt	30 July 1944
BUTLER, EDWARD L.	20424628	Pvt	11 July 1944
CHRISTOPHER, ALBERT L.	37328174	Pvt	30 July 1944
DAVIS, CHESTER B.	35327315	Sgt	24 July 1944 to 30 July 1944
Di NINO, WILLIAM	33153680	Sgt	24 July 1944 to 30 July 1944
EARNEST, CLAUD M.	34501574	Pfc	11 July 1944
EASTHAM, JOHN	15114427	S Sgt	24 July 1944 to 30 July 1944
HALL, JOHN H.	33172164	S Sgt	26 June 1944 to 14 August 1944
JOHNSON, DESSIE	34578403	Pvt	11 July 1944
KENNEDY, EDMOND L.	37152781	Pfc	30 July 1944
MANN, CHARLES R.	01821890	1st Lt	16 June 1944 to 10 August 1944
MYERS, JOHN B.	0337357	Capt	25 June 1944 to 13 August 1944
O'MALLEY, ROBERT J.	35601336	Pfc	11 July 1944 to 10 August 1944

R E S T R I C T E D

General Order citing Lieutenant I. C. Meeth and Sergeant Jerry A. Sinkule as wounded in battle.

By the end of July 1944, the 2nd Infantry Division had taken Hill 192, Saint-Lô, Saint-Georges-d'Elle, and Saint-Jean-des-Baisants, and moved in the direction of Etouvy, Coulances, Vire, and finally Tinchebray. As the infantry moved forward, the fighting was vicious. The Germans stubbornly and aggressively defended every inch of ground.

Edwards (left) and Hillis (right) in the ruins of a building in Saint-Jean-des-Baisants, July 31, 1944.

2nd Infantry Division MP James Bundschuh examines a church bell felled from its steeple, Saint-Jean-des-Baisants, July 31, 1944.

By August 16, 1944, Tinchebray was in the hands of the 2nd Infantry Division and Normandy had finally been secured by Allied forces. During the first two weeks of August 1944, the MP Platoon processed 691 prisoners of war from the Normandy region, mostly as a result of the defeat of the Germans in Tinchebray.

6

The Brest Offensive

August–September 1944

On August 16, the 2nd Infantry Division was removed from the fighting for two days of rest prior to being attached to the VIII Army Corps. On August 18, the Division began to move west some two hundred miles to a new front in the Brittany Peninsula, where they would participate in the siege of the German-held port city of Brest. In less than a week, the 2nd, 8th, and 29th Divisions would surround the ancient walled fortress and engage the German forces of Brest in some of the heaviest fighting in Division history.

On August 15 the Morning Report indicated that Corporal John P. Sears suffered an accidental gunshot wound to his right leg near the town of Maisoncelles la Jourdan. During the same episode, Private John Sheehan was listed as receiving wounds in action against the enemy to his right arm and thigh. The next day, as the Division prepared to move toward Brest, Private Dalton Lester joined the MP Platoon by way of the 3rd Replacement Depot.

The entire 2nd Infantry Division left the vicinity of Maisoncelles la Jourdan on August 18 and traveled by convoy

217 miles westward, arriving in the town of Ploudaniel, France, the following day. The Division spent time in the small French villages of Ploudaniel, Kersaint-Plabennec, and Gousenou as they worked their way closer to the port at Brest. Appearing on the next two pages are copies of a portion of General Orders Nos. 92 and 95. Evident by the large number of names listed on each document, fighting was fiercely heavy during the months of June, July, and August and accounted for many 2nd Infantry Division soldiers being cited for meritorious actions against the enemy. These two pages represent what is likely a much larger collection of documents.

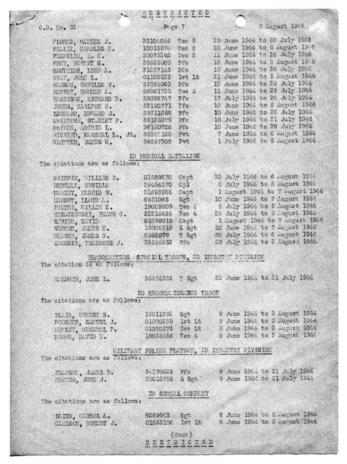

General Order No. 92; soldiers cited for medals, August 8, 1944.

RESTRICTED

G.O. No. 95   Page 14   15 August 1944

HINOJOSA, JUAN H., JR.   0370944   Capt   9 June 1944 to 5 August 1944
PESSICK, LAWRENCE   0950833   Tec 5   7 August 1944
NELSON, EVERETT J.   0363115   Capt   9 June 1944 to 5 August 1944
TOFT, RICHARD C.   33384592   Pfc   15 July 1944 to 10 August 1944

2D RECONNAISSANCE TROOP
The citations are as follows:

HEEG, EDGAR   35030496   Sgt   9 June 1944 to 13 August 1944
JOSEY, R. A.   18050305   Sgt   9 June 1944 to 13 August 1944
O'NEAL, STEVE   12042197   Tec 4   9 June 1944 to 13 August 1944

702D ORDNANCE LIGHT MAINTENANCE COMPANY
The citations are as follows:

DUNN, CARL D.   35206689   Tec 4   22 June 1944 to 23 July 1944
HOFFMANN, GEORGE D.   01552296   1st Lt   12 June 1944 to 12 August 1944
SCHOEN, JOHN   34421592   Pvt   22 June 1944 to 23 July 1944
WJHELNKTP, HERBERT T.   18013036   T Sgt   22 June 1944 to 23 July 1944

2D SIGNAL COMPANY
The citations are as follows:

HARRIS, ROY E.   18029783   M Sgt   10 June 1944 to 10 August 1944
PROFFITT, STANLEY   6986356   Sgt   1 July 1944 to 10 August 1944
SLOAN, KENNETH J.   39167344   Tec 5   10 June 1944 to 10 August 1944
ZEVELOFF, HAROLD   32021738   T Sgt   10 June 1944 to 10 August 1944

MILITARY POLICE PLATOON 2D INFANTRY DIVISION
The citations are as follows:

KEETH, IRA C.   01293085   2d Lt   28 June 1944 to 6 August 1944
SINKULE, JERRY A.   18009765   Sgt   26 June 1944 to 6 August 1944

612TH TANK DESTROYER BATTALION
The citations are as follows:

BACHORSKI, GEORGE R.   16169891   Pvt   21 July 1944
BARNOSKI, JOHN   33356286   Pfc   11 July 1944
BATTLES, WOFFORD J.   38324735   Sgt   30 July 1944
BUTLER, EDMUND L.   20424628   Pvt   11 July 1944
CHRISTOPHER, ALBERT L.   37326174   Pvt   30 July 1944
DAVIS, CHESTER E.   35327315   Sgt   24 July 1944 to 30 July 1944
Di NIDO, WILLIAM   33153680   Sgt   24 July 1944 to 30 July 1944
EARNEST, CLAUD E.   34601574   Pfc   11 July 1944
EASTMAN, JOHN   15114427   S Sgt   24 July 1944 to 30 July 1944
HALL, JOHN H.   33172164   S Sgt   26 June 1944 to 14 August 1944
JOHNSON, DESSIE   34578403   Pvt   11 July 1944
KENNEDY, EDMOND L.   37152781   Pfc   30 July 1944
MUTH, CHARLES R.   01621890   1st Lt   16 June 1944 to 10 August 1944
MYERS, JOHN R.   0337357   Capt   25 June 1944 to 13 August 1944
O'MALLEY, ROBERT J.   35501336   Pfc   11 July 1944 to 10 August 1944

RESTRICTED

General Order No. 95; soldiers cited for medals, August 15, 1944.

On the following pages are excerpts from one of the letters I received from George Swearingen in 2007. George wrote to me about the battle for Brest from his perspective. His view is somewhat different from what was officially recorded in the After Action Reports of the infantry units that engaged the Germans holed up in the fortress. However, as with any individual soldier's story, the recollection of these events was a personal journey back through time for him. This account is a treasured piece of a soldier's memory.

June 12, 2007
The Victory Bell Rang Loud

Dear James,

I heard the bell ringing loud and clear last night. I think in my sleep I found the answers to the question you are searching for. This is my story about our capture of Brest.

Brest, as you know, was a walled city. This goes back to Bible times, when most cities were walled in for protection. Brest is an ancient city. This wall goes all around the city. Where the earth and rock meet. There are big, heavy iron doors where the road entered the city. This was back years ago for protection.

The Germans used this walled city for their protection. Brest was the strongest seaport that they had. It was believed it could withstand all aggressions that could happen. Thus our army's leadership knew the only way to capture this city was to starve them out.

This method was used. We had very few casualties. This starving them out was a blessing for us. We could stay in the background and plan new strategy. It worked for us. The 2nd Division, the 8th, and the 29th Division had time to take a break, to regroup our troops, to plan our next drive. We were three months at Brest before they decided their only way to survive was to give it up and come out as prisoners of war. It was the easiest battle of all.

We had a few problems while at Brest. . . . On our first night at Brest I was asked to lead the guards to their post as I was the man that knew the roads that had been cleared. I led the way to the points in our sector that needed guards. I took Sergeant Higgins and his group on the area. . . . The map the sergeant was using showed a dirt road leading back to the campsite. The sergeant wanted to take this road back to our area. It would save about forty miles in road travel and hours time. The sergeant, a fifteen-year man, wanted to go back this way. I refused.

We argued. I could not convince him that we were not to use roads that had not been swept. He insisted. I told him I would go this *road only if I was given a direct order. His answer was, "I will give you a direct order. We go this road." We went this road.*

We had gone only a short distance. I saw a spot where the ground was different. I dodged this spot, but called his attention to it. He laughed at me. Then there were other spots. I pointed them out but would not drive over them. When we got back to camp, he said, "See there, nothing happened." I said, "It is not over yet, Sergeant, wait until tomorrow."

On to tomorrow. We made the same rounds. . . . There was a lieutenant from the mine sweepers, and a stack of mines. The sergeant asked where those mines came from. The lieutenant said, "Up that dirt road," and pointed to the road I had driven very carefully. The sergeant said, "We drove that road late yesterday." The lieutenant said, "You should thank your driver for dodging those spots."

The sergeant said, "George, I will never argue with you again."

Surrounding the city of Brest was a network of unpaved dirt roads that created perilous travel for Allied troops as they drove during the day—and not merely because there were mines. The Germans occupied Hills 90, 100, and 105, and had commanding views of the entire area. They opened fire with artillery and mortars on the roads whenever they observed dust clouds generated by jeeps, trucks, or tanks. In an effort to minimize the dust and provide for the safe movement of Allied vehicle traffic, a number of MPs decided to construct a sprinkler system out of a large water tank and hoses, which they could use to wet down the roads, thus preventing the dust clouds and saving lives.

Lieutenant Chet Meeth led the expedition to retrieve the water tank. George Swearingen, his usual driver, was replaced by Tec 4 Donald G. Wheelington. Swearingen's letter, which continues on the following page, recounts his memory of the event, recalling each detail with great clarity even after sixty-seven years.

...Now this brings me to an event that I think you will want to keep.

I have told you that the dust from this road was drawing artillery fire. A group of fellows wanted to go to this old sawmill and get a huge steel tank and make a sprinkler system to wet the roads down in our sector for our protection. This would be a good deal and possibly save some lives. I was asked to take my jeep to get this big tank, but I could not do it at the time. I had another project that I had to take care of.

They got our mechanic from the motor pool to go with them. When they got to the field road, they walked down the path to examine the tank. They thought it would do and went back for the jeep. They had also spotted some piping material for a sprinkler system.

Lieutenant Meeth led the way. Sergeant Meeker came about fifty yards [behind him]. Then the jeep, with one man following the jeep . . . Eddie Edwards brought up the rear.

The jeep ran over a mine. It was thought to be a depth charge. It had been out there so long the weed and grass hid the signs. It went off . . . the driver was killed instantly, and all the others were hit and wounded. Some were hurt bad.

They were trying to do something to help others. The man that was following the jeep was hurt bad. He died on the way to the hospital. Edwards was sent to the hospital along with Lieutenant Meeth, Sergeant Meeker.

Later the water tank was retrieved and the roads were wet down.

These people were trying to save lives, but needed more know-how.

The battle for Brest was soon over. General Patton made his drive across France. The German drive had bogged down. Many POWs were taken. Our army was bringing in fresh troops.

The improvised explosive device that caused such destruction was later determined to be an anti-ship or submarine mine or depth charge. Lieutenant Meeth was most seriously wounded, with shrapnel lodged in his neck. In my research I discovered the fifth man (whom George described as the motor pool mechanic) was Sergeant Jerry Sinkule, who was the noncommissioned officer in charge of the MP motor pool.

This photo is from George Swearingen's collection. Oddly enough there is no official record of a Sergeant Meeker in the Morning Reports of the MP Platoon. The back of this photo identifies the man only as Meeker.

Angelo Lochetto and Rocco Festa, somewhere in France, August 1944.

*1st Lieutenant Edward L. Jarczynski, outside the Ivanhoe prisoner of war enclosure
near Ploudaniel, France, 1944.*

2nd Infantry Division MP James Pearson having a smoke in Kersaint-Plabennec, France, August 23, 1944.

The 2nd Infantry Division arrived in Gouesnou, about five miles north of Brest, in late August 1944. This area was shared between the 2nd and the 8th Infantry Divisions. Gates Church, in Gouesnou, was the scene of a horrific war crime committed by the Germans against French citizens of the town. German naval personnel entering the town indiscriminately killed a number of unarmed civilians at this church in an incident later known as the Penguerec Massacre.

Gates Church, Gouesnou, France, August 28, 1944. (Photo by James Edwards.)

MPs Herring, Davidson, and Edwards (left to right) outside Gates Church in Gouesnou, France, August 28, 1944.

On September 14, the MP Platoon recorded its second loss of the month when Private First Class Joe T. Silveria was killed by artillery as he drove to Le Havre, France, for an unknown purpose.

After the German commander Colonel Erich Pietzonka finally surrendered on September 18 to Major General Walter M. Robertson of the 2nd Infantry Division, the MP Platoon secured the remainder of the prisoners from Brest in a prisoner of war enclosure one mile south of Landernau, France.

An unidentified 2nd Infantry Division MP near Brest, France, September 1944.

Another 3,313 Germans were captured from August 21 to August 31 as a result of the heavy fighting in the Brittany region of Brest. Of the 37,282 German prisoners taken captive during the Brest campaign, approximately eleven thousand were captured by the 2nd Infantry Division.

MP Paul Porter kneels beside the graves of German soldiers, Guipavas (near Brest), France, September 8, 1944.

In the foreground, two armed 2nd Infantry Division MPs escort two German officers and a German Red Cross worker who is holding a small cat. In the background are additional Germans escorted by other MPs and closely watched by the armed American soldiers at the rear of the column.

The two MPs in the foreground of the photo above are from the MP Platoon of the 2nd Infantry Division. The MP leading the way appears to be armed with an M-1 Garand rifle, a weapon normally carried by the infantry. The other MP is armed with what looks very much like an M3A1 Grease Gun, or perhaps a Thompson SMG. This is unusual because the MPs typically carried either the M-1 carbine or the M-1911 pistol, as these were their official weapons of issue.

I found the original of this photo among many other photos, documents, and personal items that belonged to my father. The same photo also appears in the *Combat History of the Second Infantry Division in World War II*, which was originally published in 1946. Although my father did not leave any clues as to the exact location where this photo was taken, the caption listed with the photo in that book states it was taken during the push to seize Brest.

Brest Picture of Ruin

Nazis Swarm From Sub Pens To Surrender

By Barbara Wace

BREST, SEPT. 18.—(Delayed)—(*P*)— A few French civilians trudged back into captured Brest today, pushing wheelbarrows piled with mattresses or riding in carts. But there was nothing to come back to in this great port city, a picture of desolation and ruin with a majority of its buildings demolished by terrific aerial and naval bombardment during the Allied siege.

Lt. Gen. Hermann Ramcke, commander of the crack German paratroopers who had been holding the port, left to his subordinates the formality of surrender.

German prisoners interviewed as they walked through the streets, said Ramcke had not been seen for several days. There were reports he had fled either by submarine or plane, and one stocky paratrooper said "he is probably in South America now—it does not matter to us here."

Brest fell at 3 p. m. after a final 24 hours of terrible artillery bombardment. Swarms of Nazis—naval personnel, paratroopers and merchant men—began emerging from the famed submarine pens.

"THERE are thousands of them in there," said one U. S. lieutenant. "I don't know how we can cope with them. They're all coming out with their suitcases—ready to go."

At the entrance to the pens was a large blue shield with the words "Torpedo Commando 1942" on it, probably the insignia of one of the submarines which had nested here after raids on Allied shipping.

We moved into one pen, past rooms filled with scattered German belongings. The narrow pen opened into the bay (30 words censored) Like the others, this pen had a 15-foot reinforced concrete roof. There was a gaping hole in the roof, however, with steel girders hanging down.

One Nazi said the damage had been caused by a British raid in June.

A sixty-seven-year-old newspaper clipping detailing the Germans' surrender of Brest.

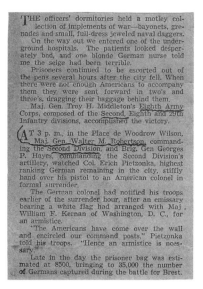

THE officers' dormitories held a motley collection of implements of war—bayonets, grenades and small, full-dress jeweled naval daggers.

On the way out we entered one of the underground hospitals. The patients looked desperately bad, and one blonde German nurse told me the selge had been terrible.

Prisoners continued to be escorted out of the pens several hours after the city fell. When there were not enough Americans to accompany them they were sent forward in two's and three's, dragging their baggage behind them.

Maj. Gen. Troy H. Middleton's Eighth Army Corps, composed of the Second, Eighth and 29th Infantry divisions, accomplished the victory.

AT 3 p. m., in the Place de Woodrow Wilson, Maj. Gen. Walter M. Robertson, commanding the Second Division, and Brig. Gen Georges P. Hayes, commanding the Second Division's artillery, watched Col. Erich Pietzonka, highest ranking German remaining in the city, stiffly hand over his pistol to an American colonel in formal surrender.

The German colonel had notified his troops earlier of the surrender hour, after an emissary bearing a white flag had arranged with Maj, William F. Kernan of Washington, D. C., for an armistice.

"The Americans have come over the wall and encircled our command posts," Pietzonka told his troops. "Hence an armistice is neessary."

Late in the day the prisoner bag was estimated at 8500, bringing to 35,000 the number of Germans captured during the battle for Brest.

A sixty-seven-year-old newspaper clipping detailing the Germans' surrender of Brest.

An officer of the 2nd Infantry Division stands in the ruins of a building in Brest holding a pair of binoculars. (From the North photo collection.)

Much of the city of Brest was demolished by the repeated bombardments of the 2nd, 8th, and 29th Infantry Divisions artillery units. Strangely enough, the sign in the photo above stands erect amidst the rubble. Not much was left of this once large city due to the Allied forces' efforts to shake the Germans from their underground hiding places.

After Brest fell, the 2nd Infantry Division took a period of rest from September 19 through September 26. Bivouacked in an area between the towns of Guipavas and Landerneau, they repaired vehicles and other equipment. This was the first opportunity since D-Day that the men of the Division were able to remove their steel helmets and use lighting at night. A blackout after sunset had been imposed since the Division left New York Harbor on October 7, 1943. In mid-September 1944, with the majority of France now in the hands of the Allied forces, the 2nd Infantry Division would travel 683 miles across France to join the Rhineland Campaign that was already under way. Leaving Brest, they headed east, passing through the small French villages of Guipavas and Landerneau as they went.

Major North, Guipavas, France, September 22, 1944.

1st Lieutenant Henry S. Kurowski, Guipavas, France, September 22, 1944.

Major North, Landerneau, France, September 25, 1944.

Lieutenant Meeth, Landerneau, France, September 25, 1944.

Corporal Willie Wilson, Landerneau, France, September 25, 1944.

Foreground, left to right: MPs Smith, Welch, and Vogel, Landerneau, France, September 25, 1944.

7

St. Vith and Wirtzfeld, Belgium

September 15, 1944–December 15, 1944

On September 27, the entire 2nd Infantry Division departed Landerneau, France, and moved by motor convoy and railcar through recently liberated northern France. Since every man in the MP Platoon had been assigned a jeep, motorcycle, truck, or other wheeled vehicle, it is likely that the MP Platoon utilized this equipment to travel from Guipavas through Rennes, Chateunef (just north of Paris), and Saint Quentin, France. They finally arrived at St. Vith, Belgium, on September 30, 1944, at 1900 hours. According to the Morning Reports, the total distance they traveled was 683 miles.

Four days later, the MP Platoon left their bivouac area in St. Vith, probably due to a shortage of available quarters, and moved to an open field two and a half miles west of the town. Based on available photographs of the area, it appears that the majority of the enlisted men were forced to pitch their tents over foxholes for protection from potential German mortar and artillery attacks.

Corporal James Pearson at the MP camp near St. Vith, Belgium, October 1, 1944.

Although there was still a chance of German counterattacks, many of the men of the MP Platoon were able to relax a little after army intelligence indicated that the threat from any offensive by the German Army was minimal. It was actually during this time that Hitler was planning his Ardennes Offensive, which he would launch on December 16, 1944, surprising the Allied Intelligence Corps.

During this lapse in combat action, however, the MPs were able to take a breather and relax whenever their duties did not require them to man a traffic post or undertake some other police action. After arriving in Belgium, the 2nd Infantry Division, functioning as rear units since the capture of Brest, had a good amount of spare time on their hands. Many of the MPs took advantage of this time to take photos with their buddies, hamming it up for the cameras.

MP Randall Cathron and Lady near St. Vith, Belgium, October 2, 1944.

MP Paul Porter and Lady near St. Vith, Belgium, October 2, 1944.

Corporal James Earl Hillis, St. Vith, Belgium, October 6, 1944.

Private First Class James Edwards, St. Vith, Belgium, October 6, 1944.

Private First Class Warren B. Ross, St. Vith, Belgium, October 6, 1944.

MP James Southall, St. Vith, Belgium, October 9, 1944.

MPs Conaway and Accetone, St. Vith, Belgium, October 9, 1944.

Sergeant Jerry Sinkule behind the MP command post in St. Vith, October 9, 1944.

From left, MPs Sinkule, Nelson, McMahan, Hillis, Davidson, Herring, and Edwards enjoy some downtime near St. Vith.

Mark Hillis, the son of James Earl Hillis, provided the above photo to me from his father's collection. His father identified each of the MPs in that photo in his own handwriting. I would later discover the same photo among my father's photos and documents as well. The MPs are having a beer party, compliments of Division Headquarters. The vehicle Edwards is sitting on is an early model Volkswagen Beetle.

Stationed at St. Vith, Belgium, for more than two months, the MPs took every opportunity to relax and enjoy the calm before the storm. By the middle of December, their lives would be changed dramatically as they participated in one of the greatest land battles during World War II. All of these men and many more would play a vital role in this historical military event.

According to the Morning Reports from October 30, Privates Linus Gittemeier and Angelo Watznauer were promoted to the rank of private first class. Two months later, Gittemeier would lose a leg at Camp Elsenborn, and Watznauer would pay the ultimate price by giving his life for freedom's cause on German soil in February 1945.

On October 31, 2nd Lieutenant I. C. Meeth was promoted to 1st Lieutenant per Special Order No. 295, HQ First US Army. At the end of October, the MP Platoon was authorized as an over-strength unit (a unit possessing more troops than they were officially allowed to have) when Privates Wahal, Ballwahn, Quail, Waldron, and Cather joined the platoon from the 23rd Infantry Regiment. That same day, Privates Wallace and Goldstein joined the platoon from the 9th Infantry Regiment, bringing the unit strength to 105 enlisted men and officers.

While the 2nd Infantry Division command post was established in St. Vith, Belgium, General Robertson and his staff devised a plan of attack to assault the German stronghold at Wahlerscheid, Germany, through the Monschau Forest. This offensive was necessary to secure the Roer River dams to prevent the Germans from destroying them, which would have delayed the Allied forces in crossing the river.

During this period, the MP Platoon was responsible for the security of rear areas and roads, guarding prisoners, conducting foot and jeep patrols, marking roads with division signs, and returning lost soldiers to their units. Furthermore, the MPs provided around-the-clock security for Generals Eisenhower, Bradley, Robertson, Middleton, and Patton, and British Army General Montgomery while they were in the 2nd Infantry Division sector.

In the first half of October 1944, the Division Headquarters was relocated from their camp two and a half miles west of the town of St. Vith to the dense Belgian forest east of the city. By mid-October, as the temperatures began to drop and the heavy rains turned the forest and surrounding area into a sea of mud, the Division moved back into St. Vith. There they utilized every available building for Division Headquarters personnel.

On October 24, while the MP Platoon was stationed in St. Vith, MPs Luther Lawrence, Randy Cathron, McNamara, George McConnell, George Conner, and Martin Davern were sent to the division clearing station to be treated for undisclosed illnesses. While they were en route, the truck they were riding in hit a slick spot on the road that was later believed to be a patch of ice. The driver of the truck, Private Warren Ross, lost control and the truck overturned, ejecting the MPs who were riding in the back onto the road. Lawrence, Cathron, and McNamara were sent to the 107th Evacuation Hospital for treatment of their injuries. The following day, Private First Class Luther A. Lawrence became the third fatal casualty of war for the 2nd Infantry Division MP Platoon when he died of his injuries.

The roads became increasingly dangerous at this time of year, when the threat of enemy activity was compounded by hazardous weather conditions. Private First Class James Edwards lost his jeep (serial number 2082774-S) when it was destroyed on a trip to Luxembourg in late October. He was soon issued a replacement, jeep 2082774-S, MP-5, which appears in the following photo.

James Edwards in his new jeep on a muddy road in late October 1944. Edwards's face and distinguishing characteristics have been removed by the army censors. The new jeep has not yet been inscribed with his wife's name.

The MPs would remain stationed at St. Vith through November and early December.

Sergeant Sinkule, James Earl Hillis, and Warren B. Ross in St. Vith, Belgium, November 8, 1944.

MP Roger Gilmore, St. Vith, Belgium, November 1944.

While on patrol in his jeep in early December, Dad stopped at a road junction and took a photo that captures the high level of alert the 2nd Infantry Division maintained during this time. The MPs had placed a sign on the pole warning drivers not to use their headlights at night.

On the highway from Liège to Verviers, Belgium, December 3, 1944. The sign on the right side of the photo reads All Vehicle Headlights Out, Cats Eyes Only.

Although the route has changed much over the last sixty-seven years, in my estimation this road junction is in the vicinity of the town of Mazures, Belgium, where highways N666 and N61 meet today. This view is looking north toward Pepinster, Belgium. The railroad tracks run east and west, connecting the cities of Liège and Verviers. Identified now as Highway N61, this route would have been the most direct connection to the two large supply depots of the US Army at that time.

A 2nd Infantry Division Engineer makes repairs on the highway from Liège to Verviers, Belgium, December 3, 1944.

From October 4 through December 11, the 2nd Infantry Division had established a 3,400-yard front along the Siegfried Line—the Belgian-German border in the Ardennes Forest. They dug in and fortified their positions in preparation for the attacks on German ground at Wahlerscheid. By December 12, the 2nd Infantry Division had relinquished its sector to the 106th Infantry Division and moved to the vicinity of Elsenborn, Belgium, in preparation for the attack toward the Roer River.

As of December 16, 1944, the US First Army Command—including the 2nd Infantry Division—was deployed north of the Belgian Ardennes region, a heavily forested area with many hills and ridges. To their rear lay the cities of Liège, Verviers, and Spa, and the massive supply installations built up through the autumn to support the advance toward the Rhine. At Spa, the First Army established its command post surrounded on every side by service installations, supply dumps, and depots. Liège, twenty miles northwest of Spa, was one of the largest American supply centers on the European continent. Verviers, an important and densely stocked railhead, lay eleven miles directly north of Spa.

Buzz bombs, also known as V-1 rockets, had been used only sporadically by the Germans against the 2nd Infantry Division previously. Their use in late 1944, however, increased dramatically and targeted the Division rear areas as German Field Marshal Gerd Von Rundstedt unleashed his great winter offensive on the American lines. Buzz bombs and V-2 rockets were not particularly accurate and accounted for very little material damage. Although more than twenty of these so-called "vengeance weapons" were launched at Liège, they were responsible for little more than a few anxious moments. Their erratic behavior often sent them spiraling out of control, and they caused few deaths on the ground.

Liège, Belgium. On the back of this photo is a simple message describing the method in which this home was destroyed: Buzz Bomb Damage.

St. Vith, Belgium, December 10, 1944. On the back of this photo is written: One of the many buildings the 2nd Division stayed in while in St. Vith.

The building in the photo above housed the 2nd Infantry Division Headquarters, Division Artillery, Provost Marshal, and the MP Platoon. After the muddy landscape the Division had occupied previously east of St. Vith in the dense Belgian forest, the move back into town was a welcome change. These accommodations were thought luxurious to some degree, as the quarters had running water and heat that was provided by steam radiators. As evidenced by the light snow that had collected on the roof of the building above, the weather was growing colder. Only a few days later, the entire region would transform into a winter wonderland.

Two days later, on December 12, the MP Platoon left St. Vith and traveled via truck a distance of fourteen miles to their new command post located in the small town of Wirtzfeld, Belgium. The Division command staff, the MP Provost Marshal, the Division Artillery personnel, and other units moved to Wirtzfeld as well. In a small farmhouse on the southern fringe of this tiny town, Major General Walter M. Robertson and his staff, including Headquarters Commandant Lieutenant Colonel Matt F. C. Konop, Commander of the Division Special Troops, and MP Provost Marshal Major William North, established their headquarters. Here they would have a better view of the entire area.

In less than a week, however, the 2nd Infantry Division would be forced to give up this tiny town to the advancing German Army and fall back to defensive positions to the north along the Elsenborn Ridge. This seemingly insignificant town and its small road network would play a deciding role in the outcome of World War II and the ultimate failure of the German Army to capture Liège and the Allied supplies it badly needed that were stored in that city.

An unidentified MP walks along a wooden sidewalk, probably toward his bivouac area, Wirtzfeld, Belgium, December 15, 1944. That same day or very early the next morning, the rain would turn into heavy snow and continue for several weeks.

Major North and Lieutenant Meeth, Wirtzfeld, Belgium, December 15, 1944.

Lieutenant Stephan Kovalyak, on detached service to the MP Platoon from the 38th Infantry, December 15, 1944.

The Wahlerscheid Offensive, also known as the Battle of Heartbreak Crossroads, was a costly four-day battle fought in freezing weather. Infantrymen of the 2nd Division ate, slept, and fought in temperatures well below zero degrees. The men of the 9th and 38th Infantry Regiments spearheaded their attack through the dense Monschau Forest toward their objective of heavily fortified German pillboxes. As they did so, they had to endure knee-deep snow and frostbitten fingers and toes while laden with heavy weapons and gear. As they pressed on, the thawing snow from tree branches overhead fell upon the troops, soaking them to the skin.

As night fell after the first day of battle, the temperatures dove from just above zero to thirty degrees below. Lacking blankets and dry clothes, the troops had to sleep in ditches or on the ground, to which their clothing froze. Due to the severe weather conditions, many of the infantry suffered trench foot and frostbite caused by their constantly wet feet and the freezing temperatures. Enduring these incredibly difficult hardships, the determined 9th Infantry breeched the concrete pillboxes of the Siegfried Line in the Wahlerscheid region of Germany and eliminated the German defenses in their sector within three days.

Acting swiftly to exploit this advantage, General Robertson ordered the 38th Infantry Regiment to proceed through the 9th Infantry lines toward its objective—Dreiborn, Germany—on December 16. Unaware that a German counterattack was already under way, the 2nd Infantry Division commander, General Robertson, prepared to move forward. He hoped to use the previous victory as an opportunity to seize the roads to Hofen, Monschau, Dreiborn, and Schleiden.

Although it was a well-deserved moment of triumph for the Allied soldiers who suffered from freezing temperatures, sleepless nights, cold food, and many casualties, their victory at Wahlerscheid would turn out to be shortlived. General Robertson was soon made aware of the situation unfolding around him. As the Germans advanced through the Ardennes region and into Belgium, he would receive orders to withdraw to a defensive position and support the holding of the small network of villages to the south.

The small sign on the building directly above this MP shows the directions to Wirtzfeld to the left or Murringen to the right. Bullingen, Belgium, December 15, 1944.

On December 15, Lieutenant Stephen Kovalyak was placed on detached service from the 38th Infantry Regiment and joined the MP Platoon when it arrived in Wirtzfeld. On December 16, the MP Platoon received a transfer when Private Lawrence B. Moore joined the platoon from the 9th Infantry where he had been assigned to a rifle company. Prior to the German thrust reaching the 2nd Infantry Division Command Post, Robert Whitney and James Moore were sent to a rear medical clearing station as nonbattle casualties. By December 22, both Whitney and Moore would be sent to the 2nd Evacuation Hospital for further treatment.

Richard Nelsion, Lieutenant Kovalyak, and Kruger, Bullingen, Belgium, December 15, 1944. This photo was taken the day before the German Ardennes Offensive began.

8

The Ardennes Offensive and the Battle of the Bulge

December 16, 1944–January 31, 1945

Still in Wirtzfeld and evidently completely unaware that the German Ardennes Offensive had already begun, James Edwards spent the evening of December 16 writing his wife, Aleta, a five-page letter, which appears on the following pages. By early the next morning, Edwards and the rest of the Division would be pressed into action to thwart the German drive to capture the great Allied supplies depots at Liège and then at Antwerp, Belgium.

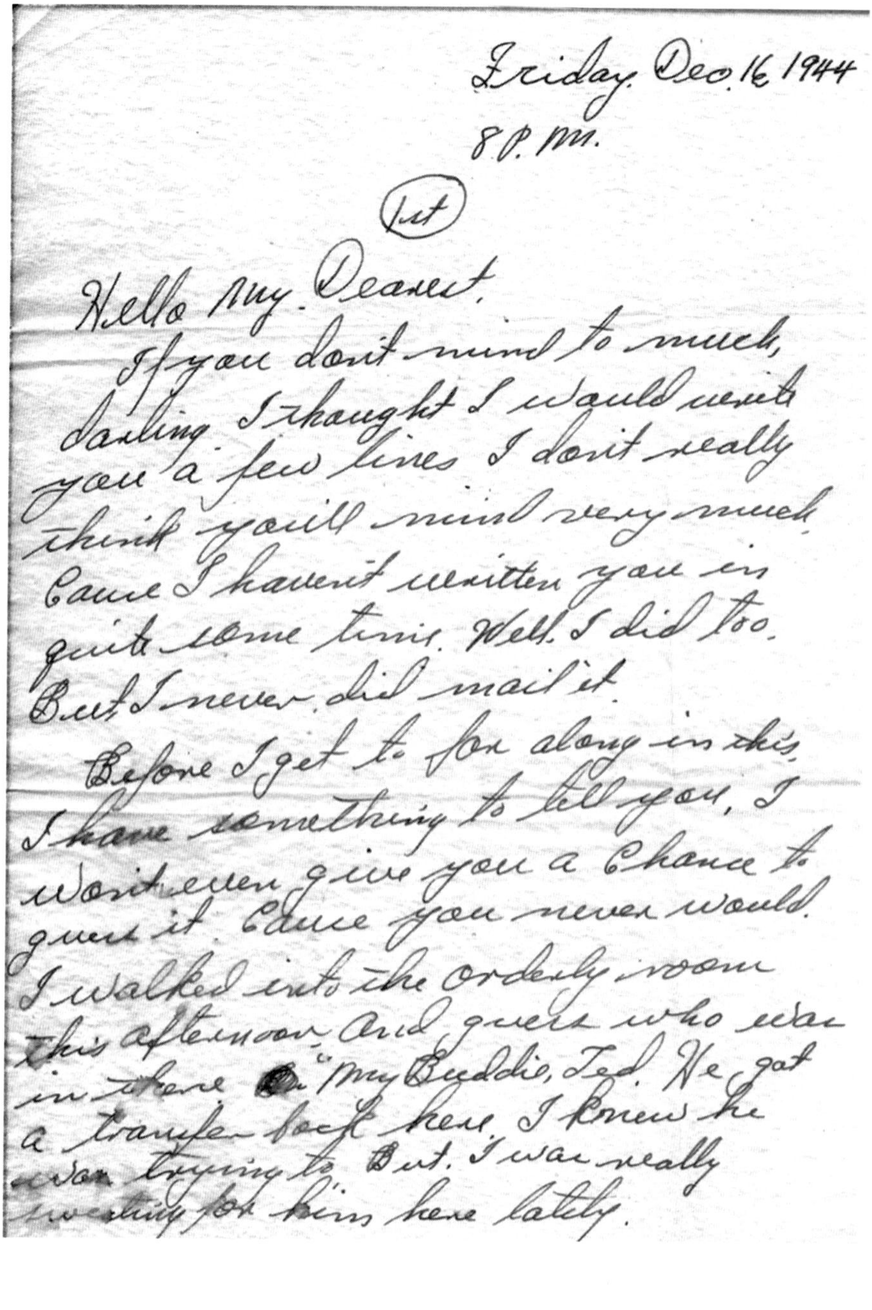

Friday. Dec. 16 1944
8 P. M.

(1st)

Hello My Dearest,

If you don't mind to much,
darling I thought I would write
you a few lines I don't really
think you'll mind very much
cause I haven't written you in
quite some time. Well. I did too.
But I never did mail it.

Before I get to far along in this,
I have something to tell you, I
won't even give you a chance to
guess it Cause you never would.
I walked into the orderly room
this afternoon And guess who was
in there "My Buddie, Ted. He got
a transfer back here, I knew he
was trying to. But. I was really
wishing for him here lately.

2nd

Darling, I'm sending you a few pictures, of some of the boys in the org. I'm in a couple of them. But they aren't very good. And speaking of pictures, honey, I got one from you the other day. And I don't like it. Do you know why I don't like it?? Well I'll tell you, it looks real tacky. All because of the way you have your hair done up. Don't be angry with me, sweetheart. I don't mean to hurt your feelings.

I got a letter yesterday from you, dear. And I wouldn't take anything for what I got out of it. It was written the 10th of Nov. Now do you know what I'm speaking of? If I had been in the soldiers place. I couldn't even have said, "Gee Hi." No kidding, darling. Thats the best thing I've seen, since I last saw you. You're still as beautiful as you ever were. But, I'm jealous as hell of the soldier, The lucky dog. Standing two ft. from my wife, and I'm three thousand miles away,

3rd.

I like that picture so well I pinned it up by my bed. So I can see it real often. I like the way you have your hair in that picture too. If in the large picture you're sending me, you have your hair fixed like the snap shot, you may as well get ready for a spanking when I come home, honey. (And I don't mean put a pillow in your pants)

Honey, "Snuffy" is in the hosp, in the States. And Roy is in Eng, Ted got a letter from Roy a few days ago. And some of the boys got one from "Snuffy."

I saw Marlene Dietrich here a few days ago. What a hag. If you ever get to the point, that you're that ugly, I'll divorce you. She had some swell fellows with her show tho. One of them went to the supply and got me a suit of O.D's. That I couldn't have

4th,

got for a month if I had put in through the supply.

They came in our room one night and we set up till nearly midnight listening to them. I laughed tell I nearly busted.

Darling, I got a package from "Mom" the other day. I don't have time to write her right now so you "Thank" her for me. And tell her I really enjoyed it all especially the fruit Cake. And tell her I also said "Hello."

I made quite a long trip yesterday and I have an Idea I was pretty close to Dennis. If it hadn't of been so Cold and the roads so bad. I would have went a little further and seen him. By the way dear. I've had two letters from Sam. Both from France. I have an Idea. That his in the 8.7th Army some where.

On the first page of the letter, James Edwards makes reference to his buddy, "Ted," who had returned to the platoon. In reviewing the Morning Reports I found that Ted Foster returned to the MP Platoon on December 10, 1944, after a short stint with the 9th Infantry as a rifleman. At that time, the 2nd Infantry Division received many replacements and there were several such references in Dad's letters about his friends coming and going from the MP Platoon. According to the same Morning Report, MPs Warren Ross and Warren Parker were promoted to the rank of private first class by 2nd Division General Order No. 48.

On the fifth page of Edwards's letter, he makes reference to "Dennis," who was Aleta's oldest brother. My uncle Dennis was a rifleman with Company K of the 334th Infantry Regiment of the 84th Division. Dennis McWilliams had been seriously wounded during the battle for Geilenkirchen, Germany, while assaulting the Siegfried Line on November 19, 1944, a quarter mile west of Immendorf.

Dennis was originally captured by German search parties who were looking for their wounded. As the Allies overran the area, the German doctor and his staff who had saved Dennis's life surrendered to him four days later on Thanksgiving Day as American soldiers took the town around them. Based on the statements in the letter, Edwards was on an assignment that brought him close to the evacuation hospital where Dennis was being treated. Due to the weather, however, he was forced to turn back before he could locate Dennis. Dennis McWilliams survived and returned home aboard the High Speed Transport ship APD-29 USS *Barry*. Once home, he raised two sons, Barry and David.

Private Dennis McWilliams, Company K, 84th Infantry Division. This photo was taken at Camp Howze, Texas, in July 1944.

By the morning of December 16, intelligence reports had started streaming into regimental and battalion command posts, announcing that a major German counterattack was imminent along the 2nd Infantry Division lines. Concerned that the 9th and 38th Infantry Regiments—now deep inside Germany at Wahlerscheid—would be cut off by advancing German forces, General Robertson requested permission from 5th US Army Corps Headquarters the night of December 16 to withdraw toward Camp Elsenborn. The 5th US Army Corps commander, Major General Leonard Gerow, delayed his decision to grant Robertson's request pending approval from General Courtney Hodges, 1st Army commander.

Based on earlier reports from army intelligence units, the Allies believed that the German activity was simply spoiling attacks, not a major counteroffensive, in which the Germans would push to regain territory in Belgium. This bloody struggle would later be known as the Battle of the Bulge.

However, with increased signs of significant German armor movements and heavy artillery shelling, and a loss of communication with some advanced units near the Belgian-German border, General Gerow finally agreed shortly after midnight on December 17 to allow Robertson to withdraw those units. Immediately, General Robertson ordered all forward units to fall back to the Division Headquarters at Wirtzfeld. Early in the morning on December 17, battalion commanders were hurriedly summoned to their command posts, where they were notified of the situation developing to the east of Krinkelt-Rocherath, Belgium, and the Lausdell Crossroads.

At this point, the majority of the 9th and 38th Infantry Regiments and their attached units were well in front of the Division Command Post—with the exception of the 2nd Battalion of the 23rd Infantry Regiment held in reserve. Thus the majority of the Division was in serious danger of being isolated from the rest of the army by the Germans approaching Wirtzfeld from Bullingen to the south and from the Lausdell Crossroads at Krinkelt. Because there were not enough troops to properly defend the Division Command Post at Wirtzfeld, the German forces were in a position to cut off or capture the 2nd and 99th Divisions—perhaps as many as thirty thousand men and their equipment.

At sunrise on the morning of December 17, German armor rolled into the town of Bullingen, where the 2nd Quartermaster Company command post was located. Although they were completely outnumbered by the men and armor of the German army, the 2nd Quartermaster Company, a portion of the 2nd Signal Company, and a company of 2nd Engineers resisted for three days until their supplies of food and ammunition were exhausted and they were overrun and captured. The Morning Reports for the MP Platoon dated December 20, 1944 reveal that Private Fred J. Marlow, the quartermaster for the MP Platoon, was listed as MIA when he was captured by the Germans as they took control of Bullingen.

At approximately 0700 hours on December 17, General Robertson made an urgent phone call to his Division Command Post in Wirtzfeld. In a near-agitated voice, General Robertson alerted Lieutenant Colonel Matt F. C. Konop, Headquarters Commandant, to assemble a defensive force and form a line on the southern fringe of Wirtzfeld in front of the command post. Alerting the headquarters units under his command by phone, Konop gave orders for the cooks, clerks, orderlies, jeep drivers, telephone and radio operators, and messengers of the Second Signal Company—along with all other able-bodied men—to take up defensive positions to counter the German thrust south of town. Additionally, Lieutenant Colonel Konop instructed Major William North, Provost Marshal of the MP Platoon, to have every available MP take up defensive positions on the Bullingen Road south of the command post as well.

Corporal J. R. Cantrell was on duty and in charge of quarters that morning in the MP command post, and was quickly alerted to the German advance. In a conversation I had with Mr. Cantrell, he informed me that my father, Private First Class James Edwards, was on duty with him that morning. Cantrell further stated, "I could hear German guns firing behind our position. At least one artillery round struck the second floor of a nearby building, which caused the sleeping MPs on the second floor of our quarters to scramble downstairs."

Well aware of the urgency of protecting the Division Command Post, MPs J. R. Cantrell, James Edwards, George Swearingen, James Earl Hillis, and Paul Porter, along with a large number of other MPs, responded by arming themselves with every available weapon. They took up defensive positions one hundred yards south of Wirtzfeld along the road from Bullingen. This impressive little defensive force assembled a battery of 105mm and 155mm howitzers, 57mm antitank guns, four half-track armored vehicles equipped with quad .50-caliber machine guns, and men armed with bazookas. In spite of this, they should have been no match for the determined armored thrust of Kampfgruppe Peiper—the German combat unit under command of Joachim Peiper, which had a task force of thirty tanks—and a battalion of armored infantry of the 1st SS Panzer Division.

Shortly after 0800 hours, the fears of the 2nd Infantry Division commanders materialized. At least five German Panther tanks and several half-track personnel carriers loaded with infantry appeared out of the fog on Bullingen road. At the top of the hill where it crossed the ridgeline eight hundred to one thousand yards south of Wirtzfeld, large German armored vehicles moved down the road toward the command post.

Fearing imminent attacks by the Panther tanks, which would have easily wiped out the small defensive force, the entire group of headquarters personnel opened fire first with their carbines and other small arms, antitank weapons, and the available battery of howitzers. A battle ensued between the two determined foes. Within moments of the headquarters personnel's initial response to the German tanks, five American tank destroyers of the attached 644th Tank Destroyer Battalion and the 2nd Battalion of the 23rd Infantry, which had been held in reserve, arrived at the battle. They quickly knocked out four of the five Panthers and one half-track vehicle. The remainder of the German units turned and withdrew over the hill.

In 2008, I asked J. R. Cantrell if he was able to share his memory of that day with me. After an emotional pause, this is what he said:

"I was in charge of quarters on the 17th [of December]. I only remember seeing ten tanks, and we knocked out one. There was also a half-track that was knocked out by our antitank guns, which were stationed at the T in the road ahead of the tanks. The other tanks turned and went back over the hill. I saw one man jump off the half-track with no legs. The whole MP Platoon was there, including your father. I remember that same night our quartermaster [Fred Marlow] was captured when the Germans took the town of Bullingen. The 2nd Division Headquarters was also at Wirtzfeld. There could have been as many as thirty tanks that morning, but I only remember seeing ten."

On pages 94 and 95 of the Infantry Division history book, *Combat History of the Second Infantry Division in World War II*, historical accounts describe this battle very much the same way as J. R. Cantrell remembered:

"Division Artillery Headquarters received word at 0640 on December 17 that 30 tanks and a battalion of armored infantry were attacking in the vicinity of Murringen and Bullingen. Having already instructed his forward combat arms, General Robertson took personal charge of organization of Division Headquarters and headquarters company for defense. He took clerks, MPs, orderlies, and cooks from headquarters group to establish an all-around defense of his command post against the armored spearheads thrusting at lines in Wirtzfeld. These troops, armed with carbines and antitank guns, took their stand there in the snow of this cold and bloody front and held firmly as the enemy surged forward and broke against the stubborn tenacity with which these men defended their line. These troops knocked out a tank and an armored car. Supporting tank destroyers and artillery accounted for others. A defensive line was established about 100 yards south of the Division Artillery command post [at Wirtzfeld] and into this line went the available men from the rear echelon."

Although the initial battle with the Germans lasted only fifteen minutes, over the course of a four-hour period the German armor and their supporting infantry viciously assaulted the defensive positions of various 2nd Infantry Division units in and around the Krinkelt-Wirtzfeld-Rocherath area. However, before noon on December 17, the 2nd Infantry Division had the situation temporarily under control. The German thrust had suffered staggering losses from division artillery that day and withdrew to Bullingen. For the majority of the men of the 2nd Infantry Division MP Platoon, this defining moment at Wirtzfeld was their "baptism of fire," as a soldier's first experience of actual combat conditions was known.

By 1230 hours on December 17, some of the MPs who had not already been reassigned to strengthen infantry units withdrew from Wirtzfeld and traveled seven miles northwest to Camp Elsenborn. Four days later their command post was established at Camp Elsenborn as well. The platoon continued to engage in battles from December 17 to 20. While fighting the German forces in and around Wirtzfeld, the following MPs were listed as wounded: Private Robert L. Whitney, Private James W. Moore, Private Herbert S. Keidan, Private James King, Private

Leon Webster, Private John P. Enos, Private Lawrence B. Moore, Corporal Sam V. Nerren, Sergeant Arie Ardoin, and Sergeant Walter D. Higgins.

The German offensive in the Ardennes region continued to grow. The necessity of countering that growing threat with more Allied troops became urgent. Immediate action was required in order to prevent the Germans from overrunning the area and cutting off the withdrawing units of the 2nd and 99th Infantry Divisions.

Major General Robertson ordered Colonel Lovless to take command of a task force of two provisional battalions formed from rear echelon personnel in an effort to bring more troops into the fight against the advancing Germans. Although the order was originally given by General Robertson late on December 16, it wasn't actually implemented until December 17 when field orders were issued to each command of the 2nd Infantry Division. Units from various companies were merged and command was restructured.

According to the 23rd Infantry unit history, this task force was formed from incomplete elements of the 741st Tank Battalion, 23rd Infantry (Assumed Tactical Command), 462nd AAA Battalion, 612th Tank Destroyer Battalion, Battalion Headquarters personnel, 197th AAA Battalion, 86th Engineer Battalion, 702nd Ordnance Company, 2nd Signal Company, 2nd Service Company, and other 2nd Infantry Division rear echelon personnel including the MP Platoon.

Initially one large force was assembled, but later they were separated into two provisional battalions. The first provisional battalion was under the command of Major Frank A. Hoke, 2nd Division Special Service Officer, and consisted of approximately three hundred men. The other, commanded by Major Turner of the 462nd AAA Battalion, comprised 180 of his own men and one company of other rear echelon personnel. On December 18, battalions under the command of Hoke and Turner moved to positions along a ridge with Berg to the south and Elsenborn to the north and dug in to form a line where a defensive stand could be made if necessary. Although Berg was the location of the 38th Regimental command post, the provisional battalions were placed under the tactical command of the 23rd Infantry.

On the night of December 18, Lieutenant Colonel Tuttle, the commander of the 3rd Battalion, arrived at the command post and was ordered by Colonel Lovless to take command of the Turner Battalion and merge it with his depleted 3rd Battalion into one unit. The company of rear echelon personnel originally assigned to the Turner Battalion then reverted to the control of the Hoke Battalion. For the next two days, these provisional units would shift between defensive lines in the Elsenborn area and fight off attacking Germans bent on breaking through the newly established front.

There is no doubt that these provisional forces, hastily assembled by General Robertson to combat the German advance into Belgium, helped save the lives of many of the 2nd Infantry Division soldiers and spared the capture or destruction of the Division's equipment. Most importantly, the fifteen-minute battle fought by the headquarters personnel near Wirtzfeld on December 17 delayed the main thrust of the 1st SS Panzer Division long enough for the bulk of the 2nd and 99th Divisions to withdraw to defensive positions along Elsenborn Ridge. Without this delay to the German armor, the outcome of the war might have been much different.

Furthermore, the assembled rear echelon personnel played a vital part in supporting the infantry by reestablishing the new Division front and participating in battle by holding off the fanatical German advances in the 2nd Infantry Division area. Their actions during each phase of General Robertson's withdrawal of 2nd Infantry Division troops allowed for a successful maneuver that saved two divisions and ultimately decided the fate of General Von Manteuffel's plan to divide Europe.

The MPs' battle at Wirtzfeld also represents a unique moment in modern US Army history, when men who were assembled from noncombat rear units fought as riflemen after they were thrust into the lines in an effort to bolster depleted infantry units. For their actions, each of these participants was awarded the Combat Infantry Badge by General Order after the war and was also presented with the Distinguished Unit Citation under the tactical command of the 23rd and 38th Infantry Regiments.

Noted in the Morning Reports for the MP Platoon for December 18, 1944, "One EM participated with other Division Rear Echelon Personnel organized in a provisional battalion under the tactical command of the 23rd Inf. Regt." Although the Morning Report does not indentify by name an MP who was attached to the provisional battalion of the 23rd Infantry Regiment for two days, I believe that MP was my father, Private First Class James D. Edwards. The special Ranger Battle Training Edwards had received at Camp McCoy—which none of the other MPs had received—would have made him a valuable frontline soldier in spite of his MOS (Military Occupational Specialty) designation as an MP. It makes sense that commanding officers would have taken advantage of his training by temporarily placing him in an infantry unit. Furthermore, James Edwards, alone among all the MPs of his platoon, later received the Distinguished Unit Citation—the same citation that was awarded to the 23rd Infantry for their performance in the battle mentioned by this Morning Report.

The Morning Report for December 20, 1944 shows the status of Private Fred J. Marlow, who had been captured by the Germans as they took the town of Bullingen. By December 19, the US 1st, 2nd, and 99th Divisions were well entrenched along the Elsenborn Ridge with their line of defense stretching from just south of the Monschau Forest to just north of Wirtzfeld. To the west they were in and around the towns of Berg and Nidrum, just north of Butgenbach and Weywertz.

COMPANY   RESTRICTED
MORNING REPORT   ENDING 2400   18 December   194 4

STATION Camp Elsenborn, Belgium K-905085
ORGANIZATION MP Plat., 2d Inf Div   CMP

SERIAL NUMBER	NAME	GRADE	CODE
	NO CHANGE		

RECORD OF EVENTS

One (1) EM participated with other
Division Rear Echelon Personnel
organised in a provisional battalion
under the tactical command of the
23rd Inf. Regt.

OFFICER STRENGTH	FLD O & CAPT		1ST LT		2D LT		WO		FLT O	
	PRES	ABS'T	PRES	ABS'T	PRES	ABS'T	PRES	ABS'T	PRES	ABS'T
ASSIGNED	1		3							
ATTACHED UNASSIGNED										
ATTACHED FR OTHER ORGN			1							
TOTAL	1		4							

AVN CADET & ENLISTED STRENGTH	AVIATION CADETS		ENLISTED MEN			
	PRESENT	ABSENT	PRESENT FOR DUTY	PRESENT NOT FOR DY	ABSENT	PRESENT AND ABSENT
ASSIGNED			112	2	1	115
ATTACHED UNASSIGNED			1			1
ATTACHED FR OTHER ORGN						
TOTAL			113	2	1	116

R A T I O N S	I	ESTIMATED NUMBER OF RATIONS REQUIRED FOR	DAY OF WEEK			NUMBER	
	II	MESS ATTENDANCE FOR DAY OF THIS REPORT			TOTAL	AVERAGE	
		BREAKFAST	DINNER	SUPPER		3	
	III	MEN AUTHORIZED TO MESS SEPARATELY	MEN ATCHD FOR RATIONS				
		MEN ATCHD TO OTHER ORGN FOR RATIONS	NET	O & OTHERS MESSED		TOTAL	
		MEN PRESENT	LESS		PLUS		

PAGE 1 OF 1 PAGES

I CERTIFY THAT THIS MORNING REPORT IS CORRECT AND
THAT RATION RECORDS IN PARS II REPRESENT AN ACTUAL

SIGNATURE ... 1st Lt CMP

MARCH 20, 1944   NO COPY THRU HRU OR SCS   2d Inf Div

RESTRICTED

COMPANY
MORNING REPORT ENDING 2400 20 December 192 4

STATION Camp Elsenborn, Belgium K-905085
ORGANIZATION MP Plat., 2d Inf Div CMP

SERIAL NUMBER	NAME	GRADE	CODE
18009706	Marlow, Fred J.	Pvt	M
Fr duty to MIA as of 17 December			
1944 ASN: 677			

RECORD OF EVENTS
One (1) EM returned from serving
in Provisional Battalion under
the tactical command of the 23rd
Infantry Regiment.

OFFICER STRENGTH	FLD O & CAPT		1ST LT		2D LT		WO		FLT O	
	PRES	ABS'T	PRES	ABS'T	PRES	ABS'T	PRES	ABS'T	PRES	ABS'T
ASSIGNED	1		3							
ATTACHED UNASSIGNED										
ATTACHED FR OTHER ORGN			1							
TOTAL	1		4							

AVN CADET & ENLISTED STRENGTH	AVIATION CADETS		ENLISTED MEN			
	PRESENT	ABSENT	PRESENT FOR DUTY	PRESENT NOT FOR DY	ABSENT	PRESENT AND ABSENT
ASSIGNED			109	4	2	115
ATTACHED UNASSIGNED ATTACHED FR OTHER ORGN			1			1
TOTAL			110	4	2	116

R A T I O N S	I	ESTIMATED NUMBER OF RATIONS REQUIRED FOR	DAY OF WEEK DATE		NUMBER
	II	MESS ATTENDANCE FOR DAY OF THIS REPORT		TOTAL ÷ 3	AVERAGE
		BREAKFAST DINNER SUPPER			
	III	MEN AUTHORIZED TO MESS SEPARATELY	MEN ATCHD FOR RATIONS		
		MEN ATCHD TO OTHER ORGN FOR RATIONS	NET	O & OTHERS MESSED	TOTAL
		MEN PRESENT LESS		PLUS	

PAGE 1 OF 1 PAGES
I CERTIFY THAT THIS MORNING REPORT IS CORRECT AND
THAT RATION REQUIRED REPRESENT AN ACTUAL

SIGNATURE 1st Lt CMP
WD COPY THRU REG OR SCO 2d Inf Div.

The Morning Reports from December 18 and 20, 1941, which provide details about
the activities of James Edwards and Fred Marlow.

Task Force - On 16 December, when the enemy counter-offensive threat developed in the 99th Division sector, General Robertson, 2nd Division Commander, ordered Colonel Lovless, commanding the 23rd Infantry, to form a task force from available personnel. As formed on paper, 16 December, the force included rear echelon personnel of the 2nd Infantry Division, elements of the 2nd Battalion, 9th Infantry, now under his control, to remain in place and improve positions on the ridge. The Hoke Battalion and 3rd Battalion, 23rd Infantry, were ordered to move to this ridge and dig positions, which would be occupied by the 2nd and 3rd Battalions, 38th Infantry. The 3rd Battalion, 23rd Infantry, and the Hoke Battalion, after digging these positions, were to withdraw to their original positions. Arriving at the forward ridge about 1500, 19 December, these two battalions dug positions until 1800 when they were withdrawn to their positions on the Berg - Elsenborn ridge. Guided by men from the 3rd Battalion, 23rd Infantry, division troops began arriving at the newly dug positions about 1800 in order, 2nd, 3rd, and 1st Battalions, 38th Infantry; 1st and 2nd Battalions, 23rd Infantry. The 1st Battalion, 38th Infantry, replaced the Hoke Battalion on the Berg - Elsenborn ridge, thus relieving the Hoke Battalion from the task force. The 2nd and 3rd Battalions, 38th Infantry, assumed positions on the forward ridge and came under command of Colonel Lovless, who was responsible for that portion of the division sector within the two ridge lines east of Berg and Elsenborn. The 1st and 2nd Battalions, 23rd Infantry, were guided to positions near Berg, where a guide from 23rd Infantry Headquarters led both battalions to a hill southeast of Nidrum.

An After Action Report from the 23rd Infantry Regiment that describes the formation and circumstances in which the provisional battalions were deployed during the German breakthrough.

Following is a letter from James Branch, who was a member of the 38th Infantry Regiment—a unit in the 2nd Infantry Division—and fought in the Battle of the Bulge along with other 2nd Infantry Division troops.

January 24, 2012

Mr. Edwards,
To try to clarify, the story is as follows. As we arrived in Krinkelt [a small village in the Ardennes region] *there were ten of us who occupied this house. In ten to fifteen minutes, this German tank motored up, one track on the sidewalk—it was that close to the window of the house.*

We had two rounds for the bazooka. Now it takes two to load and fire the bazooka, one to wire the round and one to fire the bazooka. I wired, Red (my sergeant) fired. All the time I was telling him to shoot it in the boogey wheels, and I kept repeating this as I wired the second round. "Shoot him in the boogey wheels!" And he did.

The second round set the tank ablaze and the Germans started to abandon the tank and we all were shooting at them as they exited the tank. All this drew about forty to fifty German soldiers, who began pulling the bodies away from the burning tank. Then we were thinking they were coming into the house. All of us had all windows and doors covered.

About that time a loud whistle blew and the Germans pulled out of town, only to come back at daylight with a vengeance, but we were ready for them. Our Second Lieutenant Emerich came to the house and got me and my rifle grenade launcher to go hunt tanks. We didn't get too far and we ran into one head-on as we retreated to a second-floor window. We fired all three of the grenades at the tank, which didn't faze it, so we made tracks back to the house. The story that the lieutenant told was quite different than what really happened, and he received a Silver Star for his actions, or his story. All I got out of the deal was a little experience—the rifle grenades were no match for tanks.

I drove the Ammo & Pioneer platoon truck, which had all of the ammo and explosives. This is why I had access to the ammo we had available. [There was] not much after Heartbreak Crossroads.

Hope this clears up the story for you.

—James Branch

The house in Krinkelt described in the letter from James Branch.

James D. Branch
38th Infantry Regiment HQ Co.

James D. Branch, 38th Infantry.

FORTRESS BUILT OF YANK BLOOD; COURAGE HOLDS
2D DIVISION MEETS HEAVIEST ASSAULT

By: Morley Cassidy
     North American Newspaper Alliance

WITH SECOND INFANTRY DIVISION IN BELGIUM, Dec. 19 (Delayed) --
Here stands a fortress. For the fourth successive day, Field Marshal Karl Von Rundstedt has been throwing masses of his men, tanks
and guns against this Division in its forest stronghold in one of
the major thrusts of the great German offensive.

Elsewhere along the 60-mile front in Belgium and Luxembourg the
attack continues today in great strength but nowhere with more force
than on this Division's front.

Infantry and tank attacks throughout the morning followed a
night in which there was no night -- a night when the woods and roads
were filled with the movement of patrols and the shifting of columns
while the skies flamed on every side with flares and blasts of
artillery and the sputtering light of racing V-weapons, trailed by
streaming red tracers or white blasts of ack-ack fire.

But the attacks today, like the first day's shelling and the
last two days' combined assault, are still beating in vain against
the walls of this fortress.

This is a fortress built of the blood and courage of American
men. They are fighting and dying today in this land of Christmas--
tree forests as gallantly as any Division ever fought in American
history.

They are determined to hold their bastion and seal off the
penetration made by the Germans Sunday in the area of a neighboring
division.

FIRMER THAN ROCK

No fortress built of rock and steel ever stood firmer than the
men deployed over these miles of hills and forests, rocky gorges
and villages.

17 TANKS KNOCKED OUT

From a hill outside this battalion command post I have just
seen at least 17 tanks knocked out in a single battle for a tiny
village which cannot yet be named, lest it give the Germans a clue
to their situation.

The fight for this village began at dusk last night when 1st
Lt. Albert Sheldton, blond young platoon leader from Oklahoma City,
led his platoon into positions along a village street of barns and
dung heaps.

Three of our tanks were drawn up behind the village, on their
right, as protection but were barely in position when a German force
of five Tiger tanks rumbled into position on the infantry's left.

Unspotted by the Germans, Lt. Sheldton consulted with the
American tank commander.

*A newspaper article given to Major North after the Battle of the Bulge began
detailing the activities of the 2nd Infantry Division.*

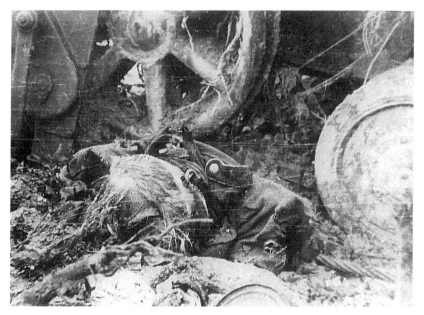

*A German soldier killed during the Battle of the Bulge, December 1944.
This photo was taken by Major North.*

*The Vielsalm railroad bridge, which was destroyed by the 508th AB Engineers,
December 23, 1944.*

George Swearingen, who witnessed many of these battles first-hand, provided me with an account of his experiences during the withdrawal of the forward infantry units from Wahlerscheid, in Germany, as the Germans pushed back into Belgium. The details he shared with me are unknown to military historians and not mentioned in any other publication.

Late in the day on December 17, after General Robertson received word to begin withdrawing the 2nd Infantry Division troops from near Wahlerscheid, a problem occurred when Robertson was unable to make contact with the 15th Field Artillery, who had been supporting the 9th and 38th Infantry during the Wahlerscheid offensive. According to George Swearingen's personal account of that day, General Robertson, concerned that the 15th Field Artillery would be trapped behind the lines and unaware of the Division's move, summoned Lieutenant Chet Meeth from the MP Platoon. He planned to give Lieutenant Meeth a special mission—to retrieve the trapped artillery unit.

But, unknown to General Robertson, Lieutenant Meeth had been placed on another assignment and was unavailable for the mission. Private First Class George Swearingen arrived in his place and informed General Robertson that Lieutenant Meeth was unavailable for the assignment, but that he was prepared to accept the mission in his place. Swearingen was able to provide another excellent account of a little-known set of events and a behind-the-scenes look at just one of many soldiers' experiences during the Battle of the Bulge. On the following pages is an excerpt from a letter that George Swearingen sent to me in 2007 detailing these events in his own words. While the exact location of the 15th Field Artillery is not mentioned in the letter, it is highly likely that since the 15th Field Artillery was supporting the 9th and 38th Infantry, the unit was somewhere east of Elsenborn Ridge on the high ground between there and Wahlerscheid.

The Second Division was moved over, east of Camp D'Elsenburg [sic] to make room for more troops. This is where the German drive fizzled out, but the 15th Field Art. [Artillery] *got trapped. General Robertson called for Lt. Meeth. Meeth was on another assignment. I answered his call.*

I told him why Meeth could not come, but I was prepared to answer his call. I was told about the 15th Field Artillery being trapped. I pointed out the field and woods road, saying we had checked it out before. That I could go get them.

I was told, "Young man, I like the way you talk. Get gassed up, get a meal, and get back before dark. If Lt. Meeth is not back, I will get another officer to go with you." I said, "Sir, I had rather do this myself. I have the training for such a deal and I'd rather do this on my own. Another officer could foul things up." He said, "Young man, I like the way you talk. I will let you do this alone."

I was ready for this mission, and was ready to go when I got back to him. It was twilight when he wished me luck. I was soon off on this mission. I went across the field into the woods. It was easy traveling, but I had to go slow. I came out of the first woods and crossed this huge field. I went around the edge of the second high ground. Across another big field, then another woody area. This woods was not so thick, and was easy to cross.

Out south of me I could see high ground. This, in my mind, was the high ground I was looking for. I parked my jeep and started walking about one hundred yards from the point of the high ground. I was within twenty yards of these woods. I was challenged. I answered their questions. I told them my mission. I asked to talk with their commander, and was taken to the colonel.

I told him my mission. He said, "I had my men open up an old road down to the field. We can move out tomorrow." I said, "No sir, the general said bring you out tonight." He hesitated and said, "If that's what the general wants, we will prepare to move out." The order was passed—we will move out tonight.

As they got their equipment ready, it was moved down in the field. This was all before midnight. I told the drivers we would move out in low-range gears, "so you can follow as close as possible." Just after midnight we were on our way. The colonel came over and asked, "Can I ride with you?" This was very unusual, as an officer does not often ask a PFC if they can do something. I said, "Yes sir," and we were on our way.

It was a long, slow ride but everything went fine. We crossed the first patch of woods and crossed a field and around below the next woods. As we approached the next woods, the moon came out from behind the clouds. This made it easier. . . . As we came out of these woods, we had the last field to cross. We were back.

Lt. Meeth and General Robertson had sat there all night waiting for my return. The general came running out. I did not have time to salute. He took me in his arms, saying, "George, you done it," and grabbed me in his arms and hugged me. What a greeting.

On December 21, while on traffic patrol duty near Camp Elsenborn, Private First Class George Swearingen came upon three MPs who had been severely wounded by artillery fire while directing traffic at a junction in the road. Swearingen leapt from his jeep and ran to help. He immediately came upon MP Linus Gittemeier, whose left leg had been severed below the knee from the shrapnel of the first round of German artillery. Fabricating a tourniquet, Swearingen applied it to the leg in an attempt to reduce the bleeding and told the wounded MP, "This is your ticket home."

As Swearingen continued to help the other wounded soldiers and get traffic moving again, he became the victim of two more rounds of artillery. By the time the shelling had ended, Swearingen, MPs George L. McConnell, Percy C. Vogel, and

Lawrence B. Moore all lay bleeding on the ground or in their jeeps. Although badly wounded and disoriented, Swearingen stayed on his feet and kept traffic moving, which was vital to prevent other soldiers from being hurt or killed by the incoming German artillery. Shortly after hearing these explosions, Corporal J. R. Cantrell arrived on the scene. His first priority was to assist Private First Class Gittemeier, still bleeding badly, and to aid his friend George Swearingen, who had severe shrapnel wounds to his face.

In 2008, J. R. Cantrell shared with me his memory of that day.

"I heard the loud explosions from the German shells and I knew that where they were landing there could be casualties. As I drove my jeep closer to the crossroads [at Camp Elsenborn], I saw that there was a big traffic jam. I got out of my jeep and ran to Pfc. Gittemeier, who was bleeding badly and missing one leg. The ambulance was there and they were loading him in it.

"I saw a jeep that wasn't moving, so I started to tell the driver to get going when I noticed that the two MPs, McConnell and Vogel, were knocked out and bleeding. I saw Swearingen after he had been hit—his clothes were torn to shreds and his face was bloody. I don't mind telling you that I was scared to death, thinking that any minute another artillery shell was going to land right on top of us."

As J. R. concluded his recollection of those events with me that day, he paused for a moment and said, "What kind of an idiot drives into oncoming artillery fire?"

I quietly responded by saying, "A very brave man."

The crossroads at Camp Elsenborn where Private George L. McConnell, Private Percy Vogel, Private First Class Linus Gittemeier, and eventually—through his act of gallantry—Private First Class George F. Swearingen were seriously wounded by incoming German artillery on the morning of December 21, 1944.

Note the large hole in the roof of one of the buildings in the background. This photo was taken on the same day that the MP Platoon's command post relocated to Ovifat, Belgium, for a safer area of operations. The German artillery continued to pour down on the Elsenborn Ridge and Camp Elsenborn. Their guns pounded the crowded rear areas behind the Division front lines, which caused extensive casualties and damage to Division Headquarters.

In addition to these heavy artillery barrages, Nebelwerfers— aka "Screaming Mimis" (a German weapon that created clouds of smoke and poison gas)—and enemy aircraft posed a serious threat to personnel. Strafing attacks, in which German planes would fly low and attack targets on the ground, resulted in a number of deaths. On one occasion, a German ME109 accounted for the death of MP Private First Class Anthony Onica, who was wounded while directing traffic on one of the Division's main supply routes. He was the fourth MP fatally wounded during the war. Onica was awarded the Silver Star posthumously for the sacrifice he made while aiding men and equipment to move through the area and head for the cover of the surrounding forest.

In the month of December, the MP Platoon had reached a high strength of 116 men. By the end of the month, they had recorded seven casualties, who were evacuated to rear hospitals. On December 30, Private Alex Staich was slightly wounded in the hip by enemy fire from a German plane strafing Camp Elsenborn but remained on duty after he was treated by a medic at that location.

Private First Class Richard Cravens and Privates Herbert Keidan and James King were among the first casualties of the 2nd Infantry Division MP Platoon, wounded on January 1, 1945. It is not known where they were stationed at the time they were hit. On the following day, Private First Class William Davidson would be sent to the hospital for a nonbattle injury.

Strangely enough, even as the Germans continued to attack the rear areas of the Division with artillery strikes and strafing attacks, the main body of the platoon took a seven-mile hike in the snow for conditioning purposes. The MP Morning Report recorded this event as taking place on January 8, 1945.

The 2nd Infantry Division MPs take a conditioning hike in the snow, January 8, 1945.

Once the MP Platoon had secured the area around Ovifat, a detail of sixteen enlisted personnel, one officer, and four jeeps were sent to Verviers, Belgium, on January 10, 1945. Their mission was to assist the Belgian police while the 2nd Infantry Division rear rest area was established in the town. The rear rest area camp had been located in Vielsalm, Belgium, in October 1944 when the 2nd Infantry Division moved to St. Vith. After the main thrust from the German 5th Panzer Army, that location was abandoned in favor of a safer location behind the new Division lines.

━━━━━━━━━━━━━━━━

The following photos were taken at various locations in and around the MPs' command posts at Wirtzfeld, Camp Elsenborn, Ovifat, and Nidrum in Belgium, and at Wahlerscheid in Germany, from January 10 to February 14, 1945. Although it appears the MPs had plenty of time on their hands, the fact is they were constantly on alert as the advancing German 6th Panzer Army was just a short distance to the southwest, moving in the direction of Malmedy. Due to the stiff resistance of the 2nd Infantry Division in the Krinkelt-Rocherath-Wirtzfeld areas, the German 1st and 12th SS Panzer Divisions and what was left of the decimated 277th Volksgrenadier Division were forced to bypass the Butgenbach area and proceed on a more westerly route than they had originally planned. While they were in the town of Verviers, it became apparent to members of the MP Platoon that the occupants of the once prosperous city had succumbed to the harsh reality of war and the lack of available food and other necessities.

Secheval, Belgium, January 10, 1945.

Street vendors in Verviers, Belgium, January 10, 1945. These hungry Belgians stand in line to buy a limited assortment of vegetables as they await their liberators' defeat of Germany.

Verviers, Belgium, January 10, 1945.

A 2nd Infantry Division MP and a Belgian police officer, Verviers, Belgium, January 10, 1945.

Rocco Festa amd Louis Pastre, Verviers, Belgium, January 10, 1945.

Corporal Paul Porter, near St. Vith, Belgium, January 11, 1945.

On January 26, 1945, while the MP Platoon's command post was located in the small town of Ovifat, Belgium, Corporal J. R. Cantrell was dropped from assignment and transferred in a group to the 2nd Evacuation Hospital. No description of his wounds or injuries was documented in the official Morning Report. Cantrell would not return to the MP Platoon from his stay in the hospital until nearly one month later, on February 23.

Corporal J. R. Cantrell, Ovifat, Belgium, January 11, 1945.

MPs Balkum and Gammons, Ovifat, Belgium, January 11, 1945.

James Edwards, Ovifat, Belgium. The words "During the Bulge" are written on the photo.

MPs Hillis, Edwards, and Lester (left to right) in Ovifat, Belgium, January 11, 1945.

Sergeant Helfer and Corporal Porter, Ovifat, Belgium, January 1945.

Paul Porter on the main supply route from Elsenborn to Wirtzfeld, January 11, 1945.

The photographs on the previous pages were taken during the Battle of the Bulge when the snow was the most abundant and the temperatures were at their lowest. No doubt the harsh winter environment was brutal for men and equipment alike. As January drew to a close, it became clear that the German Army had failed to achieve its objective. Lacking fuel, ammunition, food, and vital equipment, the German advance slowed and then literally ran out of gas after meeting with significant Allied resistance. American forces including the 2nd Infantry Division captured thousands of battle-weary German soldiers caught behind the lines when they were squeezed into surrendering the "bulge" of territory in Belgium they had pushed into in late December 1944.

By January 24, 1945, the 2nd Infantry Division received new orders to renew its push toward the Roer River and the series of dams that separated western Germany from the Rhineland. On January 30, the Division once again advanced through Nidrum, Wirtzfeld, Rocherath, and Krinkelt. They met with resistance from the remaining German units in each of those towns. Fighting from house to house, the infantry systematically expelled the German defenders from the cellars of each building as night fell and the first day of battle came to an end. At dawn on January 31, the infantry continued its advance toward the German border and Wahlerscheid. Battling stiff resistance from German mortar, rifle, and machine-gun fire, the Division fought its way across the Siegfried Line through deep snow, extreme cold, and rugged terrain. As the infantry moved forward, the MP Platoon processed German prisoners and their captured equipment.

MP Clarence Herring, Nidrum, Belgium, January 30, 1945.

MP James Earl Hillis next to the jeep "Lula Belle," Nidrum, Belgium, January 30, 1945.

A destroyed American truck, Bullingen, Belgium, January 30, 1945.

On January 31, Lieutenant I. C. Meeth was dropped from assignment and listed as a battle casualty, slightly wounded in action, and transferred to the 2nd Evacuation Hospital. The Morning Report further showed that Lieutenant Meeth was admitted to the hospital for old wounds he suffered on September 3, 1944, in the vicinity of Brest, France. The information in this report confirms the date of the water sprinkler story told by George Swearingen. Following Meeth's evacuation to the hospital, Private First Class Edward A. Podsednik was also listed as slightly wounded in action. He was sent to the 5th Evacuation Hospital for wounds sustained on January 31, 1945.

In full retreat now, the Germans grudgingly withdrew from Belgium. Any of their equipment not yet destroyed by the advancing Americans was abandoned when it ran out of fuel. The Germans also destroyed a number of bridges and railroads as they retreated in order to make the Allied advance as difficult as possible. The Vennbahn Bridge, pictured below, was destroyed by the retreating Germans near the town of Butgenbach in late January 1945. The black and white image is remarkably similar to one used in the book *Combat History of the Second Infantry Division in World War II*. It differs from that photo in that it was taken by Major North from the other side of the valley, looking in the opposite direction. The second photo that follows on this page is the bridge as it appears today.

The Vennbahn Bridge, destroyed by the Germans as they withdrew into Germany, January 1945. (From the North photo collection.)

The repaired Vennbahn Bridge in modern times.

The following photos make it fully evident that the German Army had failed to defeat the Allied forces and take control of vital American supply depots in the Battle of the Bulge at Spa and Verviers, Belgium. The images of captured German soldiers, destroyed equipment, bombed-out and bullet-riddled structures, and freshly dug graves offer the reader just a small glimpse into World War II. *Combat History of the Second Infantry Division in World War II* contains many further photos of abandoned German equipment including tanks, trucks, flak guns, antiaircraft guns, artillery, 88mm and 120mm guns, small arms and rifles of every German model, as well as ammunition of every caliber. Large caches of mortars, artillery rounds, grenades, medical supplies, and other equipment and facilities were also captured by the Americans as they advanced. After their campaign in the Ardennes failed, the German Army was in full retreat, fighting only long enough to cause delaying actions before they were quickly eliminated or withdrew from the fight.

Sergeant Welch, an MP of the 2nd Infantry Division, pauses to grin at the camera as he loads German prisoners into a truck, Bullingen, Belgium, January 1945.

Freshly dug German graves near Wahlerscheid, Germany, January 1945.

German soldiers, captured by the 2nd Infantry Division, near Wahlerscheid, Germany, January 1945.

In the photo above, captured German soldiers are the new residents of what was formerly a prisoner of war enclosure that held American POWs for a short time. Although there are no distinguishing insignia on the German prisoners, it is quite probable that many of them are from the 277th Volksgrenadier

Division. Some would likely have been from the 1st and 12th SS Panzer Divisions and the German paratrooper units dropped into the area early in the campaign. Regardless of which military unit they came from, these would all have been fierce troops who fought tenaciously to destroy the Allied forces.

A destroyed German Tiger tank, near the twin villages of Krinkelt-Rocherath, January 1945.

The Tiger tank pictured above was completely knocked over from the blast of an antitank explosive round, probably fired from an American Sherman tank or an M-36 tank destroyer. The bottom of the tank has a gaping hole where the antitank round penetrated its side and exited through the thin metal on its belly. There were many such instances of tanks destroyed in this manner—and sometimes they looked much worse. Although the German tanks had thicker armor in the front, which could stop most rounds fired from one of our tanks, they were also slow and less maneuverable. This made them vulnerable to the faster Shermans that would engage them from the side or rear.

Once past the Siegfried Line, the 2nd Infantry Division captured the German towns of Schoneseiffen and Harperscheid. They then crossed the Roer River and took Schleiden, Hellenthal, Gemund, Mechernich, Munstereifel, Ahrweiler, Sinzig, and finally the Ludendorf-Remagan Railway Bridge. From late January until early March, the 2nd Infantry Division had been in a race to secure the Roer River Dams. As the Division prepared to plunge deeper into Germany, General Robertson was awarded the Distinguished Service Cross for his heroic activities in Belgium during the Battle of the Bulge.

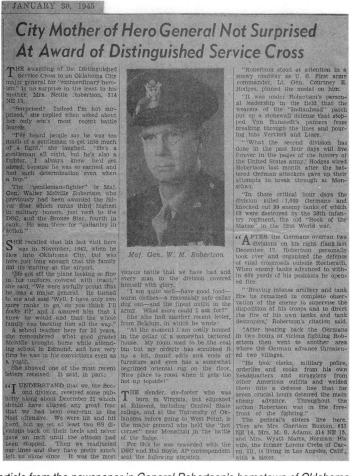

An article from the newspaper in General Robertson's hometown of Oklahoma City announcing his award of the Distinguished Service Cross.

At first glance, the following item appears to be some type of small informational pamphlet of German origin. Upon further inspection, however, it becomes clear that it was a Christmas card, evidently printed by the 2nd Infantry Division, which was made available for soldiers to mail home to family and friends. I can only assume that the rear echelon command that approved the printing of the card believed that the Division would maintain control of the German territory they had seized in December 1944.

Exterior of the 2nd Infantry Division Christmas card made in December 1944.

Interior of the 2nd Infantry Division Christmas card made in December 1944.

A variation of the Indianhead insignia displayed on the interior of the 2nd Infantry Division Christmas card made in December 1944.

After all, the 2nd and 99th Divisions had maintained the defensive positions along the Belgium-German front since October when the newly arrived 106th Division pushed into the line to relieve the 2nd Infantry Division in December. It made perfect sense that they expected Christmas would be celebrated from somewhere inside Germany. Of course, as history played out, the sliver of German soil captured by the Americans at Wahlerscheid during the battle of Heartbreak Crossroads was a short-lived victory. To the disappointment of the men who worked so hard to break the Siegfried Line, they were forced to withdraw back into Belgium almost immediately and did not step foot on German soil again until late January, a full month after Christmas Day.

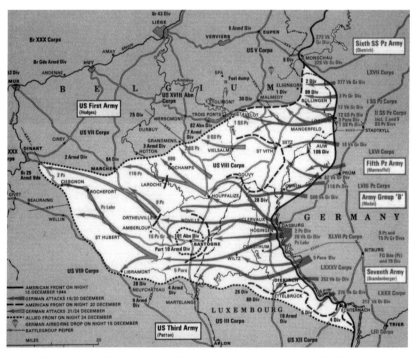

Map of the Ardennes region showing the territory reclaimed by German forces during the Battle of the Bulge. (Source: National Archives and Records Administration.)

9

Breakthrough to the Rhine

February–March 1945

On February 1, the 2nd Infantry Division Headquarters awarded Bronze Stars to one officer and six enlisted men of the MP Platoon. After several weeks of hard fighting, the bulge that the German Army had created with the Ardennes Offensive was completely gone, falling utterly short of Hitler's desired goal. Although the German drive into Belgium had failed, the remaining forces within Germany would continue to fight to the death.

The map below illustrates the extent of the penetration by the German Ardennes Offensive and the number of both American and German forces that were involved in the Battle of the Bulge. It's hard to imagine that more than one million men collectively from both sides fought during this horrendous campaign. The German army suffered one hundred thousand casualties—killed, wounded, or captured. Allied forces lost eighty-one thousand troops in the same three categories.

The arrows on the map represent the German armies that moved west in their attempt to reach the Meuse River, their first objective, and from there the city of Antwerp. Hitler's plan was to trap four Allied armies by dividing Europe all the way to the sea on the western front. By early February, after failing to achieve his objectives during what is now known as the Battle of the Bulge, the remainder of Hitler's forces who had not been captured or killed in action retreated into Germany but continued to fight viciously to defend the Third Reich.

Sergeants Helfer and Rentko, Nidrum, Belgium, February 3, 1945.

Corporal Paul Porter, Nidrum, Belgium, February 1945.

Paul Porter and Richard Magers, Nidrum, Belgium, February 1945.

German prisoners wash Sergeant Rentko's jeep, Nidrum, Belgium, February 1945.

2nd Infantry Division MP Otis Harrison, Nidrum, Belgium, February 13, 1945.

Lieutenants Jarczynski and Karowski, Nidrum, Belgium, February 1945.

Lieutenants Meeth and Karowski, Nidrum, Belgium, February 1945.

Sergeant Clifford Helfer and Corporal Paul Porter outside the Enlisted Men's Quarters, Nidrum, Belgium, February 1945.

By mid-February 1945, the 2nd Infantry Division had seen the last of the deep snow and subzero temperatures of the Belgian winter. With the Wehrmacht—Germany's armed forces—in full retreat, the Division engaged and defeated the German forces near Wahlerscheid once again. Breaking through the fortifications at the Siegfried Line once again, they recaptured the lost ground they had so grudgingly relinquished to the Germans in December.

Dragon's teeth (concrete pillars designed to impede tanks and other vehicles) at the Siegfried Line near Wahlerscheid, Germany, February 1945.

Lieutenant Meeth on the Seigfried Line near Wahlerscheid, Germany, February 1945.

2nd Infantry Division MPs Carl Kruger and Doris Bennett at a road junction near Harperscheid, Germany, February 3, 1945.

James Bundschuh in front of a Panzer IV assault gun, Schoneseiffen, Germany, February 4, 1945.

Private First Class Lefty Erwin—who replaced George Swearingen as Lieutenant Meeth's driver after Swearingen was wounded at Camp Elsenborn—stands with Meeth in Nidrum, Belgium, February 9, 1945.

Once the German Army had been forced back across the Siegfried Line, the MP Platoon advanced to a position just one and a half miles south of Heartbreak Crossroads. In the photo on the following page, MP Alex Staich guards a traffic crossroads in the area. On the pole behind Staich, signs erected by the MP Platoon point the way to the command post (which was code named "Ivanhoe") and the 45th Field Hospital.

MP Alex Staich mans a traffic post near Wahlerscheid, Germany, February 15, 1945.

In the photo below, MP Ed Cywinski is stationed at a traffic post along the road to Wahlerscheid from the twin villages of Krinkelt-Rocherath. This photo of Cywinski was taken at the same time as the one of Alex Staich and shows the view from across the road.

Private First Class Ed Cywinski, near Wahlerscheid, Germany, February 15, 1945.

The photo of the limbless trees is a grim reminder of what was left of the Monschau Forest after heavy artillery shelling. As the 9th Infantry Regiment took cover in the once dense forest, the Germans unleashed tree burst artillery, which rained down deadly shrapnel. During the ensuing explosions, pieces of hot steel would strip the branches, leaving the tree trunks bare and the entire tree devoid of any foliage. Many 2nd Division infantrymen were killed by this harassing artillery. They soon discovered that covering their foxholes with large logs already lying on the ground from previous shelling provided superior protection from all but direct hits.

Although the heavy snow appears to have melted entirely by February, Cywinski clearly decided it was still necessary to wear a long trench coat and gloves to keep away a chill in the air. It is probable that he had been there most of the night, manning his post and watching for anything unusual in his sector.

Destruction left in the wake of the Battle of the Bulge, Viesalm, Belgium, February 1945.

Through February and into early March, the MP Platoon would maintain various defensive outposts in both Belgian and German borderland towns until the forward 2nd Infantry

Division units had moved farther into Germany, into the region west of the Rhine River.

Captain Dean E. Irvin, Wirtzfeld, Belgium, February 15, 1945.

In the photo, Captain Dean E. Irvin of Headquarters Company poses in front of the building that was next door to the Division Command Post where Cantrell and Edwards were on watch.

Captain Dean Irvin on the road to Wahlerscheid, Germany, February 15, 1945.

Corporal Paul Porter on the phone in the Monschau Forest, February 18, 1945.

This photo was taken on the eastern edge of the Schnee Eifel looking east into Germany toward Mechernich. This is one of the many 2nd Infantry Division outposts the MPs maintained during this period.

An MP outpost just north of Mechernich, Germany, February 18, 1945.

An MP outpost just north of Mechernich, Germany, February 18, 1945.

A German ammo dump, Mechernich, Germany, February 1945.

*Richard Nelson stands guard on the road to Wahlerscheid, February 18, 1945.
"Insure" was the code word for the Provost Marshal. "Ivanhoe" was the code word
for the Division Command Post.*

Four days prior to the Division's crossing of the Roer River, on February 19, 1945, Private First Class George F. Swearingen returned to the MP Platoon from the hospital where he had been recovering from wounds he suffered at Camp Elsenborn.

Private First Class George Swearingen poses with the 305mm howitzer that almost took his life.

In the photo above, a solemn Swearingen stands next to the big gun and reflects on that day in December when he and three of his fellow MPs were seriously wounded. When I visited George Swearingen to celebrate his ninety-eighth birthday in September 2010, Mr. Swearingen told me that on the day he arrived back at the Division Command Post, he was personally welcomed by General Robertson, not with a salute but with a handshake and a hug. Mr. Swearingen stated that General Robertson was so relieved that George's wounds had not been so serious as to prevent him from returning to the platoon that he ordered T-bone steaks for everyone at the command post that evening for dinner as a celebration in his honor.

On February 20, in a ceremony one and a quarter miles southeast of Wahlerscheid at the Division Command Post, George Swearingen was awarded the Silver Star for his actions at Camp Elsenborn. This award, which he received due to his unselfish desire to aid his fellow soldiers, was pinned on his uniform by no less than General Robertson. During that same ceremony, those gathered also remembered the ultimate sacrifice paid by Private First Class Anthony Onica. His name was read aloud and he was awarded the Silver Star posthumously for giving his life in the line of duty. Like so many of his comrades, he gave his life in the effort to restore freedom and peace to this part of the world.

General Walter M. Robertson conducts the medals ceremony on February 20, 1945.

General Robertson pins the Silver Star on Private First Class George Swearingen,
February 20, 1945.

Major North, Private First Class George Swearingen, and Lieutenant Meeth after
the medals ceremony. February 20, 1945.

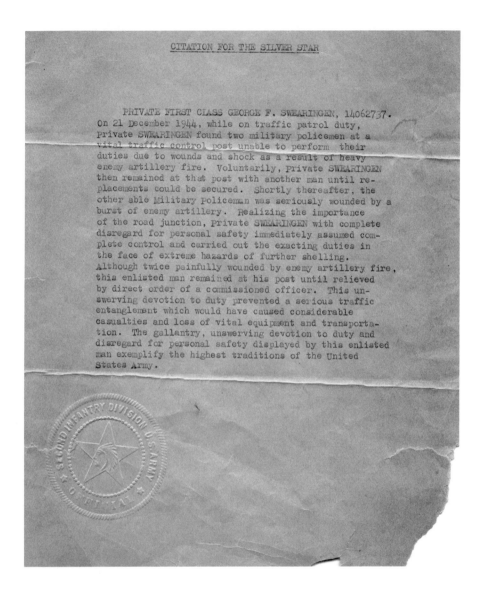

CITATION FOR THE SILVER STAR

PRIVATE FIRST CLASS GEORGE F. SWEARINGEN, 14062737. On 21 December 1944, while on traffic patrol duty, Private SWEARINGEN found two military policemen at a vital traffic control post unable to perform their duties due to wounds and shock as a result of heavy enemy artillery fire. Voluntarily, Private SWEARINGEN then remained at that post with another man until replacements could be secured. Shortly thereafter, the other able Military policeman was seriously wounded by a burst of enemy artillery. Realizing the importance of the road junction, Private SWEARINGEN with complete disregard for personal safety immediately assumed complete control and carried out the exacting duties in the face of extreme hazards of further shelling. Although twice painfully wounded by enemy artillery fire, this enlisted man remained at his post until relieved by direct order of a commissioned officer. This unswerving devotion to duty prevented a serious traffic entanglement which would have caused considerable casualties and loss of vital equipment and transportation. The gallantry, unswerving devotion to duty and disregard for personal safety displayed by this enlisted man exemplify the highest traditions of the United States Army.

George Swearingen's official citation for the Silver Star.

RESTRICTED

HEADQUARTERS
279th U. S. Station Hospital
V Hospital Group (PROV)
APO 349, U.S. Army

GENERAL ORDERS

NUMBER   —TEXT TEXT TEXT—

         x   x   x

1. By direction of the President, under the provisions of AR
600-45, 22 September 1943, as amended, the Purple Heart is awarded to:
    Private First Class George F. Swearingen, 14062737, Infantry,
United States Army, for wounds received as a result of enemy action
on 21 Dec 1944, in Belgium. Entered military service from North Carolina.

         x   x   x

             By order of Colonel DECKER:

                                        PAUL C. KELLER
                                        Captain, MAC
                                        Adjutant

OFFICIAL:

Paul C. Keller
PAUL C. KELLER
Captain, MAC
Adjutant

DISTRIBUTION:
    1 - Ea EM concerned
    1 - Ea 201 File
    3 - TAG, Wash DC
    1 - Central MRU, 887
    3 - Hq, ETOUSA

             RESTRICTED

George Swearingen's official citation for the Purple Heart.

On the following day, February 21, the MP Platoon would
suffer other losses. When the platoon sent out scouts in an effort
to locate a suitable location for their command post, Private
First Class Angelo Watznauer and Sergeant John P. Sears came
under attack by German patrols near the town of Herhahn,
Germany. In the ensuing battle, Sears was wounded by rifle fire
and Watznauer became the fifth and final MP to be killed in
action during the war.

MP Private First Class Angelo M. Watznauer, killed in action on February 21, 1945.

On February 22, the MP Platoon relocated their command post again, this time moving eleven miles east from Wahlerscheid to Einruhr, just north of Herhahn.

Paul Porter, Herhahn, Germany, February 21, 1945.

Paul Porter and Ray Gammons, Herhahn, Germany, February 21, 1945.

James Edwards and William Davidson, Einruhr, Germany, February 22, 1945.

James Edwards, Einruhr, Germany, February 22, 1945.

Private First Class James D. Edwards is pictured on page 214 leaning on his jeep while in Einruhr, Germany, during the Division's push into the Rhineland. Visible in the lower right corner of this photo is a captured German K98 Mauser battle rifle undoubtedly removed from a German prisoner. The 2nd Infantry Division Indianhead insignia is clearly seen on the spare tire cover under Dad's arm.

The white scarf Dad is wearing was a popular clothing item some of the MPs wore that was *not* furnished by the army. In a letter Dad wrote to Mom in November 1944, he asked her to send him a scarf to wear around his neck to keep the snow from falling down his shirt. It appears that Mom sent several scarves for some of the other MPs as well. Little had he and the rest of the Division realized that the snow was not the only thing to worry about in the month of December. During my research I located this same photo of Dad on the Navarro County Genealogical Society website The Men and Women of World War II.

Unit strength declined due to the number of casualties that were inflicted upon the MP Platoon in the month of February. Authorized by Field Order No. 3 of the Military Police Platoon dated February 23, 1945, Corporal Jack S. Boyd was promoted to sergeant and John H. Sheehan was advanced to the rank of corporal. During February, Private First Class Theodore C. Knecht, Private John P. Carr, Private First Class James D. Southall, Private First Class Russell V. Cather, Private First Class Orville H. Conaway, Private First Class John R. Irvin, Private First Class James D. Scalera, Private First Class Bruce L. Plyler, Corporal Joseph Accetone, and Private First Class Charles H. Waldron all became casualties and were sent to various hospitals.

Corporal Jack Boyd, who was promoted to sergeant, February 23, 1945.

After spending nearly a month in the hospital himself, Corporal James Cantrell returned to duty with the MP Platoon on February 23, 1945. Although the Morning Reports do not disclose the extent of Cantrell's injuries, his act of conspicuous gallantry displayed courage under extreme conditions. Throughout the war, many of the MPs would act bravely though many of them never received the recognition they deserved for their unselfish acts in battle.

For the entire month of February, the MPs handled traffic flow through the Division area, manned vital traffic control posts, and collected discarded weapons, ammunition, clothing, and several hundred jerry cans. All of the salvaged equipment was turned in to the quartermaster salvage area.

An MP looks on as a jeep is salvaged from a river in Germany.

Anderson, Porter, Helfer, and Bundschuh, Einruhr, Germany, February 25, 1945.

Private First Class Kermit Yandles transporting female German Auxiliary Corps (similar to the US WACs) to the PWE.

2nd Infantry Division MPs in Einruhr, Germany, February 25, 1945.

Ordensburg Vogelsang, located midway between Einruhr and Gemund in the Schnee Eifel, was an elite German SS training facility that was overrun by the 9th Infantry Division, then briefly occupied by 2nd Infantry Division rear echelon troops before they turned it over to British forces.

This photo of Ordensburg Vogelsang was taken by the 165th US Army Signal Corps as they moved along with the 2nd Infantry Division in February 1945.

MP Bruce Plyler at the entrance to Ordensburg Vogelsang, February 1945.

Rankin, Harrison, Blair, and Swearingen, Gemund, Germany, March 6, 1945.

From March 6 to 10, the MP Platoon, on the heels of the infantry, once again moved its station. The platoon traveled from Einruhr through rainy weather and on muddy roads, stopping in Vlatten, Mechernich, and Munstereifel before finally arriving at their new bivouac area in Bad-Neuenahr, Germany. Finally, on March 9 the German-organized resistance to the Allied drive to the Rhine collapsed in the face of the 9th and 23rd regimental attacks. The MP Platoon remained stationed at Bad-Neuenahr for twelve days as the 2nd Infantry Division engaged more German troops and secured further Rhineland soil en route to the next major offensive.

On March 12, 1945, while the MP Platoon was still bivouacked in Bad-Neuenahr, Major William North received word that he had been awarded the croix de guerre with palm by the French government on January 29, 1945. The croix de guerre citation that follows is a photo of the original that was sent to Major William North by the French government. Both the original citation and medal are in my possession.

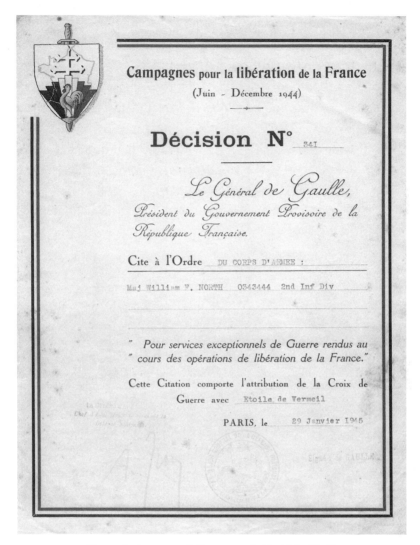

Campagnes pour la libération de la France

(Juin - Décembre 1944)

Décision N° 341

Le Général de Gaulle,
Président du Gouvernement Provisoire de la
République Française.

Cite à l'Ordre DU CORPS D'ARMEE :

Maj William F. NORTH 0343444 2nd Inf Div

" Pour services exceptionnels de Guerre rendus au
" cours des opérations de libération de la France."

Cette Citation comporte l'attribution de la Croix de
Guerre avec Etoile de Vermeil

PARIS, le 29 Janvier 1945

The croix de guerre citation presented to Major North.

During this period, Privates First Class Raymond D. Atkinson, Russell V. Cather, and Eugene M. Anderson were sent to the 102nd Evacuation Hospital for undisclosed wounds or injuries. As personnel were sent to the hospital for various reasons, the 3rd Replacement Depot made good use of troops who had healed, hurriedly placing them back into service. Many replacements were sent to the MP Platoon in an effort to bolster their strength.

At the end of March, former personnel who had been casualties but were now well enough to resume their duties began to return to the MP Platoon. Private First Class John R. Irvin, Private First Class Charles H. Waldron, Corporal Joseph O. Accetone, Corporal Stephen Wahal, Private First Class Wallace Bergman, Private First Class Dorsey Howling, Corporal Phillip Farley, Private First Class Ralph Bloom, Private First Class John Klak, Private First Class Raymond Perry, Private Floyd Russell, Sergeant William Tiernan, Private Robert McLean, Private Walter Rose, Private Glenn Schively, Private First Class Raymond Atkinson, and Private First Class Russell V. Cather would all rejoin the platoon as it raced across Germany with the rest of the Division.

Four 2nd Infantry Division MPs are having a breakfast of Wheaties, compliments of the US Army. No names were listed on the back of this photo—just "Germany, March 1945," which places this location anywhere from Vlatten to Sachsenhausen.

Until recently when I examined this photo, I had forgotten that my dad would usually buy Wheaties at the store. When my brother and I were children, he would often sit with us and eat a bowl for breakfast.

As the infantry fought forward, 5,007 prisoners of war were processed by the MP Platoon through the 2nd Infantry Division's PWE located at Bad-Neuenahr. It became apparent to the men of the Division that they had reached a turning point of the war. They witnessed the disorganized resistance of the scattered German units west of the Rhine River whose actions only bought them enough time to fall back, often without discernible battle order.

The Ludendorf Railway Bridge, also known as the Remagen Bridge, had been captured fully intact by the advancing Allied forces on March 7. However, the German Air Force continued in persistent efforts to plunge it into the Rhine River, thus denying its use to US troops. On March 8, less than thirty hours after Allied troops had captured the bridge, German artillery had opened fire on the bridge, coinciding with their attacks by air. During the twenty-four-hour assault on the bridge by German artillery, air, and V-2 rocket attacks, the MP Platoon had played a significant role in maintaining a hold on the bridgehead across the Rhine. Now that they were in control of the west bank of the Rhine River, and with the retreating Wehrmacht offering little resistance, the 2nd Infantry Division prepared to cross the river to take up new positions near the Remagen bridgehead.

In an attempt to get more troops across the Rhine River in a short period of time, the US Army erected three temporary bridges at different points on the river. These pontoon and treadway bridges crossed the river at Sinzig, Linz, and Bad-Honningen. Meanwhile, army engineers struggled to repair the Remagen Bridge, which was badly damaged by the fighting of the previous weeks. The makeshift bridges became even more vital after the Remagen Bridge collapsed suddenly on March 17. The stress on the remaining supporting structures of the bridge had caused it to crumble into the river, killing twenty-eight of the soldiers who fought gallantly to save it.

The badly damaged Remagen Bridge, under repair.

The collapsed Remagen Bridge, March 20, 1945. (From the North photo collection.)

Nonetheless, the 2nd Infantry Division had soon crossed the river using the secondary bridges and arrived at Sinzig, Germany, by March 21.

Corporal Accetone, Sergeant Rentko, and Sergeant Ciesnicki, Bad-Neuenahr, Germany (near the Remagen Bridge), March 18, 1945.

Major North, Sinzig, Germany, March 20, 1945.

Paul Porter standing on the banks of the Rhine River, Sinzig, Germany, March 20, 1945.

Sergeant George Epperly, at the Remagen Bridge, March 20, 1945.

Lt. Meeth and Lt. Jarcunski, Sinzig, Germany, March 20, 1945.

2nd Infantry Division crossing the Rhine River, Sinzig, Germany, March 21, 1945.

MPs Anderson and Segers standing on a pontoon bridge crossing the Rhine River, Linz, Germany, March 21, 1945.

A number of 2nd Infantry Division men were awarded medals for their heroic service during this time, including MP Joseph A. Beri, who received the Bronze Star on March 21.

R E S T R I C T E D

HE.DQU.RTERS 2D INFANTRY DIVISION
.FO #2, U. S. Army

0641

GENERAL ORDERS   22 March 1945
NUMBER   31

                                                                    Section
AWARD OF BRONZE STAR MEDAL —   I
AWARD OF BRONZE STAR MEDAL (MERITORIOUS) — — — — — — — — — — — — — — —   II
AWARD OF BRONZE STAR MEDAL (OAK LEAF CLUSTER) — — — — — — — — — — — — — III
AWARD OF BRONZE STAR MEDAL (OAK LEAF CLUSTER)(POSTHUMOUS) — — — — — — —   IV

I — AWARD OF BRONZE STAR MEDAL — In accordance with AR 600-45 and Circular 2, Headquarters First United States Army, dated 4 January 1945, the Bronze Star Medal is awarded to Staff Sergeant JAMES T. MINOR, 35509457, Infantry, 9th Infantry Regiment, who, while serving with the Army of the United States, distinguished himself by heroic achievements in connection with military operations against the enemy in Brittany, France, on 1 August 1944. Entered military service from Kentucky.

In accordance with AR 600-45 and Circular 2, Headquarters First United States Army, dated 4 January 1945, the Bronze Star Medal is awarded to the following named officer and enlisted men, who, while serving with the Army of the United States, distinguished themselves by heroic achievements in connection with military operations against the enemy in Belgium and Western Germany, on the dates shown:

NAME	ASN	RANK	ARM OR SERVICE	DATE	ENTERED MILITARY SERVICE FROM

37TH FIELD ARTILLERY BATTALION
The citation is as follows:

NAME	ASN	RANK	ARM OR SERVICE	DATE	ENTERED MILITARY SERVICE FROM
MOORE, KENNETH	6960064	Cpl	FA	17-18 December 1944	Texas

741ST TANK BATTALION
The citations are as follows:

NAME	ASN	RANK	ARM OR SERVICE	DATE	ENTERED MILITARY SERVICE FROM
BARCELLONA, GAETANO R.	01017167	1st Lt	Inf	18 December 1944	Texas
GALLIHER, HANSON B.	35259324	Tec 4	Inf	4 February 1945	Indiana
GOETZ, EVERETT D.	16053939	Sgt	Inf	2 February 1945	Illinois
SHORT, ESTLE I.	36311225	Sgt	Inf	6 February 1945	Illinois

II — AWARD OF BRONZE STAR MEDAL (MERITORIOUS) — In accordance with AR 600-45 and Circular 2, Headquarters First United States Army, dated 4 January 1945, the Bronze Star Medal is awarded to Private First Class JOSEPH A. BERI, 36179606, Corps of Military Police, Military Police Platoon, 2d Infantry Division, while serving with the Army of the United States, for exceptionally meritorious achievements in performance of outstanding service against the enemy in Belgium, for the period 17 December 1944 to 7 February 1945. Entered military service from Michigan.

In accordance with AR 600-45 and Circular 2, Headquarters First United States Army, dated 4 January 1945, the Bronze Star Medal is awarded to Captain JAMES W. BRYAN, 01685123, Medical Corps, 2d Medical Battalion, while serving with the Army of the United States, for exceptionally meritorious achievements in performance of out-

DECLASSIFIED
DOD Dir. 5200.9, Sept. 27, 1958
NNW by _____ date _____

— 1 — (Over)

R E S T R I C T E D

General Order No. 31, citing MP Joseph A. Beri for the Bronze Star.

By March 22 the MP Platoon was on the move once again, this time traveling thirteen miles along the river to Honningen, Germany, located on the east bank of the Rhine. The 2nd Infantry Division moved at a hurried pace now, hoping to quickly neutralize the remaining German defenses. Within nine days, they passed through the towns of Niederpeiper-Segendorf, Hohr-Grenzhausen, Hadamar, Homberg, and Sachsenhausen.

MPs crossing a treadway bridge, Honningen, Germany, March 22, 1945.

MPs Helfer and Porter standing on a treadway bridge over the Rhine River, Honningen, Germany, March 22, 1945.

In the last days of March, the infantry moved at an even more accelerated pace in an attempt to keep up with the armored spearheads, which had covered two hundred miles in three days. During this quick advance through the Rhineland, the MP Platoon had to deal with the large number of prisoners who surrendered or were captured. Because they lacked sufficient equipment and manpower to transport the vast numbers of German soldiers now in their custody, the remainder of the prisoners were disarmed and instructed to march to the rear of the advancing US Army. Eventually they would come upon units who could process them into prisoner of war enclosures.

A snapshot of the German autobahn found in my father's collection of photos.

Hitler's paved highway, the autobahn, was the preferred route for sending the defeated German soldiers to the rear. The wide lanes and long stretches of the highway allowed for large numbers of POWs to march toward the rear while American troops and equipment moved forward at the same time. The autobahn made it possible for this process to take place without the delays normally associated with the narrow roads encountered throughout most of Europe.

Three German prisoners captured at Homburg. A copy of this photo was found in the collection of Major William North, but it also appears in the book Combat History of the Second Infantry Division in World War II. *An inscription on the back of the photo identifies the date as March 30, 1945. It is also marked "Cleared by US Army Censors."*

Reverse of the previous photograph, marked by the Field Press Censor.

Dozens of captured German prisoners listen to instructions from 2nd Infantry Division MPs, Ruddinghausen, Germany, March 30, 1945. This photo was given to Major North by Sergeant A. T. Martin of the 165th Signal Corps.

Reverse of the previous photograph, marked by the Field Press Censor.

10

The Pursuit through Germany

April–May 1945

Although they were in full retreat by the first week of April, German forces continued to defend every inch of the German homeland, many fighting to the death. As the Division moved quickly, the MP Platoon spent less than a day at each of their stations of Niederlistingen, Grebenstein, Veckerhagen, and Dransfeld. Upon reaching the Weser River, elements of the 23rd Infantry crossed in assault boats and secured the opposite bank at Veckerhagen.

In the final days of what became known as "the pursuit across Germany," the 2nd Infantry Division and other Allied forces launched another major offensive. They advanced at a rate of twenty to thirty miles a day, seizing town after town and capturing thousands of German prisoners. During the month of April, the MP Platoon processed 18,773 prisoners of war and an additional 313 Nazi Party leaders through the 2nd Infantry Division PWEs. Due to the large number of prisoners on hand, the MP Platoon was forced to utilize every facility. American troops continued to move forward, seizing large towns such as Giessen and Warburg en route to their next destination, Gottingen and Sonderhausen, both of which lay on the other side of the Leine River.

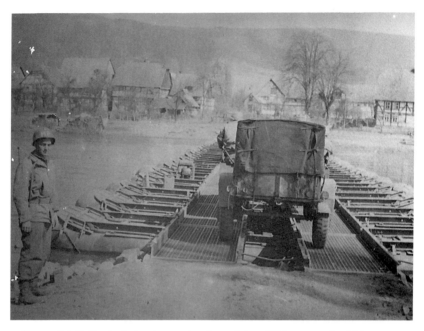

Corporal J. R. Cantrell stands guard as he watches US troops and vehicles cross the Weser River on a treadway bridge built by the 2nd Division Engineers.

Cantrell remembered the moment portrayed in the photo above very well, and shared with me that he had been forced to avoid sniper fire directed at him from Germans hiding in the buildings on the other side of the river earlier in the day. That night the 23rd Infantry secured a firm hold on the temporary treadway bridgehead and neutralized the enemy resistance in the town of Veckerhagen. In spite of the tense situation, the MPs still found opportunities to capture memorable moments on film, as seen on the following page where Joseph Accetone poses with a stuffed bear outside a building in Veckerhagen.

Joseph Accetone, Veckerhagen, Germany, April 7, 1945.

By April 8 the 2nd Infantry Division had secured the town of Gottingen with little enemy resistance. Here they found a German hospital unit fully intact, containing both German and Allied patients. As a bonus, the Division also captured an abandoned and fully intact German airfield.

Jeep No. 5, driven by Private First Class James Edwards, sits just off the road next to the small shack on the right. Behind the camera, Edwards takes a moment to capture history as it unfolds.

Bosch prisoners, Gottingen, Germany, April 8, 1945.

A captured German hospital unit, Gottingen, Germany, April 8, 1945.

German ME 109s, captured at the Luftwaffe airfield near Gottingen, Germany, April 8, 1945.

Major North and Corporal Joseph Accetone, near the runway of a captured Luftwaffe airfield, Gottingen, Germany, April 8, 1945.

Private First Class Kenneth Segers, Gottingen, Germany, April 9, 1945.

MPs looking relaxed in Gottingen, Germany, April 9, 1945.

There is a noticeable difference in the mood of many of these MPs as they recognize their time left in Germany is short. As they obviously are aware, the defeat of the German Army is imminent. According to a portion of the After Action Reports below, the improving weather conditions were also responsible for the jovial mood of the MPs in April.

> During the month of April roads were found in excellent condition, usually hard surfaced, two-way. Weather conditions changed from preceeding month, most of the month being cold and raining. In the early part of April the Division crossed the Weser River. By-passes had to be used to the approach of the bridges and the far side. Four (4) SCR 610 radios, mounted on LAC M-8s, were used at critical road junctions to restrict non-essential traffic from hampering traffic conditions over the Weser River. The Division moved on the average of four (4) times per week. Total distance covered by the Division was two hundred and ninety-nine (299) miles during the month of April. Traffic control was provided the Division on each of its moves. In its pursuit of the enemy the Division captured great numbers of Prisoners of War. Traffic posts were used for apprehension and guarding of Prisoners of War and the Traffic Section was used to supplement the regular Police Section due to the large numbers of prisoners. In addition of handling of regular traffic posts, the Traffic Section also handled the police of the town of Bad Lausick, Germany, arresting all violators of the non-fraternization policy and curfew violation. Several reconnaissances were completed the latter part of April for future moves of the Division.

According to other reports from this period, Corporal Paul M. Porter was promoted to the rank of sergeant by platoon order No. 9 on April 9. The following day, Sergeant John P. Sears was mentioned in the Morning Reports as returning to the MP Platoon after recovering from his injuries. He had been wounded in action on February 21 by the same German patrol that had killed Private First Class Angelo Watznauer at Herhahn.

Sergeant Paul Porter celebrates his promotion in Wollmarshausen, Germany, April 9, 1945.

While bivouacked at Wollmarshausen, Germany, from April 8 to 10, the MP Platoon stayed busy processing the vast number of prisoners. In many cases the Division only took as many prisoners as necessary, which generally included SS troops fanatically loyal to Hitler and still too dangerous not to be in a prisoner of war enclosure. By now the 2nd Infantry Division was forced to move quickly to keep up with the rest of the advancing American troops. They still met with various grimly determined enemy groups, but none of them delayed the advance until they moved into the industrial area of Merseburg on April 13.

It was in Merseburg that the Germans turned more than one thousand guns normally employed as antiaircraft batteries upon the Allied ground forces with remarkable accuracy. The flat shooting trajectory of this weapon—as opposed to the arc of an incoming artillery shell—meant that the target had no warning of its approach until the projectile exploded upon impact.

Although this was very effective at slowing the Allied advance, a large part of that effectiveness was attributable to the shock factor these weapons initially provided. Their limited mobility, however, proved to be their Achilles heel. Since these large guns were stationary ground weapons, they were susceptible to the Division's artillery, which dealt with them easily from a safe distance.

As the 2nd Infantry Division moved forward into this area under the cover of darkness, the infantry units engaged the antiaircraft gunners in ground fighting and hand-to-hand combat. Not trained in ground fighting combat techniques, the antiaircraft gunners were no match for the well-trained infantry of the 2nd Division. The Division moved swiftly during this night maneuver, neutralizing each battery of the German antiaircraft weapons and capturing or killing their gunners. The 2nd Infantry Division captured or destroyed more than five hundred antiaircraft heavy weapons during their drive around Merseburg and into Leipzig. By April 18, the Division had captured an additional eight thousand German prisoners, many of whom were recovering from battlefield wounds and other injuries, along with at least one German car, seen in the following photo.

Private First Class James Edwards driving a German car in Markrandstadt, Germany, April 18, 1945.

By mid-April the MP platoon had completed ten station changes as they moved along with the infantry through the heart of Germany. With each day's advance, the loss of key personnel hampered their efforts to maintain peak efficiency. Since April 1 the MP Platoon had lost another six men to a variety of battle and nonbattle related wounds and injuries. Private First Class Adolf Meier, Private First Class Nathan Hibbert, Private First Class Clarence Herring, Private First Class John Klak, Tec-5 James Sullivan, and Private First Class Stephen Wahal were all sent to rear hospitals for treatment during this period.

MP Ray Gammons leans against a crashed German JU88 bomber, near Leipzig, Germany, April 19, 1945.

German POWs captured by the 2nd Infantry Division. An unidentified MP keeps a watchful eye. Leipzig, Germany, April 19, 1945.

Sergeant Walter D. Higgins, Leipzig, Germany, April 19, 1945.

Richard Nelson, Leipzig, Germany, April 19, 1945.

In the final days of April 1945, the Military Police Platoon continued to process and intern prisoners of war, keeping up with the advance of the infantry as they moved from Schladebach to Markrandstadt, and then onto Bad-Lausick by April 20, 1945.

Bruce Plyler, Bad-Lausick, Germany, April 21, 1945.

246

American Red Cross workers in Bad-Lausick, Germany, April 1945.

Private First Class Okley White and Staff Sergeant John Rentko, Bad-Lausick, Germany, April 21, 1945.

Tec-5 Richard Magers, MP Platoon barber and orderly, Bad-Lausick, Germany, April 21, 1945.

Private First Class George Swearingen, Bad-Lausick, Germany, April 21, 1945.

Private First Class William Davidson, Bad-Lausick, Germany, April 21, 1945.

2nd Infantry Division Counterintelligence Corps, Bad-Lausick, Germany, April 21, 1945.

On April 24, the MP Platoon received word that it had been awarded the Meritorious Service Unit plaque per paragraph IV General Order No. 48 Second Infantry Division, for outstanding service rendered for the Allied cause—an award similar to the Legion of Merit for an individual soldier. The following day in a ceremony, the MP Platoon acted as the guard of honor during the presentation of awards.

––––––––––––––––––

In an effort to delay the advance of the American army units moving east toward the Elbe River, German engineers had destroyed two sections of the Elbe River bridge at Torgau, even as the Russians (now American allies) moved west toward the same destination. No doubt the destruction of the bridge proved to be an inconvenience to both US and Russian forces; its destruction, however, merely delayed the inevitable.

On April 25, at a meeting that took place on the Elbe River twenty miles east of the 2nd Infantry Division's Command Post, the Russian and American soldiers met for the first time to shake hands and exchange congratulations. Although history identifies the 69th Division as the first US troops to make contact with the Russians, several members of the MP Platoon arrived at the Elbe River that day as well. By evidence of the photos appearing on the following pages, it is quite clear that the 2nd Infantry Division shared a portion of that important historical moment with the 69th Division.

Given the explanation on the back of each of the following photos, there is no doubt that a contingent of MPs from the 2nd Infantry Division including Major William North and Private First Class James D. Edwards were present when the Russians crossed the Elbe River to meet the US forces in Torgau, Germany, on the west bank. Following is an excerpt from a letter written by Glynn Raby from Company H, 9th Infantry detailing his memory of these events:

In late April 1945, the 2nd Infantry Division's eastward advance halted at the Mulde River as the Russians neared the Elbe River, some twenty miles further east. For two great armies, advancing toward each other to meet head-on could have been chaotic. The 9th Regiment was at the town of Colditz, about fifteen miles southeast of Leipzig.

On April 25, the regiment sent a mounted patrol east across the Mulde in an attempt to make contact with the Russian forces. With an artillery observation plane overhead, the patrol consisted of a light tank, one or more recon cars, jeeps with .50 cal and .30 cal MGs, and 2½-ton trucks carrying riflemen. We departed after breakfast and drove through several villages. I don't remember seeing any civilians.

Colonel H. sent two jeeps with .30 cal water-cooled MGs. Arnold Yager drove one, Virgil Monroe was the gunner, another man and I were also aboard. Late morning we stopped in a village and found some "unattended" apple cider, which soon replaced the water in the cans, which was meant for cooling the MG barrels. Later in the day, some of it was used for that purpose.

Early afternoon the road we were on approached a wooded ridgeline, and beyond that was a large open plain and then a canal. Beyond that was a small town. As soon as the leading elements of the patrol passed the ridge, we began receiving small arms fire from somewhere in the town. A large red cross was painted on the side of one building—presumably a hospital—and the firing seemed to come from that building or close by. When we returned fire, they ceased.

We went no further, as word from the observation plane was that the bridges across the canal had been blown. We reversed our route and returned to Colditz in late afternoon. We were told that the Russian forces were spotted just beyond the town. We also learned that just to our north, a patrol from the 69th Division had contacted the Russians at Torgau and made history that same day.

—Glynn Raby

Elbe River bridge, Torgau, Germany, April 25, 1945.

Dad wrote, "That's my jeep in front!" Torgau, Germany, April 25, 1945.

"Long live the victory of the military alience of Amerika, England and the Soviet Union over the German Facist occupants [sic]." April 25, 1945.

Russian soldiers crossing the Elbe on a rope-drawn ferry to meet the Americans coming from the west, April 26, 1945.

253

An unidentified 2nd Infantry Division officer, possibly Major General Robertson, wearing glasses on the Elbe River, April 26, 1945.

A female Russian MP in Torgau, Germany, April 26, 1945. This photo was taken by Private First Class James Edwards.

Private First Class Zane Tugman poses with a Russian Army doctor somewhere between Bad-Lausick, Germany and the Elbe River. Tugman wears the typical headgear and goggles the MPs wore when riding their motorcycles.

Major North confers with two Russian officers near the 2nd Infantry Division frontier on April 26, 1945. Written on the back by the unknown photographer are the words, "Curly North attempting to explain to a Russian Major and a Captain how excruciating their cigarettes are."

V Corps Commander Major General Clarence Huebner and his Russian counterpart, Major General Balankov, commander of the 34th Corps, meeting in Torgau, Germany, April 27, 1945.

Reverse side of the previous photograph with a notation written by the photographer, Major William North.

It is likely that during this time the commanding officers of each army spent some time discussing the territorial dividing lines that would determine the future of many Germans at the end of the war. Since April 20, scores of German troops and civilians had been fleeing across the Mulde River at Grimma in an effort to escape the life that would await them under the Russian rule of communism. The 38th Infantry, which was stationed at Grimma, had to place ladders on the blown apart bridge, which had fallen virtually intact onto the riverbank below. In spite of this, German troops trying to surrender as well as displaced persons used this bridge as a means to cross the river to the American-held territory.

At the end of April, the 1st and 9th Armies completed mop-up operations. US forces encircled the Ruhr Gap—an industrial area in western Germany that still contained thousands of German soldiers. More than three hundred thousand German prisoners were captured as the Ruhr Gap was closed, cutting off the Germans from their supply lines and communications. With the disintegration of the German armed forces complete, it was painfully obvious to the Nazi Party and Adolf Hitler that they had been defeated and the fall of Berlin was imminent. As Russian soldiers stormed the city and overwhelmed its heavily entrenched defenders, Hitler committed suicide on April 30, 1945, ending the tyrannical rule he had held over Germany and the European continent for more than a decade.

With Hitler dead, most of the Wehrmacht destroyed or captured, and Berlin in the hands of the Russian armies, one last campaign lay ahead for the 2nd Infantry Division. On May 1, as the 3rd Army under General George Patton advanced toward Czechoslovakia, the 2nd Infantry Division was swiftly transferred from the 1st Army to the 3rd Army. They were tasked with holding territory already gained by Patton's rapidly advancing armor. After traveling 205 miles south from Bad-Lausick in a serpentine motor convoy, the 2nd Infantry Division arrived at a sector near the Czechoslovakian border where it began its final campaign.

11

The Czech Offensive

May 1–June 18, 1945

En route to Czechoslovakia, the MP Platoon reached the town of Ober-Viechtach, Germany, on May 1, 1945, where they posted routes to direct the 23rd and 38th Regimental Combat Teams to their new assembly areas. On May 2, 1945, the 38th Infantry took control of the Waldmunchen-Domazlice sector and the roads leading to Pilsen, Czechoslovakia. The remaining pockets of German resistance in the area crumbled. On May 4, in the vicinity of Ober-Viechtach and Rotz, lead elements of the German 11th Panzer Division—which had already surrendered to Lieutenant General Horace McBride through their commander, General Hermann Balck—began arriving in the 3rd Army sector and the 2nd Infantry Division's area of responsibility. Lieutenant General McBride was division commander of the 80th Infantry Division when General Balck surrendered to him.

The German 11th Panzer Division surrenders to the 2nd Infantry Division, Rotz, Germany, May 4, 1945. (Photo by Private First Class James Edwards.)

The German 11th Panzer Division surrenders to the 2nd Infantry Division, Rotz, Germany, May 4, 1945. (Photo by Private First Class James Edwards.)

As they neared Czechoslovakia, the 3rd Army also encountered a number of Allied POWs who had been liberated as the Germans retreated into Bohemia.

POWs liberated by the 2nd Infantry Division, May 4, 1945. The Indianhead insignia on the sign marks the way for 2nd Infantry Division troops. The sign indicates to the advancing units that they are entering the town of Waldmunchen, Germany.

The back of the photo indicates that these are two British soldiers and one American. These men would have been sent to the rear for health care, food, and rest, as all liberated Allied POWs were before being processed out of the war.

The 3rd Army, with the 2nd and 90th Infantry Divisions attached, continued to move southeast toward Czechoslovakia, crossing the mountains and going through the Bohemian Forest. Here they closed the noose on the remainder of the German forces, encircling and trapping sixty German divisions. Although the united German troops still made up a formidable force capable of inflicting heavy casualties on the advancing Allied army, instead they made a desperate lunge toward American lines, surrendering by the thousands in an effort to avoid being captured by the advancing Russians. The lead elements of the 16th Armored Division, supported by the 2nd Infantry Division, entered Pilsen on May 4, 1945, and were greeted by crowds of Czechs eager to welcome their liberators.

The 16th Armored enters Pilsen, May 4, 1945.

Pfc. Edwards's jeep and an unidentified MP in Pilsen public square, May 7, 1945.

Pilsen public square. George Swearingen captured this moment on film in May 1945 at the end of the war. The poor quality is due to copying of the original at low resolution.

George Swearingen directing traffic, Pilsen, Czechoslovakia, May 7, 1945.

The Skoda Works—a manufacturing facility that produced weapons for the German Army until the liberation of Czechoslovakia—May 7, 1945.

The Skoda Works, Pilsen, Czechoslovakia, May 7, 1945.

On May 7, 1945, in Reims, France, at 2:41 a.m., German General Alfred Jodhl signed the unconditional surrender of all German forces on all fronts, ending the European phase of World War II.

A copy of the act of surrender signed May 7, 1945, on behalf of the German High Command. (Source: National Archives and Records Administration.)

For nearly a month, numerous parades, medal ceremonies, and other official functions would be held in the Pilsen public square after the surrender of Germany. Throngs of grateful Czech citizens crowded the streets to witness historic events unfold.

A formal ceremony held on May 8, 1945, in the main public square of Pilsen, where the 2nd Infantry Division conducted a parade in front of thousands of Czech citizens, who looked on as Major General Walter M. Robertson decorated General Salvan, commanding officer of the 5th Russian Tank Corps, with the Legion of Merit.

Major North receives a medal from a Czech official in Pilsen.

Major North is shown here third from the left.

NÁRODNÍ VÝBOR V PLZNI   NATIONAL COMMITTEE AT PLZEŇ

Bojovník   **The fighter**

Maj. North

II. armádní divise U. S. A. byl za zásluhy při osvobození Plzně (Č S R) dekorovám odznakem svobodné PLZNĚ.	of the 2nd Army division of U. S. A. has been decorated for merit on the occasion of the liberation of Plzeň (Czechoslovakia) with the emblem of the liberated city of PLZEŇ.
Plzeň, 2. června 1945.	Plzeň, the 2nd of June 1945.
Předseda Národního výboru: President of National Committee:	Primátor města Plzně: Prime-major of Plzeň:

A document recording Major North's Czech award.

US Army Commanders and Pilsen city leaders during formal ceremonies, May 8, 1945.

Major North wearing his new "Ike jacket," May 8, 1945.

On the previous page, Major William North of the MP Platoon shows off his newly issued "Ike jacket," which was approved by General Eisenhower for wear by all officers and enlisted men in lieu of the longer service coat.

2nd Infantry Division headquarters, Pilsen, Czechoslovakia, May 8, 1945.

Although the German High Command had signed the instrument of surrender on May 7, word of the formal cessation of hostilities would not reach German troops until May 8. The 2nd Infantry Division was enjoying a banquet at the Slavia Building in Pilsen when the formal orders declaring Germany's capitulation were delivered. As the good news spread throughout Pilsen, throngs of Czechs ran into the streets in celebration. They greeted American soldiers with a passionate show of appreciation and showered their liberators with gifts, hugs, and Czech hospitality.

The 2nd Infantry Division celebrates the surrender of Germany and their victory in Europe in the Slavia Building, Pilsen, Czechoslovakia.

Major General Walter M. Robertson is seated at his table in the Slavia Building with whom I believe is his replacement, Brigadier General W. H. Harrison. Although only partially visible, the man sitting next to General Harrison (a colonel by his uniform) shares a striking resemblance with Colonel O. M. Barsanti.

This photo of Major North and several other officers was provided by Max North, Major North's son, and were part of the collection of personal items his father brought home from the European theater.

It is also important to note that all of the enlisted men shown in the previous photos are wearing newly issued Ike jackets, whereas the officers are wearing the traditional length service coat.

Czech soldiers, Domazlice, Czechoslovakia, May 8, 1945.

MP Platoon traffic post, Pilsen, Czechoslovakia.

2nd Infantry Division MP jeep bearing the Czech flag, May 8, 1945.

On May 9, 1945, 337 days after the Allied invasion force landed on Omaha Beach, victory in Europe was finally proclaimed. The relaxed, cheerful atmosphere in Pilsen is evident in the following photos of the MPs, who continue to carry out their duties.

MP Clarence McCormick also appears in several of the next few photos. Here McCormick poses for a snapshot with two Czech citizens and their dog.

Shortly after the surrender of the German Army, most of the men of the MP Platoon who were not on duty were no longer required to carry their sidearm or wear their steel helmets.

Private First Class James D. Edwards poses for the camera dressed in his Ike jacket, armed with his pistol, and standing next to his jeep "Leta."

MPs Anderson, Bundschuh, Erickson, and Bennett, Pilsen, Czechoslovakia, May 10, 1945.

276

MP Private First Class Calvin Hall, Pilsen, Czechoslovakia, May 1945.

Private First Class James Brown.

By this time in May and with the surrender of Germany formally accomplished a few days earlier, the complete cessation of hostilities created a more normal environment where armed troops were no longer necessary. Clarence McCormick, seen in the following photos, was probably responsible for the safety of a division officer while he transported that officer to various functions in and around the 2nd Infantry Division sector.

Clarence McCormick, Pilsen, Czechoslovakia, May 1945.

Clarence McCormick, Pilsen, Czechoslovakia, May 12, 1945.

McCormick is armed with his pistol in this photo, but many of the MPs who were not actively on duty in Czechoslovakia were not required to arm themselves with their pistols as they would have been earlier in the war. McCormick's MP brassard is plainly visible along with his 2nd Infantry Division patch. His jeep is clearly marked and appears to be parade ready, clean and decorated with a flag, which may be that of a ranking division officer or the Czech colors mounted as a symbol of friendship.

On May 14, the Morning Report would reflect that the status of the MP Platoon was soon to change and a major reorganization of the unit was under way. By May 16, 1945, orders arrived at

Division headquarters that would send a large number of men to the United States for R&R and reunions with their families. Additional orders would soon follow each of these men once they arrived home, informing them of additional training and potential deployment to the Pacific theater in anticipation of an invasion of the Japanese mainland.

Each man in the MP Platoon received orders with the date of their departure, mode of travel, and waypoints on the route back to the United States. From May 16 until June 18, several men each day said their goodbyes to their friends and boarded trucks for the long journey across Europe to the point of embarkation in France. The photos on the next few pages reflect the various attitudes of the MPs as they await their orders to return home to the United States and their families. For the most part they appear relieved that the war in Europe is over, but anxiety also appears to remain among the soldiers as they fear there might be yet another series of battles to fight on the other side of the world.

MPs Erickson, McCormick, Smith, and Cravens, Pilsen, Czechoslovakia, May 12, 1945.

MPs standing in line for chow, Pilsen, Czechoslovakia, May 1945.

2nd Infantry Division MPs loading German soldiers who had surrendered onto trucks, Pilsen, Czechoslovakia, May 12, 1945.

George Epperly and Clifford Helfer, Pilsen, Czechoslovakia, May 12, 1945.

George Epperly and his Czech interpreter, Pilsen, Czechoslovakia, May 13, 1945.

Dickerson, Pilsen, Czechoslovakia, May, 1945.

MP Eugene Anderson and friends, Domazlice, Czechoslovakia, May 23, 1945.

Porter and Davidson in Pilsen, Czechoslovakia, May 1945.

George Swearingen, Pilsen, Czechoslovakia, June 2, 1945.

During the month of May, the MP Platoon made corrections to several Morning Reports dating as far back as July 1944. As the amount of time the MP Platoon had left in Czechoslovakia was quickly coming to an end, headquarters utilized this time to acknowledge those MPs who had sustained wounds in action that were never reported, recognize men who had never received their medals for meritorious acts in combat, and tie up other loose ends in paperwork. The platoon also promoted enlisted men to higher ranks and shifted responsibilities to those who had not departed the unit. Weapons and other equipment not necessary for the return to the US were turned in to the 2nd Infantry Division Quartermaster.

On May 16, Staff Sergeant John P. Sears received orders to return to the US and Reception Station 18, Camp Chaffee, Arkansas. Private First Class Robert Holcomb left for Reception Station 10, Fort Sam Houston, Texas, the same day. For a little more than a month the MP Platoon continued to lose one or two men each day until the remaining soldiers were all ordered to depart for France and then home to the United States. On May 24, after five months in the hospital, the Morning Report showed Private First Class George McConnell, who was seriously wounded with George Swearingen at Camp Elsenborn, returning to the MP Platoon.

J. R. Cantrell was asleep in his quarters on the morning of May 28, 1945, when the door to his room opened suddenly and a fellow MP shouted, "Come on, Cantrell, they're waiting for us, we're going home!" Startled by the sudden interruption, he sprang to his feet and ran out the door of his quarters where he stood in the street with the other MPs pictured on the next page.

MPs receive some good news, May 1945.

One by one, these happy men received their orders from Major North that would send each of them home. On June 1, 1945, as he gathered his gear, Cantrell returned the pistol he had carried throughout the war to the quartermaster in a final act of obedience and respect to the MP Platoon—never even thinking that he might have been able to take it home with him as a keepsake. Later that same morning, J. R. Cantrell departed Pilsen, on his final journey as an MP, sharing his ride with Howard Parker, Robert Whitney, Clifford Helfer, and Earnest Lee.

Since he was ordered to return home three weeks earlier than most of the MP Platoon, this departure turned out to be the last time he saw many of the men he had so proudly served with since the early days of Fort Sam Houston, including one of his good friends, my father, James Edwards. On the day that Cantrell was quickly rushed to a waiting truck and headed home, James Edwards was probably on assignment somewhere in Pilsen, Czechoslovakia. I can only imagine what my father thought once he discovered that his friend J. R. had left for home without a final farewell. This day mixed sadness with joy. As he drove away from his friends and comrades, his travel afforded him time to reflect on the sense of relief that came after the constant fear that he might not survive the war that claimed the lives of more than four hundred thousand of his comrades.

After a four-day trip from Pilsen, Czechoslovakia, to Le Havre, France, Cantrell arrived at the Assembly Area Command near Reims. For approximately three days Cantrell had time to clean up, eat hot meals, rest, and recuperate. Cantrell probably sailed home aboard the USS *Admiral Benson* along with former American POWs, as this was the only ship to leave the port of Le Havre on or near June 5, 1945, according to records (made public on the Internet) tracing World War II troop ship movement.

Arriving at New York Harbor on June 17, 1945, J. R. Cantrell would billet once again at Camp Shanks for a few days before he received his final orders to board a train destined for San Antonio, Texas. After he arrived at Fort Sam Houston a few days later, Cantrell underwent a discharge physical examination, completed his Enlisted Record and Report of Separation, and received his final pay of $115.30. He was issued his honorable discharge and a lapel button, and perhaps exchanged a handshake with Major C. F. Arnold, who approved his discharge form. On June 27, 1945, after serving four years, eight months, and twenty-three days, J. R. Cantrell said goodbye to Fort Sam Houston, the MP Platoon, and the United States Army in his official capacity for the last time, and turned to the next chapter of his long journey in life.

The next photo shows the 2nd Infantry Division headquarters staff in Pilsen before they are reassigned or sent home. This photo was taken almost one year to the day after the original staff photo taken in May 1944 while the 2nd Infantry Division was in Tenby, Wales.

A number of staff officers who appeared in the original photo had left the Division, some by promotion or reassignment, others having been wounded or killed in action. The list that appears on page 290 displays the names of those officers who were still with the Division in May 1945.

2nd Infantry Division staff, Pilsen, Czechoslovakia, May 1945.

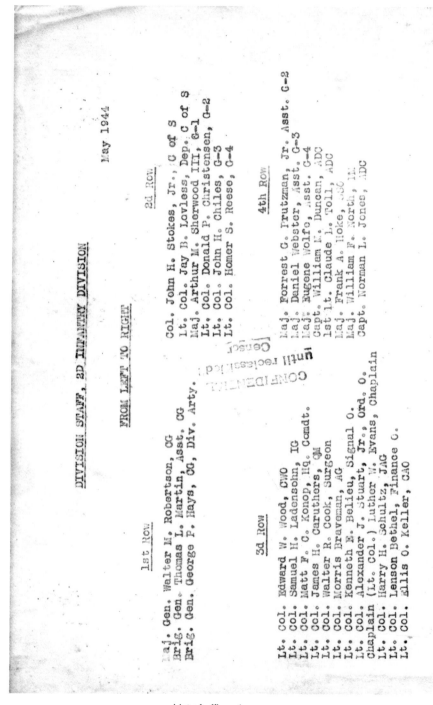

DIVISION STAFF, 2D INFANTRY DIVISION

May 1944

FROM LEFT TO RIGHT

1st Row

Maj. Gen. Walter M. Robertson, CG
Brig. Gen. Thomas L. Martin, Asst. CG
Brig. Gen. George P. Hays, CG, Div. Arty.

2d Row

Col. John H. Stokes, Jr., C of S
Lt. Col. Jay B. Lovless, Dep. C of S
Maj. Arthur M. Sherwood III, G-1
Lt. Col. Donald P. Christensen, G-2
Lt. Col. John H. Chiles, G-3
Lt. Col. Homer S. Reese, G-4

3d Row

Lt. Col. Edward W. Wood, CWO
Lt. Col. Samuel H. Ladensohn, IG
Lt. Col. Matt F. C. Konop, Hq. Comdt.
Lt. Col. James H. Caruthers, QM
Lt. Col. Walter R. Cook, Surgeon
Lt. Col. Morris Braveman, AG
Lt. Col. Kenneth E. Belieu, Signal O.
Lt. Col. Alexander J. Stuart, Jr., Ord. O.
Chaplain (Lt. Col.) Luther W. Evans, Chaplain
Lt. Col. Harry H. Schultz, JAG
Lt. Col. Lenson Bethel, Finance O.
Lt. Col. Ellis O. Keller, CAO

4th Row

Maj. Forrest G. Trutzman, Jr. Asst. G-2
Maj. Daniel Webster, Asst. G-3
Maj. Eugene Wolfe, Asst. G-4
Capt. William K. Duncan, ADC
1st Lt. Claude L. Toll, ADC
Maj. Frank A. Hoke, ADC
Maj. William F. North, IG
Capt. Norman L. Jones, ADC

CONFIDENTIAL until reclassified: Censor

List of officers' names.

Evidently by June 1945 James Edwards anticipated his return to the United States. He was probably advised by his commanding officer that if he intended to return home with Lady, it would be necessary for him to have the dog vaccinated for rabies. The document below proves that he did so. Since I am not remotely fluent in the Czech language, Bob Balcar, a good friend of the American people and the US 2nd Infantry Division, as well as a citizen of Czechoslovakia, was kind enough to translate this document for me.

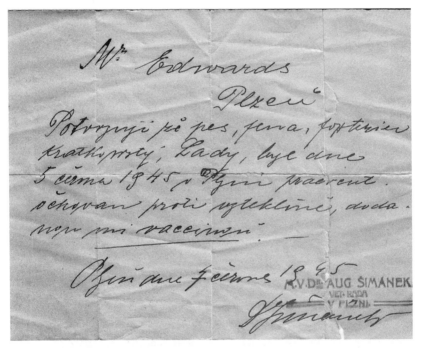

Certificate from the Czech veterinarian who vaccinated Lady for rabies.

Dear Mr. Edwards,

I am very glad to get this e-mail from you and to have a chance to help you. Please accept my best regards from our country—from the Czech Republic your father had helped to liberate. The document you have sent me is a certificate issued by a Czech veterinarian in Pilsen concerning vaccination of a female dog named Lady.

Here is the exact translation:

Mr. Edwards, Pilsen

I confirm hereby that the female dog, shorthaired fox terrier, named Lady, was preventive vaccinated against rabies on 5 June 1945 with a vaccine delivered to me.

Pilsen, 7 June 1945

—Augustin Šimánek, DVM, Veterinary councilor

Have a pleasant Advent time!

—*Bob Balcar*

Edwards and Swearingen in front of Edwards's jeep, MP-5, Domazlice, Czechoslovakia, June 8, 1945.

George Swearingen and Sergeant Farr, Domazlice, Czechoslovakia, June 8, 1945.

```
                                      Domazlice, Czech.
                                      Sat. June, 9, 1945     II P.M.


     Hello Darling,
     Darling If you dont mind, Ill try to write you a few lines,
     I dont really know anything to write but Ill try any way.

          I havent had a letter from you in so long it isnt
     even funny, I know it isnt your fault, But it still doesnt
     keep me from being lonely and blue.
          Honey guess where im going? Thats right you e wrong,
     Im moveing to Paris, Well close to Paris any way. Maybe ill
     get to see some of the place before i come home. I hope so.
          I went into the dance tonight but i didnt dance a
     time, I didnt have a woman, Baby. I wasnt interested, Im
     only interested in one thing, darling. And thats getting
     home to my baby. YOU. I never was so tired of a place in
     all of my life
          I saw a little girl killed to day, Every time i think
     of it it makes me sick. I went through all this over here
     and i never saw anything that i hated so much, Or made me
     feel any worse.
          I was reading one o  your old letters to day honey,
     You were probly feeling well when you wrote it, Cause you
     really sounded that way. But Ill tell you  now, If you are
     si ck when i come home, Ill go over the hill. That darling,
     would be the last straw, I just wont stand for any tricks
     like that. Youll probly wish after the first week that you
     could get sick and stay that way. If you dont wish it, youre
     a better woman then i gave you credit for being.
          Baby i have  our rolls of film I think ill send you,
     maybe you can find a camera to take them in. I dont have one
     any more. And i also have some more pictures im going to
     send you.
          Do you know a tailor there in in cleburne that you
     might be able to talk into giving you a rush order on a suit
     of clothes for your old man whenhe gets home? Maybe you
     might throw a real sweet smile in his direction if you would
     think of me when you do it. I wouldnt mind to much. not for
     just one time.
          Well darling i guess you had better kissme good night
     for this time, And tell Mom I said hello. Bye be real sweet
     just for me, And dont do anything i wouldnt want you to.
     I love you, Darling, Youd be terribly nice to come home to.


                                      Love always
                                      Your loveing hubby
                                      Eddie
```

*Letter from James Edwards to his wife, Aleta, written in Domazlice,
Czechoslovakia, June 9, 1945.*

Domazlice, Czech.
Wed. June, 13, 1945   9'45 P.M.

Hello Darling

Honey I dont Know a darn thing to write tonight
But if my bab y doesnt mind to much, Ill try,which will
be about all. I didnt get a letter from you to day so
that will make it that much harder. Ive only had one
letter from you in a week or more. We have the poorest
mail service going, I do believe. One minute youget it
all and the next you dont get any. Dont pay any attention
to me tonight darling, I feel like the north end of a
South bound Jackass. You can imigine what your old man
looks like now or feels like, Cant you, Honey?
          I went to thedan ce tonight, But i didnt dance any
The music wasnt so hot, And besides I was kindly peed off.
So I just drank beer, (Water) Thats what its like.I
guess a man would be better off if he would take it to
the latrine and pour it out, Instead of acting as the in
between man. It hasnt any achohol in it at all.
          I ha d aletter from Sam This morning, Hes worring
about getting back to the states, So he can get married,
Can you Imigine any one wanting to get married??? I dont
want to, But i would like to get back to the darling
little wife that I already have.Honey you dont know what
I would give to be able to hold you in my arms tonight.
Its been so long since i had a beauti ful doll like you
in my arms, I wouldnt know what to do if i ever got a hold
o' you. I was telling one of the boys tonight about
wanting to gethome, And he said, " I cant blame you for
wanting to get home, If I had what you have, I would want
to get home too. He said. " I saw her over at the service
club one day, And i was e yeing Her up for a date, Then
some one had to tell me she was your wife? He said that
really was disgusting to see a beautiful baby like you
then find out you were married." I dont really know how
lucky I am? Darling. I always did expect to marry a girl
that i thought was preety good looking, But I never once
thought Id marry an angle.Maybe your legs are alittle
bowed, But then that doesnt worry me, Cause honey your
face will make up for that,That with a few other things
you have, Dont you thi k! im silly, honey? Dont answer
that you might tellthe truth,
          Sweetheart hows the weather over there now? Gosh!
baby, I hope its better when i get there than it has been
over here, Its really miserable. And its worse than La.
for rain, It will be my luck tho. to get there some time
in Dec. Or Jan. Well then we can sleep real close to g
gether, Cant we darling??? Hello sleep!
          Well Darling I guess This willhave to be all for this
time. Tell Mom I said Hello. Good night Honey. Sweet dreams
I love you and how much i miss you?, Youll never know.

                    Love Always
                    Your Loving Hubby
                    Eddie

*Letter from James Edwards to his wife, Aleta, written in Domazlice,
Czechoslovakia, June 13, 1945.*

Almost three weeks after J. R. Cantrell departed from Czechoslovakia, Edwards left Pilsen on June 19, 1945, in a convoy of trucks destined for France. However, in Ansbach, Germany, he was separated from the 2nd Infantry Division and transferred to the 3rd Army, 512th MP Battalion, Company C, by way of the 99th Division. He would continue his service in Germany with the remaining members of the military police still serving in Europe.

Morning report form, 2d Inf. Div., CMP, 16 June [194]5, 1/2 miles East Ansbach, Germany.

NAME	SERIAL NUMBER	GRADE	MOS	CODE
...il, Robert L	36105316	Pfc	677	X/
...sednik, Edward A	38035196	Pfc	677	/
...rley, George R	18220304	Sgt	652	
...vens, Richard C	18050270	Pfc	677	
...ggins, Walter D	6246991	Sgt	677	
...Donnell, George L	6276793	Pvt	677	
...rring, Clarence R	6955490	Pfc	677	
...berts, John C	18007305	Sgt	677	
...ards, James D	18005119	Pfc	677	
...ndley, Kermit C	18029375	Pfc	677	
...air, Dan C	18035771	Pfc	677	
...chetto, Angelo L	33025393	Pfc	677	
...Geary, George R	6852343	Cpl	677	
...lum, Wilmer F	18013966	Pfc	521	
...dia, Rocco	32021828	Cpl	677	
...rison, Otis L	6261938	Cpl	677	
...ckson, George W	36033089	Cpl	677	
...al, Heinz W	32060291	Sgt	821	

	ATCHD THRUD (2)	TOTAL (4)	RECD FROM DY'S (5)	FOR DUTY (6)	NOT FOR DUTY (7)	L.D. (8)	AW (9)	CONF POK (10)	AB POK (11)	AWOL (12)	MISS (13)
1		1		1							
3		3	1	4							
4		4	1	5							
1		1		1							
6		6		6							
4		4		4							
78	5	83		82		1					
8	3	11		11							
97	8	105		104		1					

I CERTIFY THAT THIS MORNING REPORT IS CORRECT.   PAGE 1 OF 2 PAGES

[signature] W. F. North

W. F. NORTH

Major   CMP

The Morning Report in which thirty MPs received their orders for occupation duty and their transfer to the 3rd Army, 512th MP Battalion, by way of the 99th Infantry Division.

12

Last Stop Le Havre and the Voyage Home

June 19, 1945–

On June 19, 1945, a platoon order was read aloud at an army camp near Ansbach, Germany, by the newly promoted Sergeant Willie Wilson. This order listed the names of all of the MPs who had been selected to return home, as well as those who were assigned to occupation duty. The army had devised a point system that would—in theory—allow soldiers with more points to return home before those with fewer points. Many of those who stayed a few months longer, however, were high-point men, but in the long run, they may have benefited from remaining in Europe rather than returning home and then being sent to face the Japanese in the Pacific.

Sergeant Willie Wilson reads the names of those going home and those continuing their duty, near Ansbach, Germany, June 19, 1945. Somewhere in the crowd of men is Private First Class James D. Edwards.

The MPs at a camp near Ansbach, Germany, June 19, 1945.

R-E-S-T-R-I-C-T-E-D

PARAGRAPH 1, SPECIAL ORDERS NO. 70, HEADQUARTERS 512TH MILITARY POLICE
BATTALION, APO 403, U.S. ARMY, 19 JUNE, 1945.(CONT'D)

COMPANY "C" (CONT'D)

GRADE	NAME	SERIAL NUMBER	MOS	PROFILE	ADJUSTED SERV SCORE
CPL	BARR, ALBERT C.,	33269410	677	A	90
CPL	ERICKSON, GEORGE W.,	36033089	677	B	92
CPL	FESTA, ROCCO	32021828	677	A	85
CPL	HARRISON, OTIS L.,	6261936	677	A	94
CPL	HEGEDUS, ANDREW S.,	32068472	677	A	37
CPL	OGLESBY, LINDSAY W.,	14032135	677	A	90
CPL	SHEEHAN, JOHN H.,	19075175	504	A	90
PFC	BALKUM, WILMER R.,	18013966	677	A	88
PFC	BLAIR, DAN C.,	18035771	521	C	86
PFC	BOTTANDO, JOSEPH L.,	16001573	677	A	88
PFC	BOUCHER, PAUL W.,	32023556	677	A	87
PFC	BURGER, HENRY A.,	33076986	677	A	87
PFC	CRAVENS, RICHARD C.,	18050270	521	A	90
PFC	CYWINSKI, EDWARD J.,	33031981	677	B	90
PFC	DAVIS, ELBERT C.,	14024432	677	A	90
PFC	EDWARDS, JAMES D.,	18005119	677	A	87
PFC	FLETCHER, HOWARD W.,	7024147	677	A	89
PFC	HART, HARRY R.,	32132578	677	A	87
PFC	HERRING, CLARENCE E.,	6955490	677	C	89
PFC	HOLMES, HOWARD E.,	6395706	677	A	89
PFC	HOYT, FRED L.,	6283546	677	A	87
PFC	KLINE, ANDREW E.,	33010447	677	A	89
PFC	KOEPPE, GEORGE	32173475	677	A	85
PFC	LAWLESS, EARNEST G.,	18012124	677	A	87
PFC	LOCHETTO, ANGELO L.,	33035398	677	A	90
PFC	HARCZINKO, GEORGE J.,	32067665	677	A	06
PFC	MCAULEY, CLOYD M.,	34116949	745	A	87
PFC	MICHITSCH, ALOYSIUS W.,	32023551	677	A	83
PFC	PAIGE, MERLE G.,	7032729	677	A	86
PFC	PARKER, WARREN D.,	18010047	677	A	87
PFC	PODSEDNIK, EDWARD A.,	39035106	677	C	89
PFC	RHODEN, CLIFTON A.,	38050300	677	B	93
PFC	ROBERTSON, RAY	35136620	677	A	86
PFC	SMITH, JAMES D.	20403359	677	A	87
PFC	STINE, W.L. (IO)	7008155	651	B	85
PFC	TUGMAN, ZANE	18020749	521	A	87
PFC	WALLACE, OSCAR	18035831	677	A	90
PFC	WOOD, ROBERT L.,	36105318	677	D	87
PFC	YANDLES, KERMIT O.,	18029375	677	B	94
PVT	ELLSWORTH, BRIGHAM E.,	19115816	377	UNKNOWN	88
PVT	GALLIMORE, CONNIE B.,	7024028	651		90
PVT	KALENISH, JOHN M.,	7025822	677	A	89
PVT	MCDONNELL, GEORGE L.,	6276793	677	A	88
PVT	PARSONS, LOUIS J.,	7026259	677	A	90
T SGT	GILER, WILLIAM F.,	32067655	651	A	92

BY ORDER OF MAJOR ALLGEIER:

OFFICIAL:

WILLIAM R. KESLER
1ST LT., 512 MP BN
ADJUTANT.

WILLIAM R. Kesler
WILLIAM R. KESLER
1ST LT., 512 MP BN
ADJUTANT.

DISTRIBUTION A

—4—

R-E-S-T-R-I-C-T-E-D

Special Orders No. 70 from June 19 listing the names of those MPs who would continue service with the 512th MP Battalion. Note James Edwards is among them.

Although the majority of the 2nd Infantry Division had already been ordered home, James Edwards had been notified that his service would continue with the 3rd Army, 512th MP Battalion. On June 19, as my father prepared to be separated from the 2nd Infantry Division MPs, he hurriedly wrote all thirty of the names listed in the Morning Report that day in his address book. In addition to those thirty names, he listed another thirty-seven men who had survived the past twenty-three months with him and would return to the United States.

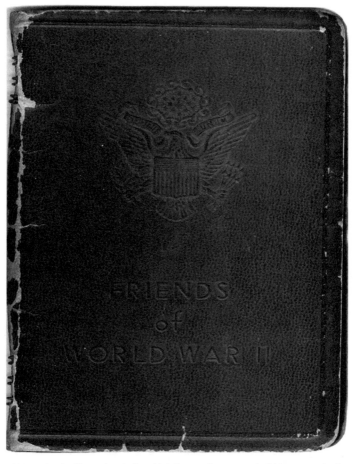

James Edwards's address book, in which he made a record of his comrades' names.

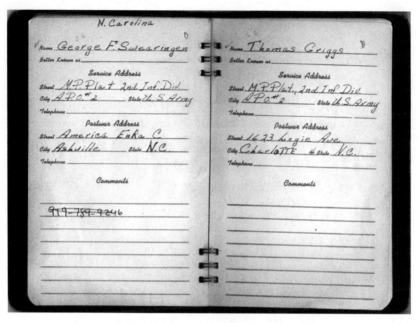

Interior of the address book belonging to James Edwards.

George Swearingen and Thomas Griggs are just two of the MPs whose names were listed in Dad's address book. Beginning with the first page, this is the order in which Dad wrote them: Warren B. Ross, Alfred J. Merrymen, Warren D. Parker, Wilbert R. Balkum, Robert J. Walker, Earnest G. Lawless, Edward A. Podsednik, Zane Tugman, Eugene H. Cooper, Ted Foster, Okley G. White, Joe N. Beckwith, Jimmie Rankin, Dan C. Blair, Glen F. Smith, Richard C. Cravens, Paul Porter, Randy Cathron, Ray W. Gammons, Howard F. McMahan, Howard Moore, William L. Davidson, Willie R. Wilson, James B. Pearson, James E. Hillis, Leonard E. Dixon, Kermit Yandles, Warren D. Parker, George L. McConnell, Carl C. Ballwahn, Russell V. Cather, Willie Taylor, Robert L. Woods, Doris H. Bennett, Edwards Reeve, John W. Ciesnicki, Edward L. Jarczynski, John J. Rentko, James F. Bundschuh, Francis E. Welch, I. C. Meeth, Glenn Schively, Joseph Accetone, Edward J. Cywinski, Francis Cook, Angelo L. Lochetto, Andrew E. Kline, Robert W. Pitts, I. C. Meeth, Ray Hall, Charles H. Waldron, Bruce Plyler, J. R. Bonds, George

Swearingen, Thomas Griggs, Carl Kruger, Norman D. Kent, Walter H. Rose, George Erickson, Clarence McCormick, Richard M. Nelson, Louis Pastre, Charles W. Irvine, Rocco Festa, Richard E. Magers, Eugene Anderson, and M. E. Gibson Jr.

Although J. R. Cantrell's name did not originally appear in the address book above, on one of my visits to his home several months before he passed away, I asked him if he would write his name on the last page. Surprised by my request, he gladly accepted when I expressed to him that Dad would have wanted it that way.

The members of the MP Platoon who were headed home climbed into trucks that same day and departed Germany for France. Along with the majority of the 2nd Infantry Division, they arrived at Camp Norfolk, forty miles southeast of Reims, France, on June 20, 1945.

Lieutenant Thomas J. Cagle, Camp Norfolk, near Reims, France, June 21, 1945.

Frank J. Peters and Clarence Pass, Camp Norfolk, June 21, 1945.

It is important to note that once the MPs arrived in France, the 2nd Infantry Division patch was removed from their uniforms, probably in an attempt to disguise the movements of the Division from any would-be Japanese spies. For two weeks the men of the Division enjoyed a period of rest before being alerted that they would soon board ships for their long voyage back across the Atlantic Ocean. On July 5, the Division moved by rail to Camp Old Gold near Yvetot, France, where they made final preparations for shipment home to the US.

In a ceremony held on July 7, 1945, the United States Army relinquished control of the building that had housed the Headquarters Assembly Area Command of the European theater back to the city of Reims, France. Throughout the war this location served as the war room for the Supreme Headquarters Allied Expeditionary Force (SHAEF) and the planning center for General Eisenhower and his staff. This building was also the meeting place for the surrender negotiations of the German forces in May 1945.

HEADQUARTERS
ASSEMBLY AREA COMMAND
Theater Service Forces
European Theater
United States Army

SHAEF WAR ROOM AT REIMS, FRANCE

The room in which the Germans capitulated in World War II was partitioned off from what was once a large assembly room on the first floor of the Ecole Professionelle in Reims. When Supreme Headquarters moved to Reims, it became the WAR ROOM of SHAEF Forward-the brain center of the Allied Forces and work-shop of General Eisenhower and his staff.

With the exception of minor changes in furnishings, the room as turned over to the city of Reims in a ceremony on July 7, 1945, is the same as it was on May 7, 1945, when surrender negotiations were in progress. Maps, charts and figures have been restored as they existed on that date.

Upon entering the WAR Room one sees on the right a large geographical survey map showing terrain elevations in color. This is called the "Installations Map" and is spotted with small squares of colored cardboard representing supply depots in northern France, Belgium and Luxembourg. It also shows pipe-lines feeding gasoline to the front lines from the Boulogne-Calais coastal area and from Cherbourg. There are notations showing the terminals of underwater pipelines extending from England to France. These are identified as "Plutos" -- a code name. A third row of pipelines extends northward into the combat zones from Marseilles, with a smaller inset map showing the southern part of this line. Fuel and oil storage dumps are designated on the map with a card showing the quantity of supplies on hand.

Walking counter-clockwise around the room, one sees on the next wall a railroad map showing in black lines the routes of all single and double track railroads on the continent. Red lines designate railroads under repair on May 7th. Two charts flank this map on the left. One lists the number of imported and captured locomotives and freight cars being used by the Allied Forces on April 19, 1945. The other lists the military tonnage transported by rail on May 6, 1945.

Perhaps the next chart is the most striking of all. It is a grim black swastika with a red thermometer in the center showing the number of German soldiers captured by the Allied Forces. The chart disclosed that 161 German divisions, representing 4,055,051 troops, had been captured from June 6, 1944, to May 7, 1945.

Directly beneath the swastika are two statistical charts. One shows U.S. and British planned and actual unloadings of supplies at the French channel ports. The second chart is subdivided into three sections; one a breakdown of the number of Germans captured by each Allied Army Group; the second a "Stores Discharged" chart listing the volume of troops, vehicles and supplies unloaded on the continent; and the third listing Allied Ground Forces casualties on the Western Front, showing total casualties up to May 7th as 661,900.

The remaining information on this wall consists of another transportation chart listing ship tonnages arriving, unloaded and cleared at the various ports, and two navigation charts showing the mined areas of the English Channel and the North Sea, with an open line leading to Sweden.

The next wall is completely covered by two large battle maps and a small inset map. One map shows from Budapest to Danzig on the east; from Berchtesgarden on the south to the German-Danish border on the north; and to Paris on the west. This map shows the location of all Allied troop units and headquarters on the Western Front, with string marking the dividing lines between Army Groups, Armies and Army Corps areas.

The second battle map shows the southern Germany-Austrian-Italian "Redoubt" sector. The small inset map shows the La Rochelle coastal zone of western France.

The next wall has Air Force Maps locating all British and American air fields and headquarters on the continent. A "Lay On" board lists the missions assigned to Air Forces on May 6th. There are also Air Force weather maps and charts. A casualty chart lists 197,461 Air Force personnel killed, missing and wounded for the period of September 3, 1939, to February 28, 1945. There is also a score card showing the results of the previous day's operations. The last entry on this board reveals that the RAF Coastal Command, on May 5th, attacked two U-boats. One was listed as a probable while no results were recorded on the second.

The wall above the doorway leading into the War Room is covered with maps of the Pacific; a map showing the German pockets in Western France, and a chart showing the bridges over the Rhine.

In the center of this historic, colorful, map-lined room is a large oak table, 70 inches wide by 190 inches long. Its bare top is begrimed and scarred as if it too had suffered from the ravages of war.

During the discussions and the signing of the surrender, the three German officers sat facing the Allied officers, whose backs were to the battle maps. Thus, the Germans could see at a glance the hopelessness of their military situation. They also could note the vast strength of Allied military power against them.

At that time, the British-American forces were united with the Russians almost the entire distance from Wismar, on the Baltic coast, to Dessau, where the U.S. line swung west and the Red Army line cut sharply to the east. In the south, the map showed the American and Russian forces about 35 miles apart west of Vienna. Thus, when the Germans took their places at the table, the Allies had virtually surrounded all that was left of the once powerful Wehrmacht in Czechoslovakia.

Colonel General Gustaf Jodl, Chief of Staff of the German Army, sat in the center chair on the enemy side of the table. Major G.S. Wilhelm Oxenius, his aide, sat on his right, with General Admiral Hans Georg von Friedsburg, commander-in-chief of the German Navy, on his left.

Across the table from Jodl sat Lieutenant General Walter Bedell Smith, Chief of Staff, SHAEF. To the left of General Smith was a vacant chair, placed there for Major General K.W. Strong, SHAEF G-2, who during the signing, stood behind the Germans and acted as interpreter. Next were Major General of Artillery Ivan Susloparoff, Chief of the

Document describing the SHAEF war rooms in Reims, France.

Paul Porter and George Swearingen, Camp Old Gold, July 9, 1945.

In the photo above, a somewhat disappointed George Swearingen poses for one last photo while still a member of the 2nd Infantry Division. In one of the last letters I received from George in 2008, he told me that after he had reached Camp Old Gold, he was ordered to remain in France. He then was assigned to drive for an officer of the remaining US Army Command. Like Swearingen and Edwards, many of the MPs stayed in Europe after the war had officially ended, continuing their service in various capacities. Swearingen would not return home until October 1945.

Sergeant Sam V. Nerren, Camp Old Gold, July 9, 1945.

The 2nd Infantry Division MP Platoon at Camp Old Gold, July 9, 1945.

The 2nd Infantry Division MP Platoon at Camp Old Gold, July 9, 1945.

On July 11 and 12, the units who still remained with the 2nd Infantry Division boarded ships and sailed from Le Havre, France, for the United States.

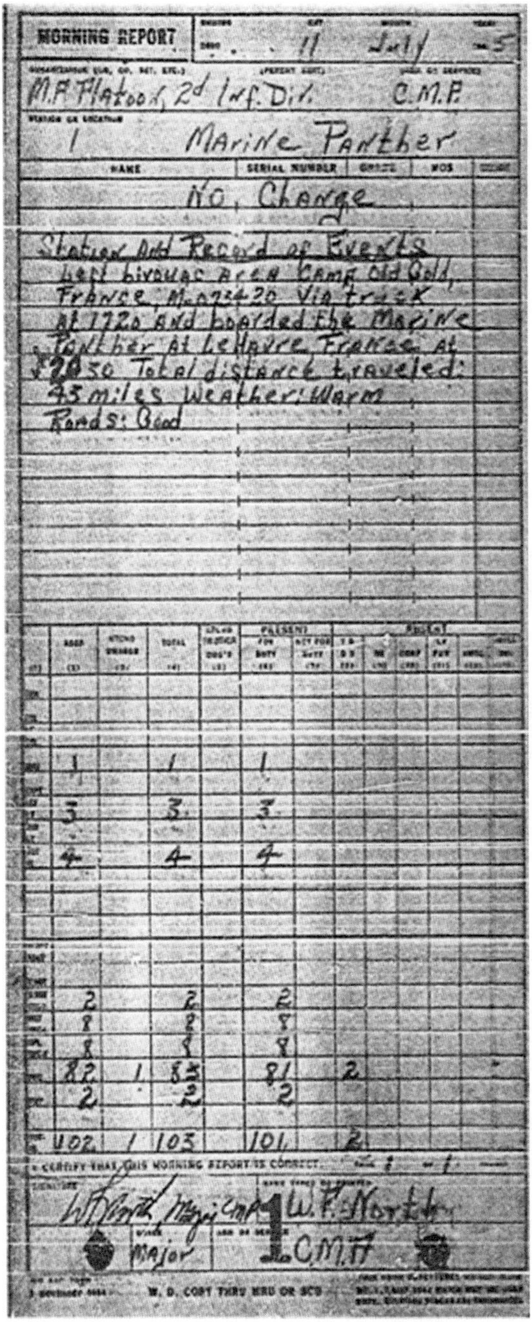

MORNING REPORT | 11 July –5

M.P. Platoon, 2d Inf. Div. C.M.P.

1 Marine Panther

NAME | SERIAL NUMBER | GRADE | MOS

No Change

Station and Record of Events
Left bivouac area Camp Old Gold, France, M.022420 via truck at 1720 and boarded the Marine Panther at Le Havre France at 2050 Total distance traveled: 45 miles Weather: Warm Roads: Good

1		1		1		
3		3		3		
4		4		4		
2		2		2		
8		8		8		
8		8		8		
82	1	83		81		2
2		2		2		
102	1	103		101		2

I CERTIFY THAT THIS MORNING REPORT IS CORRECT.

W. F. North, Major CMP | W. F. North

Major | C.M.P.

W. D. COPY THRU HRU OR SCU

2nd Infantry Division MP Platoon's Morning Reports for July 11 and 12, 1945.

The two Morning Reports above offer details relevant to the MP Platoon's preparations for embarkation including the time and their mode of transportation back to the United States.

Although the platoon had recently lost several men to transfers and occupation duty—including James Edwards, George Swearingen, and many high-point men—the platoon left France with approximately the same complement of enlisted men and officers as they had when coming ashore at Omaha Beach in June 1944. This was due in large part to the number of replacements who had joined the platoon prior to its leaving Czechoslovakia, and to a smaller extent the number of men who joined the unit after it arrived at Camp Old Gold.

Although some historical records state that the MP Platoon was originally assigned to the USS *Monticello*, the photographs that were taken by Major William North and the accompanying Morning Reports show that he and the rest of the MPs were actually aboard the USS *Marine Panther* with other officers and headquarters personnel.

Aboard that same ship was Battery C, 38th FA Battalion, which had adopted Joseph Poremba, an orphaned twelve-year-old Polish boy. "Little Joe" was smuggled aboard the ship in a duffle bag prior to embarkation.

The USS Marine Panther *at sea, July 1945.*

2nd Infantry Division soldiers aboard the USS Marine Panther, *somewhere in the mid-Atlantic Ocean, July 1945.*

2nd Division troops heading home to the United States crowd the decks of the
USS Marine Panther, *July 1945.*

Major North captured a photograph of "Little Joe" as he stood on the deck of the
USS Marine Panther, *July 1945.*

315

JOSEPH RITCHEY (G.I. JOE), one of the most often told stories of the 2nd Div. is that of a 12-year old Polish refugee named Joseph Poremba. He became attached to Btry. C, 38th FA Bn. when they passed through Freienhagen around Apr. 1, 1945, and soon won the hearts of all the men.

He remained with the Battalion throughout the rest of the campaign, acting as interpreter, since he spoke several languages, and eventually returned to the U.S. with them in July, 1945.

After Poland was invaded in September, 1939, Joe was orphaned and was placed in a German forced labor camp, where he remained until he was liberated by 2nd Div. troops.

When the 38th boarded the U.S.S. *Marine Panther* in Le Havre for the U.S.A., one of the duffle bags carried aboard contained "Little Joe," minus his combat boots—the bag would not hold him **and** his boots! He was not discovered until about the second day out of port, and as one might imagine, his discovery caused quite a commotion. In fact, U.S. Immigration officials met the ship in New York Harbor and Joe was taken to Ellis Island where he spent four days awaiting a decision on his "fate."

Lee Roy Ritchey had been designated by men of Btry. C to be Joe's adoptive father and, after several sessions of interrogation by U.S. Immigration and Naturalization officials, Attorney General Tom Clark interceded and waived deportation proceedings, granting Joe a temporary visa, or visitor's permit.

Meanwhile the Division was sent to Camp Swift, TX, awaiting transfer to the Pacific. During this time, Joe was placed in Philadelphia under the supervision of I. & N. service—**and** V-J Day occurred, thus ending the necessity of the 2nd Div.'s shipment to the Pacific.

In September, 1945, Joe was sent to Tulsa, OK, where Anita Ritchey lived and was awaiting Lee Roy's discharge from Camp Swift. Joe remained with the Ritcheys, was formally adopted by them in July, 1947, the same month their son Wendall was born. Joe attended school wherever Lee Roy and Anita taught, graduating from high school at Tishomingo, OK, in 1953, whereupon he was drafted into the U.S. Army, the highest compliment his new country could have bestowed upon him.

Upon discharge in 1956, Joe enlisted in the Oklahoma National Guard, enrolled in college, and received his B.A. degree from East Central St. University, in Ada, OK, in 1960. He married Virginia Stearman of Tishomingo in 1956. They have two daughters: Celeste Price of Seminole, OK, and Regina Frederick of Savannah, GA. Celeste has a three-year-old daughter, Afton.

Joe is presently teaching industrial arts in the Lindsay, OK, school system, and serves with the National Guard unit in Sulphur, OK, having 33 years credit in the Guard. Three times in the past several years his unit spent two weeks on maneuvers in Germany and Belgium. He has never located any of his Polish relatives, but hopes to someday return to Europe as a teacher of children of American servicemen in Europe.

A newspaper article detailing the activities of "Little Joe" after he arrived in the United States with the 38th Field Artillery.

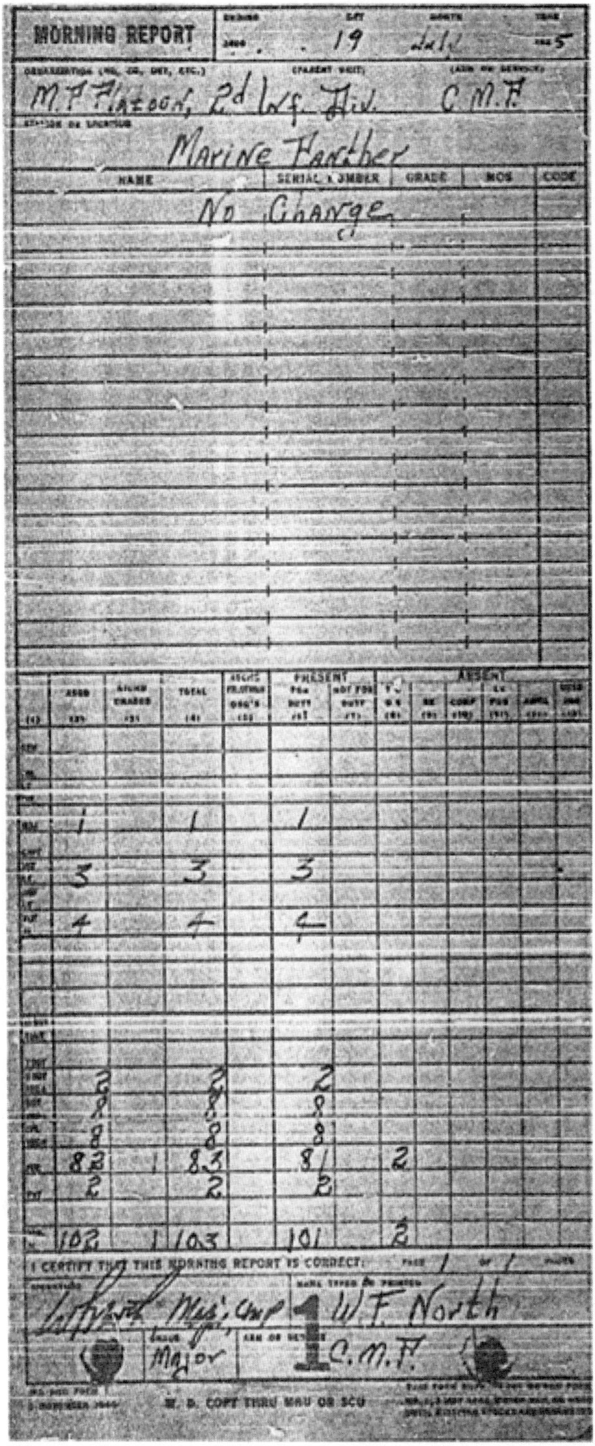

MORNING REPORT

19 July 1945

M.P. Platoon, 2d Inf. Div. C.M.F.

Marine Panther

NAME | SERIAL NUMBER | GRADE | MOS | CODE

No Change

(1)	Assd (2)	Atchd (3)	Total (4)	(5)	For duty (6)	Not for duty (7)	(8)
	1		1		1		
	3		3		3		
	4		4		4		
	2		2		2		
	8		8		8		
	8		8		8		
	82	1	83		81		2
	2		2		2		
	102	1	103		101		2

I CERTIFY THAT THIS MORNING REPORT IS CORRECT. PAGE 1 OF 1 PAGES

W.F. North Maj. CMP

Major C.M.P.

W. D. COPY THRU MRU OR SCU

2nd Infantry Division MP Platoon Morning Reports from July 19 and 20, 1945.

The 2nd Infantry Division was still at sea on July 19, and the Morning Report indicates there was "no change" in personnel—obviously there was nowhere to go. The Morning Report dated July 20, 1945, states that the USS *Marine Panther* had arrived at NYPE (New York Port of Entry) from Camp Old Gold, France. It further states that the officers and enlisted men departed for and arrived at Camp Shanks, New York, via truck by 2400 hours. Camp Shanks was the last point in the United States that the Division had seen prior to leaving for Europe in October 1943 and the first they would see upon arriving home.

"Home Never Looked So Good"—Major North photographs the Statue of Liberty from onboard the USS Marine Panther, *July 20, 1945.*

Major North photographs New York Harbor from onboard the USS Marine Panther,
July 20, 1945.

Meanwhile, James Edwards was still in France. He was actually in Paris on a two-day pass on the last day that the 2nd Infantry Division MP Platoon spent at sea.

An exhausted James Edwards photographed while on furlough in Paris, France, July 19, 1945.

Clearly visible in the previous picture are the 3rd Army patch on Dad's left shoulder, his private first class chevron, Overseas Bars, 3-Year Service Chevron, and French Fourragère. On his right shoulder is the Indianhead patch, and above his right pocket is the Distinguished Unit Citation ribbon. Dad received the Distinguished Unit Citation while under the tactical command of the 23rd Infantry Regiment from December 17 to 19, 1944.

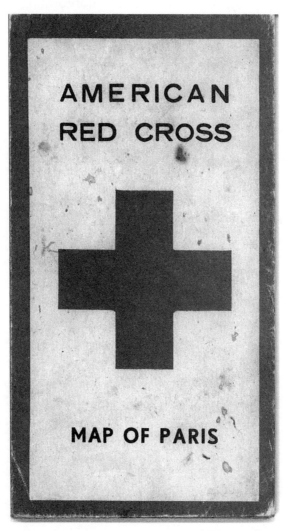

The Red Cross map Edwards used to navigate Paris in July 1945.

In a letter he wrote to his wife from Paris, Edwards mentioned that he had seen $147 worth of the city and was ready to leave and come home. Unfortunately, he remained in service in Germany until the end of August when he received orders to return to the United States.

As soon as Edwards was aware that his return to the States was imminent, he utilized a piece of modern technology at the time and wrote Mom a V-mail—short for "Victory Mail"—from Munich, Germany, on August 23, 1945, informing her that he would be home soon.

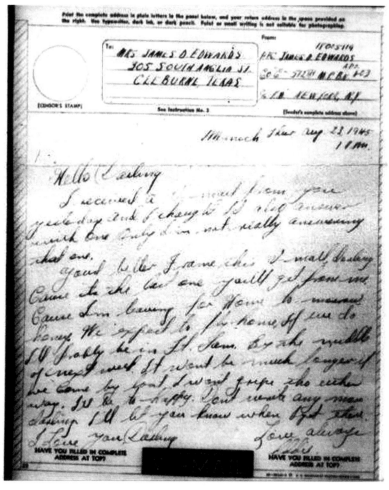

V-mail sent to Mrs. James Edwards from her husband on August 23, 1945.

RESTRICTED

HEADQUARTERS 87TH REPLACEMENT BATTALION
EUROPEAN THEATER
APO 583   U S ARMY

SO NO 6   EXTRACT   31 August 1945
                            ****

   17. (STAT CODE PKA) PAC WD Ltr, File AG 200.4 (14 May 45)
OB-S-E-M, SUBJECT: "Instructions for Return of Individuals from
the European and Mediterranean Theaters of Operation to the United
States on the 'Green Project'", dtd 15 May 45, the individuals named
below are reld fr AU 87th Repl Bn, Repl Co ind, and are asgd to
Separation Center under which their names appear.

   Individuals will travel under the "Green Project", and
w/p o/a 1 Sept 45 by rail and/or motor T to Staging Area No 1, Pas
de Lanciers, France, for forwarding to the United States by air. At
the United States port of aerial debarkation the individuals will
report to the ATC Debarkation Officers for certain processing and
will then move to a port staging area or other installation as
designated by the Commanding General, Army Service Forces.

   Baggage to accompany individual will be kept to a minimum
and in no case will exceed 35 lbs for enlisted personnel. Total
baggage, accompanied and unaccompanied will not exceed 60 lbs per
individual. Unaccompanied baggage will be processed in accordance
with Cir 72, HQ ETOUSA, dtd 30 May 45.

FOR SEPARATION CENTER NO 38, FORT SAM HOUSTON, TEXAS

NAME	GRADE & ARM OR SERVICE	ASN	CC	MOS NO	ASR SCORE	ADDRESS
GRAFTON, James J Jr	Tec 3 Ord	38031259	485	413	110-NV-Q	Kilgore, Texas
SCHOENEMANN, Otto E	Tec 3 CMP	30050656	485	816	97-NV-Q	Spring, Texas
FARRIS, Marion H	Sgt CE	6282558	486	121	100-NV-Q	Gainesville, Texas
HIGGINS, Walter D	Sgt CMP	6246991	485	677	100-NV-Q	Lufkin, Texas
GRIFFITH, Nuel W	Tec 4 Ord	38053701	485	348	104-NV-Q	Newsome, Texas
MARTINEZ, Diego M	Tec 4 MC	38120620	486	409	101-NV-Q	El Paso, Texas
JOHNSON, A. J.	Tec 4 Sig C	38132265	485	238	89-NV-Q	Comanche, Texas
HARRISON, Otis L	Cpl CMP	6261938	485	677	104-NV-Q	Huntington, Texas
CREWS, Roy H	Tec 5 Ord	38054828	485	965	104-NV-Q	Houston, Texas
GODWIN, Joe C	Tec 5 Ord	38037146	485	965	106-NV-Q	Princeton, Texas
GREENOUGH, William H	Tec 5 QMC	38408257	484	345	105-NV-Q	Galveston, Texas
MCCASLAND, William A	Tec 5 Ofd	18048738	485	835	105-NV-Q	Simonton, Texas
VAUGHT, Charlie C	Tec 5 MD	6955946	486	060	90-NV-Q	Wellington, Texas
BRITIAN, Elbert R	Pfc Sig C	18008117	484	345	104-NV-Q	Center, Texas
COOPER, Eugene H	Pfc CMP	6290158	485	677	97-NV-Q	Dallas, Texas
EDWARDS, James D	Pfc CMP	18005119	485	677	99-NV-Q	Richland, Texas
HERRING, Clarence E	Pfc CMP	6955490	485	677	99-NV-Q	Tyler, Texas

R E S T R I C T E D

Par 17 SO NO 6, HQ 87th RD, Eur Thtr, dtd 31 Aug 45, cont'd

FOR SEPARATION CENTER NO 38, SAM HOUSTON, TEXAS (Cont'd)

LANDIN, Frank	Pfc 38027053 Sig C	485	238	101-NV-Q	New Braunfels, Texas
PARKER, Warren D	Pfc 18010047 CMP	485	677	99-NV-Q	Henderson, Texas
PAULK, Thomas J	Pfc 38220811 MD	486	345	92-NV-Q	Dallas, Texas
PODSEDNIK, Edward A	Pfc 38035106 CMP	485	677	103-NV-Q	Waco, Texas
SLATER, William D	Pfc 18062408 CMP	485	745	103-NV-Q	Houston, Texas
VAN WINKLE, Loid T	Pfc 38134271 Sig C	484	345	101-NV-Q	Lamesa, Texas
VICK, Royce A	Pfc 38141425 Sig C	484	345	93-NV-Q	Pittsburg, Texas
WALLACE, Oscar	Pfc 18035831 CMP	485	677	97-NV-Q	Morton, Texas
WATSON, Arnold R	Pfc 6290136 FA	230	641	122-NV-Q	Wallis, Texas
LAWLESS, Earnest G	Pvt 18012124 CMP	485	677	100-NV-Q	Deleon, Texas
MCCONNELL, George L	Pvt 6276793 CMP	485	677	100-NV-Q	Corpus Christe, Texas

Per diem allowance for reimbursement for quarters and rations while on travel status is atzd in accordance w/AR 35-4810, dtd 19 Apr 45 for Enlisted personnel.

Travel by belligerent Vessel, commercial steamship, Army transport, Naval vessel, Military, Naval or commercial aircraft and/or rail, and motor T is atzd. PCS. TDN TCNT 60-114, 136, 500, P 431-02, 03, 04, 07, 08, A 212/50425. EDCMR: 21 Sept 45.

* * * * * * *

By order of Major LUCKETT:

MARCUS VOSK
1st Lt, AGD
Adjutant

OFFICIAL:

Marcus Vo H
MARCUS VOSK
1st Lt, AGD
Adjutant

DISTRIBUTION:
2-CG, USFET
3-CG, GFRC
1-CO, 23rd BPO
3-6936 APU

15-CA&M Sec, 14th RD
3-AG, 14th RD
1-Med Sec, 14th RD
21-Ea individual on order

R E S T R I C T E D
- 2 -

The original orders that James Edwards received and carried on his person as he traveled across Europe and over the Atlantic Ocean on his way home.

While I am not sure of the exact route my father took back to the States, according to his discharge papers he arrived on September 10, still accompanied by the dog Lady. From his point of arrival, he flew to Miami, Florida, where a newspaper listed his name—incorrectly as James O. Edwards—and confirmed his arrival there on September 14, 1945.

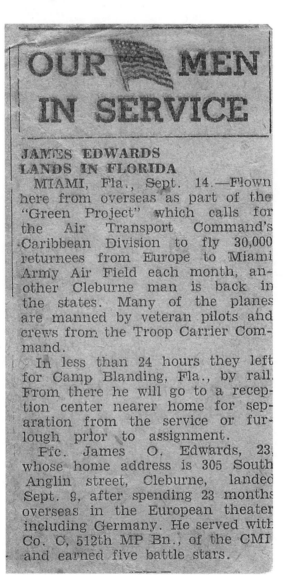

OUR MEN IN SERVICE

JAMES EDWARDS LANDS IN FLORIDA

MIAMI, Fla., Sept. 14.—Flown here from overseas as part of the "Green Project" which calls for the Air Transport Command's Caribbean Division to fly 30,000 returnees from Europe to Miami Army Air Field each month, another Cleburne man is back in the states. Many of the planes are manned by veteran pilots and crews from the Troop Carrier Command.

In less than 24 hours they left for Camp Blanding, Fla., by rail. From there he will go to a reception center nearer home for separation from the service or furlough prior to assignment.

Pfc. James O. Edwards, 23, whose home address is 305 South Anglin street, Cleburne, landed Sept. 9, after spending 23 months overseas in the European theater including Germany. He served with Co. C, 512th MP Bn., of the CMI and earned five battle stars.

Article from a Miami newspaper announcing James Edwards's arrival.

Within three days, on September 17, 1945, he was honorably discharged from military service at the Separation Station, Fort Sam Houston, Texas. That same night he celebrated his safe return with his wife, along with MP Eugene Cooper and his wife, at the Seven Oaks Club in San Antonio. Cooper served with Edwards on occupation duty in Germany, and the two arrived at home on the same flight.

(Left to right) MP Eugene Cooper, Cooper's wife, Aleta Edwards, and James Edwards at the Seven Oaks Club, September 17, 1945.

Incredibly, the small dog named Lady, who had accompanied the MP Platoon since their arrival in Europe, survived all the fighting and hardship to return with Edwards to his home in Texas.

Aleta Edwards and Lady in Rio Vista, Texas, June 1946.

After the war, James Edwards would often tell how Lady's keen hearing would warn the MPs of incoming artillery without fail, as she picked up on the hypersonic whistle that approaching bullets made. During one of my conversations with J. R. Cantrell, he confirmed that Lady could indeed hear the sound of approaching bullets and other ordnance. Lady was one of the few canines that participated—completely as a volunteer—in five battle campaigns with the MP Platoon during World War II. It only seems fair that we should accept her as a member of the Military Police Platoon of the 2nd Infantry Division and award her the respect appropriate for her years and devotion to service. Her simple loyalty and the duty she performed in protecting my father and the other soldiers in the MP Platoon may have saved many lives.

After settling in Johnson County, Texas, with my mother, Aleta McWilliams Edwards, James Edwards went to work for the Santa Fe Railroad for a few years. As was the case with many young people in those days—when many returning soldiers quickly got married, went to work, and started a family—Aleta soon gave birth to her first son, Michael Douglas Edwards, late in 1946. She was still only eighteen years old, but she and her husband, having grown up in the years of the Depression and lived through World War II, were ready to create a better life and a future for the next generation.

Epilogue

Recently I shared the story of the MP Platoon with a young man who is a junior at a Dallas high school. When I was finished, he asked me, "So, did these men from your father's story really live?" My reply: "Yeah, they really lived . . ."

There have been thousands of books printed on various military subjects for as long as there have been wars. In most cases the information in those books is derived from expert sources that outline specific battles and military events. I have several well-written military accounts that detail many of the battles in which the 2nd Infantry Division participated. These books are all excellent reads for the history buff, high school student, or college history major, but I have found that the personal stories written about the veterans themselves by their children or another relative are the history books I enjoy the most.

As we move further and further away from the Greatest Generation years, our children today and in the future will not have a firsthand reference to World War II, and certainly no concept of any of the most recent wars outside of the immediate sphere of influence it has had on them. This lack of knowledge and understanding comes as no fault of their own, but in my opinion results from our failure as a country to preserve and reinforce the traditional values these men and women fought and died trying to protect. I pray that this book will one day find its way into the classrooms and libraries of all of our public and private schools, colleges, and universities for the purpose of giving our children an opportunity to view our military history from the perspective of their ancestors, and not from the sterile, watered-down, and politically correct versions available today.

On March 14, 2011, my wife Marsha and I flew to Washington DC during spring break in order to visit the National Archives. The following day, we left our hotel in Alexandria, Virginia, and made the morning rush hour drive to College Park, Maryland, arriving at the National Archives and Records Administration (NARA) by 9 o'clock. After we were issued our official researcher identification cards, we were allowed to enter the secure section of the modern facility. For the next six hours, Marsha and I spent every minute going through and scanning After Action Reports, General Orders, and other documents relative to the 2nd Infantry Division in search of information on Dad's service. Many of the declassified documents that appear in this book are from our efforts spent at the Archives that day.

At the national World War II memorial, Washington DC.

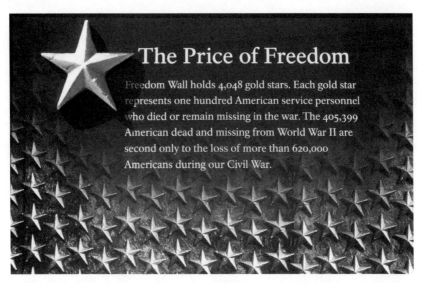

The Price of Freedom

Freedom Wall holds 4,048 gold stars. Each gold star represents one hundred American service personnel who died or remain missing in the war. The 405,399 American dead and missing from World War II are second only to the loss of more than 620,000 Americans during our Civil War.

The sign on the Freedom Wall in Washington DC, detailing the "Price of Freedom."

After a thirty-minute drive back in the direction of our hotel, we made a spur-of-the-moment decision to visit Arlington National Cemetery. We arrived at the cemetery at about three o'clock that afternoon. My wife had never been to the capital before so I decided my only real goal was to spend enough time to make the long walk to the Memorial Amphitheater before the cemetery closed for the day. During our trek to the Tomb of the Unknown Soldier, we had to avoid several military police in the process of gaining access to that part of the cemetery.

The purpose of their presence later became obvious when, unbeknownst to us, a once-in-a-lifetime event occurred. Frank Buckles, the last American doughboy of World War I, was being laid to rest at Arlington with full military honors that day. We felt a tremendous amount of pride to have witnessed that event honoring one of America's heroes. Frank Buckles, a devout American patriot at the age of sixteen, convinced an Army captain that he was eighteen in order to enlist in military service. Like all of our veterans, we are honored by his courage and commitment to the United States of America, and we are grateful that we were able to witness this moment in history.

The funeral of Frank Buckles at Arlington National Cemetery, March 15, 2011.

In some small way, all of the MPs in Dad's unit unknowingly contributed to the creation of this book. A number of them, including Dad, had the foresight to bring a camera into the largest war zone on earth at that time and capture history as it unfolded each day. While it was unusual to see a camera with anyone other than a Signal Corps photographer, sometimes—as in Dad's case—rear echelon troops had more time and were a little safer, which allowed them to make notes and other recordings. Of course, a soldier, if given the choice to defend himself, will always choose his weapon first. The main reason why many who were in the infantry and fought on the line didn't have a camera is obviously apparent; survival in combat takes precedence over everything, including going to the bathroom and eating. Though none of the photos in this book are of direct engagements with the enemy—as very few ever are—the real story lies in the relationships and the camaraderie the MPs shared with each other.

The collective efforts of George Swearingen, Major North, and my father, James Edwards, in cataloging the events that they witnessed during World War II through the lenses of their cameras were part of the catalyst for my inspiration to write this book. The phrase "a picture is worth a thousand words" certainly applies in the case of the story regarding the MP Platoon of the 2nd Infantry Division. Ultimately, I must thank my father specifically for going to the trouble of keeping up with another piece of nonessential equipment, while at the same time protecting himself from harm and completing his daily duties. Without his efforts, there would have never been a reference for me to start from.

Furthermore, there is no possible way Dad could have foreseen that his photos would have been of any personal or historical value. Separately the photos tell a story all their own, but joined with the personal testimonies of the veterans, along with the vast assortment of other materials, a true picture of the events of which they were a part comes into focus as a living chronological portrayal of the men of the MP Platoon during World War II.

Freedom is never more than one generation away from extinction. We didn't pass it to our children in the bloodstream. It must be fought for, protected, and handed on for them to do the same, or one day we will spend our sunset years telling our children and our children's children what it was once like in the United States where men were free.

—Ronald Reagan
Fortieth president of the United States of America

Appendix: True American Heroes

The Second Division MP Platoon

U. S. Second Division Is Cited by Belgium

WASHINGTON, April 1 (AP). — The 2nd "Indian Head" Division and five units that were attached to it in the Ardennes Forest fighting have been cited by Belgium.

The War Department said Monday that Count Yvan Georges du Monceau de Bergendal, Belgian military and air attache, would present the Belgian Fourragere to the division and the 462nd Anti-Aircraft Air Warning Battalion; 741st Tank Battalion; Company C, 86th Chemical Mortar Battalion; 612th and 644th Tank Destroyer Battalions. The presentations will take place at Fort Lewis, Wash., April 5.

The 2nd Infantry was stationed for many years at Fort Sam Houston, Texas, and after its return from action in the European theater in World War II was stationed at Camp Swift, Texas.

This article of significant importance appeared in a Washington newspaper on April 1, 1946. Fourteen months after the 2nd Infantry Division helped to liberate Belgium from

German occupation, the Belgian military and air attaché, Count Yvan Georges du Monceau de Bergendal, presented the Belgian Fourragère to the Division; the 462nd Anti-Aircraft Battalion; the 741st Tank Battalion; Company C, 86th Chemical Mortar Battalion; and the 612th and 644th Tank Destroyer Battalions for their actions in combat during the Battle of the Bulge.

Most of the subordinate units mentioned in the article were formed together to make up two provisional battalions during the German armored assault on the Twin Villages and Wirtzfeld in December 1944. Additionally they are mentioned in the 2nd Infantry Division history book, After Action Reports, and on page 159 of this book. In order to receive the Belgian Fourragère, these units had to distinguish themselves in combat and be cited twice in the Orders of the Day by the Belgian Army. The presentation of the award took place on April 5 at Fort Lewis, Washington, the new home for the 2nd Infantry Division. The decree No. 2509 was signed by the Belgian government on June 17, 1946.

MP Platoon Roster

Accetone, Joseph Cpl/Sgt
Allen, Albert M Pfc.
Anderson, Eugene M P
Ardoin, Arie Sgt.
Arrowood, Earl Pfc.
Asinofaky, Louis W. Pfc.
Atkinson, Raymond D. Pfc.
Balkum, Wilmer R. Pfc.
Bollwahn, Carl C. Pfc.
Beasley, Waldo D. Pfc.
Beckwith, Joe N. Sgt.
Bennett, Doris H. Pfc.
Benoit, Vardon L. Pfc.
Bergman, Wallace W. Pfc.
Beri, Joseph A. Pfc.
Blair, Dan C. Pfc.
Bloom, Ralph U. Pfc.
Bollwahn, Carl C. Pfc.
Bonds, James R. Pfc.
Bowling, Dorsey Pfc.
Boyd, Jack S. Sgt.

Czyzniewki, Chester J. Pfc.
Davern, Martin L. Pfc.
Davidson, William L. Cpl
Devlin, Neal A. Pfc.
Dilgard, William A. Pfc.
Dixon, Leonard E. Tec 4
Edwards, James D. Pfc.
Enos, John P. Pfc.
Epperley, George K. Sgt.
Erickson, George W. Cpl.
Erwin, Lefty Pfc.
Farley, Philip G. Cpl.
Farr, Unknown. Sgt.
Festa, Rocco Cpl.
Foster, Ted Pfc.
Gammons, Ray W. Pfc.
Gariham, Bruce Pfc.
Gibson, Moscoe C. Jr. Pfc.
Gilmore, Roger E. Pfc.
Gittemeier, Linos J. Pfc.
Ghormley, Unknown Pvt.

Jainnini, Alfred
Jarczynski, Edward 1st Lt
Jones, Harvey Pfc.
Jones, Malcolm
Kovalyak, Stephen 1st Lt
Keidan, Herbert S. Pvt.
Kent, Norman D. Pfc.
Kichn, Gordon M. Pfc.
King, James Pvt.
Kingery, George R. Cpl.
Klak, John F. Pfc.
Kline, Andrew E. Pfc.
Knecht, Theodore C. Pfc.
Kruger, Carl H. Pfc.
Kurowski, Henry S. 1st Lt
Lane, Hugh S. Jr. Pfc.
Lawless, Earnest G. Pfc.
Lawrence, Luther A. Pfc.
Lee, Earnest P. Pfc.
Lester, Dalton J. Cpl.
Lochetto, Angelo L. Sgt.

Boyt, Fred Pfc.
Breslin, John F. Pfc.
Brown, James L. Pfc.
Brubaker, Unknown Pvt.
Bundschuh, James Pfc.
Burditt, Murrel. Pvt.
Cagle, Thomas J. !st Lt.
Cantrell, James R. Cpl.
Carr, John P. Pfc.
Carter, Charles D. Pfc.
Cates, Robert N. Pfc.
Cather, Russell V. Pfc.
Cathron, Randy Pfc.
Catterall, John Pfc.
Cavansgh, John J. Pfc.
Ciesnicki, John W. Sgt.
Cochran, Max D. Cpl.
Conaway, Orville H. Cpl.
Conner, George Pfc.
Cook, Francis W. Pfc.
Cook, Robert N. Pfc.
Cooper, Eugene H. Pfc.
Cravens, Richard C. Pfc.
Cywinski, Edward J. Pfc.

Oppenheim, Alfred
Osborne, Charles H. Pfc
Oster, Adam A. Pfc.
Parker, Howard A. Pfc
Parker, Warren D. Pfc.
Parr, Everett, Sgt.
Pass, Clarence.Tec4
Pastre, Louis A. Pfc.
Pearson, James, Sgt.
Perkins, George A. Pfc.
Perry, Raymond, Pfc.
Peters, Frank J. Sgt.
Pickel, Gerald B. Pfc.
Pitts, Robert W. Pfc.
Plyler, Bruce L. Cpl.
Podsednik, Edward A. Pfc.
Porter, Paul M. Sgt.
Quail, David G. Pfc.
Raffarty, Gerald J. Pfc.
Rankin, James E. Pfc.
Ratushny, Joseph, Pfc.
Reeve, Edward J. Pvt.
Rentko, John J. S/Sgt.
Rhoden, Clifton A. Pfc.
Rigsby, John L. Sgt.
Robb, Alden M. Pfc.
Roberts, John C. Sgt.
Robertson, Linn S. Pfc
Ross, Walter H. Cpl.

Goldstein, Phillip Pfc.
Gonzalez, Salvador H Tec5
Grau, Bryson L.
Griffin, Unknown
Grizzle, Oscar L. Pfc.
Hall, Andrew H. Pvt.
Hall, Calvin C. Pfc.
Harper, Malcolm H. Pfc.
Harrison, Otis. Cpl.
Helfer, Clifford G. Sgt.
Henry, Howard L.
Herring, Clarence E. Pfc.
Hibbert, Nathan J. Pfc.
Higgins, Walter D. Sgt.
Hill, Henry R. Pfc.
Hill, William M. Pfc.
Hillis, James Earl. Cpl
Holcomb, Robert N. Pfc.
Hopkins, Thomas A. Pvt
Hopkins, Garret H. Pfc.
Houghtaling, Earl A. Pfc
Hoyt, Fred L. Pfc.
Irvin, John R. Pfc.
Irvine, Charles W. Pfc.

Ross, Warren B. Pfc.
Rupek, Edward J. Pfc.
Russell, Floyd K. Pfc
Scalera, James D. Pfc.
Schively, Glenn C. Pfc.
Sears, John P. Sgt.
Segers, Kenneth Pfc.
Sendre, Harry Pfc.
Shea, James B. Pvt.
Sheehan, John H. Cpl.
Short, Robert, Pfc.
Shrout, Thomas, Pfc.
Sides, Thomas R. Pfc.
Silveria, Joe T. Pfc.
Sinkule, Jerry A. Sgt.
Smith, Glen F. Pfc.
Smith, Jack W. Cpl.
Smith, William, Pfc.
Snyder, James, Pfc.
Southall, James, Pfc.
Sowers, Merion A. Pfc.
Staich, Alexander, Pfc.
Sterneski, Leonard C. Pfc.
Stewart, Erlin E. Pvt.
Stoffers, Henry B. Pfc.
Sullivan, James B. Jr. Tec5
Swearingen, George F. Pfc.
Taylor, Willis A. Pfc.
Tenoper, Lewis, Sgt.

Magers, Richard E. Tec
Malcolm, James Pfc.
Marlow, Fred J. Pvt.
McAllister, Morgan B.
McCall, Arthur W. Pfc
McColl, Bernard S/Sgt
McConnell, George L.T
McCormick, Clarence I
McGuire, Homer W. Pf
McLean, Robert W. Pfc
McMahan, Howard T. I
McNamara, Unknown I
Meeth, Ira Chet. 1st Lt.
Meier, Adolf Pfc.
Mereck, Louis F. Tec5
Merrymen, Alfred J.
Moore, Howard A. Pfc.
Moore, James W. Pvt.
Moore, Lawrence B. Pv
Nelson, Richard M.
Nerren, Sam V. Sgt.
North, William F. Majo
O'Neill, Raymond D. P
Onica, Anthony Pfc.

Theobald, Lawrence A.
Theil, Heinz W. Sgt.
Tiernan, William G. Sg
Traynor, Francis E. Pfc
Tugman, Zane, Pfc.
Turner, Robert M. Pfc.
Visnofsky, Nicholas, Pv
Vogel, Percy C. Pvt.
Wahal, Stephen, Cpl.
Waldron, Charles H. Pf
Wallace, Oscar, Pfc.
Waller, Robert J. Pfc.
Waters, Billy W. Pfc.
Watznauer, Angelo M.
Webster, Leon, Pfc.
Welsh, Francis E. Sgt.
Welsh, Loy H. Pfc.
Welsh, Richard C. Tec5
Wheelington, Donald J.
White, Okley G. Pfc.
Whitley, Tobe L. Pfc.
Whitney, Robert L. Pfc.
Wiedarmeyer, Fred W.
Wilson, Willie R. S/Sgt
Woods, Robert L. Pfc.
Wright, Herbert L. Pvt.
Yandles, Kermit O. Pfc

James Randolph Cantrell

Corporal J. R. Cantrell in Pilsen, Czechoslovakia, May 1945.

James Randolph Cantrell, at the age of 86, in his home in Johnson County, Texas.

I went to visit J. R. Cantrell shortly after I learned that he was a survivor of World War II and living in adjacent Johnson County, a mere twenty-five–minute drive from my home. Even though my father spent much of his life only a short distance from his friend J. R. Cantrell, the two never saw each other again after the war.

On a visit to J. R.'s home, I had an opportunity to talk with him for nearly three hours at which time he shared with me many of the facts that appear in this book. In the photo above, J. R. is holding a small shadow box I constructed for him, which contains a Combat Infantry Badge, miniature medals, Shooters Bar, collar brass, the Ruptured Duck lapel pin, and the Meritorious Unit Commendation ribbon bar, which I used instead of the actual patch that was proper for the World War II era. J. R. previously had revealed to me that his medals and other items from his days with the 2nd Infantry Division were lost over time. Using his honorable discharge and the circumstances surrounding his service during the Battle of the Bulge, I was able to reconstruct what he was entitled to wear on his uniform.

Over the next couple of years, J. R. and his wife, Helen, invited me to their home on special occasions where we were able to communicate on a level that J. R. felt comfortable with. As is the case with all of our veterans, it is still emotionally painful for them to share their experiences of battle, death, and mental anguish with family or friends even after other parts of their memories have faded. The ravages of time have not for any of these men diminished the horrible things they witnessed or were called upon to do.

In September 2010, J. R. celebrated his ninetieth birthday among his large family and close friends. I was thankful to be there to celebrate that special moment with him. Sadly, however, J. R. passed away on March 1, 2011. To commemorate his life and his service to our country, I honor him—and all the men of the MP Platoon—by producing this book of their story of which I pray they would be proud.

J. R.'s life was marked with examples of commitment, perseverance, determination, hard work, love of family, and many other redeeming qualities that he and his Greatest Generation Americans imparted to us, their children, the Baby Boomer generation. He, like the other World War II veterans, will be sorely missed by those of us who know their journey. I will miss my friend J. R. Cantrell. He, probably more than anyone, gave me a glimpse into his personal past and that kind of an opportunity is a once-in-a-lifetime event.

Honorable Discharge

This is to certify that

JAMES R CANTRELL 18 021 450 Corporal

Military Police Platoon 2d Division

Army of the United States

is hereby Honorably Discharged from the military service of the United States of America.

This certificate is awarded as a testimonial of Honest and Faithful Service to this country.

Given at Separation Center
Fort Sam Houston, Texas

Date 27 June 1945

C. F. ARNOLD
Major AUS

1. LAST NAME - FIRST NAME - MIDDLE INITIAL
CANTRELL JAMES R

2. ARMY SERIAL NO. 18 021 450
3. GRADE Cpl
4. ARM OR SERVICE MP
5. COMPONENT RA

6. ORGANIZATION
MP Platoon 2d Division

7. DATE OF SEPARATION 27 June 45
8. PLACE OF SEPARATION Separation Center Fort Sam Houston, Texas

9. PERMANENT ADDRESS FOR MAILING PURPOSES
General Delivery, Handley, Tarrant Co, Texas

10. DATE OF BIRTH 21 Sept 1920
11. PLACE OF BIRTH Camo, Texas

12. ADDRESS FROM WHICH EMPLOYMENT WILL BE SOUGHT
See 9

13. COLOR EYES Blue
14. COLOR HAIR Black
15. HEIGHT 5'10"
16. WEIGHT 145 LBS.
17. NO. DEPEND. 2

18. RACE WHITE X
19. MARITAL STATUS SINGLE X
20. U.S. CITIZEN YES X
21. CIVILIAN OCCUPATION AND NO. Laborer 9-64.06

MILITARY HISTORY

22. DATE OF INDUCTION -
23. DATE OF ENLISTMENT 5 Oct 40
24. DATE OF ENTRY INTO ACTIVE SERVICE 5 Oct 40
25. PLACE OF ENTRY INTO SERVICE Rctg Sta, Fort Worth, Texas

26. REGISTERED YES/NO
27. LOCAL S.S. BOARD NO. -
28. COUNTY AND STATE -
29. HOME ADDRESS AT TIME OF ENTRY INTO SERVICE See 9

30. MILITARY OCCUPATIONAL SPECIALTY AND NO.
Military Police 677

31. MILITARY QUALIFICATION AND DATE (i.e., infantry, aviation and marksmanship badges, etc.)
Marksmanship Carbine 7 Feb 43

32. BATTLES AND CAMPAIGNS
Normandy Northern France Rhineland Central Europe GO 33 WD 45

33. DECORATIONS AND CITATIONS
EAME Campaign Medal with 4 Bronze Stars Good Conduct Medal American Defense Service Medal

34. WOUNDS RECEIVED IN ACTION
None

35. LATEST IMMUNIZATION DATES
SMALLPOX 15 Feb 44
TYPHOID 24 Feb 44
TETANUS 14 Jun 43
OTHER (specify) Typhus 3 Dec 44

36. SERVICE OUTSIDE CONTINENTAL U.S. AND RETURN

DATE OF DEPARTURE	DESTINATION	DATE OF ARRIVAL
8 Oct 43	EAME	20 Oct 43
Unknown	US	17 Jun 45

37. TOTAL LENGTH OF SERVICE
CONTINENTAL SERVICE: YEARS 3 MONTHS 0 DAYS 12
FOREIGN SERVICE: YEARS 1 MONTHS 8 DAYS 10

38. HIGHEST GRADE HELD Cpl

FOR CONVENIENCE, A CERTIFICATE OF ELIGIBILITY NO. 917765 HAS BEEN ISSUED BY THE VETERANS ADMINISTRATION TO BE USED FOR THE FUTURE RECEIPT OF ANY GUARANTY OR INSURANCE BENEFIT UNDER TITLE III OF THE SERVICEMEN'S READJUSTMENT ACT OF 1944, AS AMENDED, THAT MAY BE AVAILABLE TO THE PERSON TO WHOM THIS SEPARATION PAPER WAS ISSUED.

39. PRIOR SERVICE
None

40. REASON AND AUTHORITY FOR SEPARATION
Convenience of the Government
(RR 1-1 Demobilization) AR 615-365 15 Dec 44

41. SERVICE SCHOOLS ATTENDED
None

42. EDUCATION (Years)
Grammar 8 High School 3 College 0

PAY DATA

43. LONGEVITY FOR PAY PURPOSES YEARS 4 MONTHS 8 DAYS 23
44. MUSTERING OUT PAY TOTAL $300 THIS PAYMENT $100
45. SOLDIER DEPOSITS None
46. TRAVEL PAY 14.15
47. TOTAL AMOUNT 50.00 Cash 65.30 Check
NAME OF DISBURSING OFFICER CARLOS DELIMA Capt FD
Vou. 7565

INSURANCE NOTICE

IMPORTANT IF PREMIUM IS NOT PAID WHEN DUE OR WITHIN THIRTY-ONE DAYS THEREAFTER, INSURANCE WILL LAPSE. MAKE CHECKS OR MONEY ORDERS PAYABLE TO THE TREASURER OF THE U. S. AND FORWARD TO COLLECTIONS SUBDIVISION, VETERANS ADMINISTRATION, WASHINGTON 25, D. C.

48. KIND OF INSURANCE Nat. Serv. X U.S. Govt. None
49. HOW PAID Allotment Direct to V.A. X
50. EFFECTIVE DATE OF ALLOTMENT DISCONTINUANCE 30 Jun 45
51. DATE OF NEXT PREMIUM DUE (One month after 50) 30 Jul 45
52. PREMIUM DUE EACH MONTH 6.60
53. INTENTION OF VETERAN TO Continue / Continue Only / Discontinue

54.

55. REMARKS (This space for completion of above items or entry of other items specified in W.D. Directives)
Lapel button issued

6 X 9
1-25-46

56. SIGNATURE OF PERSON BEING SEPARATED
J R. Cantrell

57. PERSONNEL OFFICER (Type name, grade and organization - signature)
SCHULTZ, 2d Lt., CAC Asst Mil Per Officer

WD AGO FORM 53-55
1 November 1944

This form supersedes all previous editions of WD AGO Forms 53 and 55 for enlisted persons entitled to an Honorable Discharge, which will not be used after receipt of this revision.

Mistakes did happen in processing paperwork. The clerk who prepared J. R.'s documents completely omitted the Ardennes Offensive from his honorable discharge.

George Swearingen

George Swearingen, Fort Sam Houston, Texas, summer 1942.

There are truly no words that can express my feelings and the admiration I have for George Swearingen. A few years ago, I came across his name in my dad's address book with other members of the MP Platoon. But George was not simply another name without a face. George was more to me than just a character from a war fought long ago. George became my friend literally overnight and he would have it no other way. From my perspective, I appeared as a new stranger in his life, linked only by the name of a former army buddy he hadn't heard from in more than sixty-seven years. Now, all of a sudden, this name from the past would eventually stimulate memories George had long forgotten; forgotten, that is, until I forwarded a list of questions that I prayed George could answer about my dad.

Like an old friend, George's first letter to me was full of enthusiasm and excitement, as if he had known me all his life.

George revealed to me that because of my questions, he was able to recall things he had forgotten years ago. From that moment on, and like a kid with a new toy, George spent many hours in front of his typewriter answering my questions as fast as he could remember by putting them onto paper. When he finished each letter, George stuffed every envelope, licked every stamp, and always closed his letters with an invitation to come see him. Like Mr. Cantrell, neither of these men owed me anything, but George was willing to share his experiences of World War II with the son of his friend Private First Class James D. Edwards. Of course the honor was all mine; after all, how many people can claim to have a pen pal who also happens to be a surviving decorated World War II veteran?

George and those who sacrificed so much for the freedom of our world in the 1940s are larger than life and true American heroes. But the notion that someone would place upon them such a lofty title would only bring about silence, and then a simple statement that they were just doing their jobs and felt blessed to have survived. These character traits of humility and selflessness were the identifying marks of those who had looked death in the eye, fought their battles with the demons bent on killing them, and were fortunate enough to prevail and live another day. George had his days with those demons, probably more than once, but perhaps none more than the day he was seriously wounded just trying to do his job and save his friends from certain death.

Like it was just yesterday, George recalled the day— December 21, 1944—with vivid clarity when a German artillery battery was bombarding the rear areas at Camp Elsenborn, Belgium, with perhaps the largest caliber weapon on dry land. Not once but twice did George survive very near misses by a 305mm shell that upon explosion sent shrapnel the size of a man's fist in every direction. In both instances, George miraculously avoided the larger pieces of metal, but the concussion from the blasts of two rounds catapulted him high into the air both times, shredding his uniform to the point it was falling off of him. Undeterred by his wounds and while suffering from severe shock, George instinctively helped others first and saved many lives before he collapsed.

Sadly my friend George F. Swearingen passed away on August 14, 2011, at the age of 98. George had told me that he had hoped to reach the century mark, but God had other plans for him. George didn't realize that his time may have been up long ago, but in God's ultimate wisdom, God knew that he needed to keep George on this earth to make a difference in people's lives by impacting them in a positive way, just a little longer. In my opinion, God allowed George to remain on this earth long enough for us to meet. Probably unaware that his timely friendship with me would help to carry on his legacy of helping others, his contributions to this book and his stories of friendship will have a lasting effect on the lives of many people, and perhaps the generations of Swearingens, as well as the children and grandchildren of those he honorably served with during World War II. We will miss him and the other heroes like him. His desire to help people turned out to be his legacy in life; I know because he helped me.

God bless you, George, and thank you.

WISHING YOU A VERY

Merry Christmas

GEORGE SWEARINGEN
HOPING YOU HAVE A
MERRY CHRISTMAS
AND A
HAPPY NEW YEAR

Army of the United States

Honorable Discharge

This is to certify that

GEORGE F SWEARINGEN   14 062 737   PRIVATE FIRST CLASS
MILITARY POLICE PLATOON 2ND INFANTRY DIVISION

Army of the United States

is hereby Honorably Discharged from the military service of the United States of America.

This certificate is awarded as a testimonial of Honest and Faithful Service to this country.

Given at   SEPARATION CENTER
FORT BRAGG, NORTH CAROLINA

Date   10 OCTOBER 1945

Ben B Mabson Jr
BEN B MABSON JR.
LT COL   CE.

347

ENLISTED RECORD AND REPORT OF SEPARATION
HONORABLE DISCHARGE

1. LAST NAME - FIRST NAME - MIDDLE INITIAL	2. ARMY SERIAL NO.	3. GRADE	4. ARM OR SERVICE	5. COMPONENT
SWEARINGEN GEORGE F	14 062 737	PFC	CMP	RA

6. ORGANIZATION	7. DATE OF SEPARATION	8. PLACE OF SEPARATION
MP PLAT 2ND INF DIV	10 OCT 45	SEPARATION CENTER FT BRAGG NC

9. PERMANENT ADDRESS FOR MAILING PURPOSES	10. DATE OF BIRTH	11. PLACE OF BIRTH
WAYNESVILLE HAYWOOD CO NC BOX 100	3 SEP 12	VIENNA GA

12. ADDRESS FROM WHICH EMPLOYMENT WILL BE SOUGHT	13. COLOR EYES	14. COLOR HAIR	15. HEIGHT	16. WEIGHT	17. NO. DEPEND.
SEE 9	BLUE	BROWN	5'11½"	174 LBS.	0

18. RACE	19. MARITAL STATUS	20. U.S. CITIZEN	21. CIVILIAN OCCUPATION AND NO.
WHITE X NEGRO OTHER (specify)	SINGLE X MARRIED OTHER (specify)	YES X NO	POLICEMAN (2-66.23)

MILITARY HISTORY

22. DATE OF INDUCTION	23. DATE OF ENLISTMENT	24. DATE OF ENTRY INTO ACTIVE SERVICE	25. PLACE OF ENTRY INTO SERVICE
	20 FEB 42	20 FEB 42	CHARLOTTE NC

SELECTIVE SERVICE DATA	26. REGISTERED YES NO X	27. LOCAL U.S. BOARD NO. UNKNOWN	28. COUNTY AND STATE BUNCOMBE CO NC	29. HOME ADDRESS AT TIME OF ENTRY INTO SERVICE ASHEVILLE NC

30. MILITARY OCCUPATIONAL SPECIALTY AND NO.	31. MILITARY QUALIFICATION AND DATE (i.e., infantry, aviation and marksmanship badges, etc.)
MILITARY POLICEMAN (677)	MM CAL 30 RIFLE M1

32. BATTLES AND CAMPAIGNS

NORMANDY; NORTHERN FRANCE; RHINELAND; ARDENNES; CENTRAL EUROPE

33. DECORATIONS AND CITATIONS MERITORIOUS SERVICE UNIT INSIGNIA GO 48 HQ 2ND INF DIV 45; EAMET CAMPAIGN MEDAL WITH 5 BRONZE STARS; GOOD CONDUCT MEDAL AR 600-68; PURPLE HEART GO 3 279TH STA HOSP 44; SILVER STAR MEDAL GO 17 HQ 2ND INF **

34. WOUNDS RECEIVED IN ACTION

EAMET 21 DEC 44

35. LATEST IMMUNIZATION DATES				36. SERVICE OUTSIDE CONTINENTAL U. S. AND RETURN		
SMALLPOX	TYPHOID	TETANUS	OTHER (specify)	DATE OF DEPARTURE	DESTINATION	DATE OF ARRIVAL
25FEB44	25FEB44	9AUG44	TYPH 3DEC44	8 OCT 43	EAMET	20 OCT 43
				NO RECORD	USA	5 OCT 45

37. TOTAL LENGTH OF SERVICE						38. HIGHEST GRADE HELD
CONTINENTAL SERVICE			FOREIGN SERVICE			PRIVAT
YEARS	MONTHS	DAYS	YEARS	MONTHS	DAYS	FIRST CLASS
1	7	23	1	11	28	

39. PRIOR SERVICE
NONE

40. REASON AND AUTHORITY FOR SEPARATION
CONVENIENCE OF THE GOVERNMENT RR1-1(DEMOBILIZATION) AR 615-365 15 DEC 44

41. SERVICE SCHOOLS ATTENDED	42. EDUCATION (Years)		
NONE	Grammar	High School	College

PAY DATA

43. LONGEVITY FOR PAY PURPOSES			44. MUSTERING OUT PAY		45. SOLDIER DEPOSITS	46. TRAVEL PAY	47. TOTAL AMOUNT, NAME OF DISBURSING OFFICER
YEARS	MONTHS	DAYS	TOTAL	THIS PAYMENT			
3	7	21	$300	$100	NONE	$	A CALPESTRI MAJ FD

INSURANCE NOTICE

IMPORTANT — IF PREMIUM IS NOT PAID WHEN DUE OR WITHIN THIRTY-ONE DAYS THEREAFTER, INSURANCE WILL LAPSE. MAKE CHECKS OR MONEY ORDERS PAYABLE TO THE TREASURER OF THE U. S. AND FORWARD TO COLLECTIONS SUBDIVISION, VETERANS ADMINISTRATION, WASHINGTON 25, D. C.

48. KIND OF INSURANCE			49. HOW PAID		50. Effective Date of Allotment Discontinuance	51. Date of Next Premium Due (One month after 50)	52. PREMIUM DUE EACH MONTH	53. INTENTION OF VETERAN TO		
Nat. Serv.	U.S. Govt.	None	Allotment	Direct to V.A.				Continue	Continue Only	Discontinue
X			X		31 OCT 45	30 NOV 45	$7.18		$5000	

54.	55. REMARKS (This space for completion of above items or entry of other items specified in W. D. Directives)
RIGHT THUMB PRINT	**ITEM 33; DIV 45 NO TIME LOST UNDER AW 107 LAPEL BUTTON ISSUED ASR SCORE (2 SEP 45) 93 World War II Victory Medal issued at Asheville, N. C. on 17 Sept 47 issuing agent

56. SIGNATURE OF PERSON BEING SEPARATED	57. PERSONNEL OFFICER (Type name, grade and organization - signature)
George F. Swearingen	L V MORAN CAPT AUS

WD AGO FORM 53-55

348

GOOD MORNING

DEAR JAMES

      THIS IS FOR TOU MY CHILE,
IT IS YOURS FOR A GOOD START.
    WITH YOUR HOPES AND YOUR DREAMS TAKE
         THIS FROM ME.
     AND BE GOOD TO THE OLD MAN YPU HOPE TO BE

YOU ARE BUILDING A HOUSE WHERE THE OLD MAN WILL ABIDE.
   YOU ARE HANGING PICTURES THAT TIME WILL NOT HIDE.
YOUR ARE CHIZZLING THE WALLS WITH LONG MEMBEREES
   BE GOOD TO UOUR SELF AND LIVE LIKE ME.

   A HAPPY OLD MAN YOU WILL BE.

FROM THE WINDOW OF YOUR CASTLE THEIR SHINES A LIGHT,
   A BEACON TO OTHERS BOTH DAY AND NIGHT.
TO HELP THEM TO FIND THEIR WAY,
   WILL MAKE YOU A HAPPY DAY

   GROWING OLD LIKE ME

HELPING OTHERS IS THE KEY,
   TO A LONG AND HAPPY LIFE YOU WILL SEE.

AND WHEN YOU GET OLD AND GREY,
   YOU CAN SAY GRAND PA GEORGE MADE IT THIS WAY.

I THOUGHT THIS WOULD BE SOME THING YOU WOULD LIKE.

AND I HAVE ANOTHER THAT I HAVE LIVED BY ALL MY YEARS.

I AM NOT A POET OR A WRITER. BUT I TRY TO DO SOME OF BOTH.

I FEEL MY POEMS AND MY STORIES ARE WORTH A LOTS TO OTHERS.

AS THEY ARE ALL TRUE THINGS THAT HAS HAPPENED IN MY LIFE?

I THINK I AM DOING GOOD FOR YOUNG PEOPLE TO TELL OF MY
EXPERIENCES. I THINK IN THIS WAY I COULD BE HELPING CHILDREN

LONG AFTER I HAVE GONE AS FOR ME THEY ARE PRECIOUS MEMBEREESS?

   HERE IS ANOTHER I LIVE BY

"MY DAILY ROUTEENE"   IS HER

I WAKE UP EACH MORNING IN A GOOD WARM BED.

   WITH A NICE SOFT PILLOW UNDER MT HEAD.
MY FIRST DUTY IS TO PREY,
   TO THANK THE "LORD" FOR A GOOD NIGHTS SLEEP AND ANOTHER DAY.

THEN I AM OFF TO THE BATH ROOM FOR A SHOWER,
   THE WARM WATER FEEL SO GOOD I COULD STAY FOR AN HOUR.
BUT FOR AN OLD MAN LIKE ME THIS CAN NOT BE,
OTHER THINGS HAVE NEEDS OF ME.

I GET DRESSED FOR THE DAY,
AND ANY THING THAT COMES MY WAY.
I MAKE MY BED FOR ANOTHER NIGHT
         and get my dirty clothes out of sight.

THEN I"M OFF TO THE KITCHEN AT TOP SPEED,
   I HAVE TO SATISFY MY HUNGER NEEDS.
A GLASS OF JUICE I HAVE AT THE START.
WHILE I PREPAIR THE OTHER PARTS.

GRITS ,SCRAMBLE EGG, WITH BEACON SAUSAGE OR HAM.
   AND I TOP IT OFF WITH BUTTERED TOAST AND JAM.
I WASH UP MY DISHES AND CLEAN UP MY MESS.
   I'NOT A GOOD HOUSE KEEPER, BUT I DO MY BEST.

THEN I AM ALL SET FOR THE DAY AND ANYTHING THAT COMES MY WAY.
   AND ANY THING THAT COMES MY WAY.
I THANK THE "LORD" FOR THE BLESSINGS I HAVE RESCIEVED
   WHILE DOWN ON MY KNEES.

THE "LORD" HAS BEEN GOOD TO ME,
   THIS I AM SURE ALL CAN SEE.

  AS I HAVE GROWN OLD IN HIS CARE,
   AND I SPEND MY TIME IN A WHEEL CHAIR

         BY GEORGE SWEARINGEN

William North

Major William North.

There is no doubt that Major William North contributed heavily to the creation of the story of the MP Platoon through the photos and documents his son Max North so graciously donated to the cause of writing this book. Of course, Major North was the foundation of the platoon as the commanding officer charged with the enormous responsibility of coordinating the duties of his men to assist in supporting the 2nd Infantry Division and the Allied cause in its goal of defeating Germany.

An essential participant in charge of well over one hundred men at any given time, Major North was a true field commander. Not merely satisfied with issuing orders from the safety of an office desk, Major North was prepared to do anything he asked his men to do. And like his men, Major North armed himself with a rifle and fought side by side with his MPs in defending the Division Command Post at Wirtzfeld during the Ardennes Offensive. During the Allied invasion of France, he came ashore under fire on June 7, 1944, at Omaha Beach, where he coordinated the duties of the MPs and secured vital areas on the beach, for which he received the Bronze Star Medal for meritorious conduct during the first month of battle in the Normandy campaign. On January 29, 1945, he was awarded the French croix de guerre by the provisional government of France and in June 1945 he received a meritorious decoration by the Czech Republic for his part in the liberation of Czechoslovakia. An undeniable leader, it is obvious that Major North had the respect and admiration of his men and his superiors.

At the close of the war, Major North returned home with the MP Platoon aboard the USS *Marine Panther* to a grateful America through New York Harbor amidst a flotilla of watercraft displaying an Indianhead banner where thousands of people lined the docks. As he made his way back to Texas and his wife, Marilee, who like so many other wives waited anxiously for her man to return home safely, Major North's journey, which seemed like a lifetime, was almost over.

Although the war ended for many of the officers and enlisted men who were mustered out and discharged under Article 615-365, it is evident that Major North still had a desire to serve in the Army. Upon his return to Texas, he remained on active duty as part of the Officers Reserve Corps until January 14, 1946. At some point after he arrived home, he was promoted to lieutenant colonel, a rank appropriate for his honorable service to the Army of the United States and the Military Police Corps. Major North did an excellent job of preserving the photos, documents, and other items he brought home with him in 1945.

Army of the United States

CERTIFICATE OF SERVICE

This is to certify that

LT COL WILLIAM F NORTH   O- 343 444   CORPS OF MILITARY POLICE

honorably served in active Federal Service

in the Army of the United States from

7 February 1942   *to*   14 January 1946

Given at   Separation Center Camp Fannin Texas

on the   14th   *day of*   January   19 46

PAUL G BELL   COL   FA

MILITARY RECORD AND REPORT OF SEPARATION
CERTIFICATE OF SERVICE

JHM

1. LAST NAME - FIRST NAME - MIDDLE INITIAL	2. ARMY SERIAL NUMBER	3. AUS. GRADE	4. ARM OR SERVICE	5. COMPONENT
NORTH WILLIAM F	O- 343 444	LtCol	CMP	ORC

6. ORGANIZATION	7. DATE OF RELIEF FROM ACTIVE DUTY	8. PLACE OF SEPARATION
MP PLT 2d Inf Div	14 Jan 46	Camp Wolters Tex

9. PERMANENT ADDRESS FOR MAILING PURPOSES	10. DATE OF BIRTH	11. PLACE OF BIRTH
2849 Fondren Drive Dallas 5 Texas	3 Apr 13	Houston Tex

12. ADDRESS FROM WHICH EMPLOYMENT WILL BE SOUGHT	13. COLOR EYES	14. COLOR HAIR	15. HEIGHT	16. WEIGHT	17. NO. OF DEPENDENTS
See 9	Brown	Brown	5'9"	140 lbs.	0

18. RACE			19. MARITAL STATUS			20. U.S. CITIZEN		21. CIVILIAN OCCUPATION AND NO.
WHITE	NEGRO	OTHER (specify)	SINGLE	MARRIED	OTHER (specify)	YES	NO	
X				X		X		Manager Installment Finance Co

MILITARY HISTORY

SELECTIVE SERVICE DATA ▶	22. REGISTERED		23. LOCAL S. S. BOARD NUMBER	24. COUNTY AND STATE	25. HOME ADDRESS AT TIME OF ENTRY ON ACTIVE DUTY
	YES	NO			
		X	None	None	5911 Morningside Dr Dallas Tex

26. DATE OF ENTRY ON ACTIVE DUTY	27. MILITARY OCCUPATIONAL SPECIALTY AND NO.
7 Feb 42	Provost Marshal Field

28. BATTLES AND CAMPAIGNS

Normandy North France Rhineland Ardennes Central Europe

29. DECORATIONS AND CITATIONS EAME Campaign Medal with 5 Br Strs Al'Ordre DU Corps D'Armee & Croix de Guerre Avec Etoile de Vermiel by Provisional Gov't of France #841 29 Jun 45 Br Star Medal GO 65 Hq 2d Inf 22 Jul 45 World War II Victory Medal American Theater Campaign Medal

30. WOUNDS RECEIVED IN ACTION

None

31. SERVICE SCHOOLS ATTENDED	32.	SERVICE OUTSIDE CONTINENTAL U. S. AND RETURN		
Command and General Staff School Ft Leavenworth Kansas	DATE OF DEPARTURE	DESTINATION	DATE OF ARRIVAL	
	8 Oct 43	EAME	Unknown	
33. REASON AND AUTHORITY FOR SEPARATION	Unknown	US	20 Jul 45	
RR 1-5 Demobilization				

34.	CURRENT TOUR OF ACTIVE DUTY					35.	EDUCATION (years)		
CONTINENTAL SERVICE			FOREIGN SERVICE						
YEARS	MONTHS	DAYS	YEARS	MONTHS	DAYS	GRAMMAR SCHOOL	HIGH SCHOOL	COLLEGE	
2	1	25	1	9	12	8	4	4	

INSURANCE NOTICE

IMPORTANT IF PREMIUM IS NOT PAID WHEN DUE OR WITHIN THIRTY-ONE DAYS THEREAFTER, INSURANCE WILL LAPSE. MAKE CHECKS OR MONEY ORDERS PAYABLE TO THE TREASURER OF THE U. S. AND FORWARD TO COLLECTIONS SUBDIVISION, VETERANS ADMINISTRATION, WASHINGTON 25, D. C.

36. KIND OF INSURANCE			37. HOW PAID			38. EFFECTIVE DATE OF ALLOTMENT DISCONTINUANCE	39. DATE OF NEXT PREMIUM DUE (one month after 38)	40. PREMIUM DUE EACH MONTH	41. INTENTION OF VETERAN TO		
NAT. SERV.	U.-S. GOVT.	NONE	ALLOTMENT	DIRECT TO V.A.					CONTINUE	CONTINUE ONLY	DISCONTINUE
X				X		31 Jan 46	28 Feb 46	'7 00	X		

42.	43. REMARKS (This space for completion of above items or entry of other items specified in W. D. Directives)
RIGHT THUMB PRINT	Lapel Button Issued ASR Score 2 Sep 45 - 99

44. SIGNATURE OF OFFICER BEING SEPARATED	45. PERSONNEL OFFICER (Type name, grade and organi...)
William F North	PAUL WORDEN Capt Inf Paul Worden

WD AGO FORM 53 - 98
1 November 1944

This form supersedes all previous editions of WD AGO Forms 53 and 280 for officers entitled to a Certificate of Service, which will not be used after receipt of this revision.

IN REPLY REFER TO:

WAR DEPARTMENT
THE ADJUTANT GENERAL'S OFFICE
WASHINGTON 25, D. C.

AGPD-B 201 North, William F.
(17 Apr 46) O 343 444

20 May 1946

. Major William F. North
2849 Fondren Drive
Dallas, Texas

Dear Major North:

By direction of the President, in addition to the Bronze Star Medal awarded to you, a bronze Oak Leaf Cluster was awarded to you by the Commanding General, European Theater, for your services from July 1944 to May 1945.

The Commanding General, Eighth Service Command, Dallas, Texas, has been directed to present the Bronze Star Medal (Oak Leaf Cluster) to you with suitable ceremony.

Sincerely yours,

Edward F. Witsell

EDWARD F. WITSELL
Major General
The Adjutant General

An appreciative Major General Edward F. Witsell notifies Lieutenant Colonel North that he had earned a bronze Oak Leaf Cluster in addition to the Bronze Star Medal he had already received in France. This was a fitting final tribute to Lieutenant Colonel North for his dedication to the Army, the United States of America, and the MP Platoon of the 2nd Infantry Division and for a job well done.

355

Glynn Raby

Glynn Raby.

Although my friend Glynn Raby was not a member of the 2nd Division MP Platoon, as a rifleman with the 9th Infantry his footsteps covered much of the same ground as other soldiers of the 2nd Infantry Division did in their concerted efforts to destroy the German Army. Glynn's recollection of the events he faced during the war reinforces not only certain historical accounts but detailed memories that thousands of soldiers shared with each other during and after the war. Specific details that Glynn wrote about in his letter from January 2010 coincide with many of those shared with me by J. R. Cantrell and George Swearingen and evidenced by the stories recalled by Faye Young and Mark Hillis as told to them by their fathers and which appear in this book. Glynn was very gracious in providing his personal account of the events he witnessed in order to help me tell the story of the MP Platoon and the 2nd Infantry Division as a whole.

January 2010
Normandy to Pilsen
June 6, 1944, D-Day—the day that Allied forces stormed ashore on the NORMANDY coast to begin the invasion of mainland EUROPE, I was in a replacement camp in southern ENGLAND. I had entered the US Army in March 1943, at age 18, trained for over a year with the 106th Infantry Division in SOUTH CAROLINA, TENNESSEE, and INDIANA. Thousands of us had been selected to become replacements for the men who became casualties as the war progressed. That day, we were asked to donate blood, and most did, joking that we might get our own blood back.

Within a short period of time, I was in NORMANDY and joined "H" Company, 9th Regiment, 2nd Infantry Division, near the town of ST. LO. The fighting was difficult, and progress was slow in the "hedgerow" country. Mounds of earth, up to 6 feet high, with trees and shrubs growing on them, surrounded each field and provided excellent defense for the enemy. Finally, about August 1st, our armor was able to start moving, and rapidly attacked south, east, and west.

While the main thrusts were to the east and south, our armored units also went west into BRITTANY, and the German troops withdrew into the larger towns and cities—mostly seaports. In mid-August the 2nd Division moved west and joined with the 8th and 29th Divisions to capture the seaport of BREST. Outside the city, we found hedgerow country similar to NORMANDY. Progress was again slow. I held the rank of Corporal and was assigned to assist our company communications sergeant. We laid telephone lines between our units and operated radios. When not moving forward, we always "dug in"—holes in the ground to get into for some protection from shrapnel. One unforgettable day we were being shelled and were in our holes. A direct hit from a mortar shell landed on Sgt. Thomas, perhaps 15 feet from me. He died, almost instantly.

A day or two later, I had just completed a radio transmission to our Battalion HQ, when someone called our code name. He had what I thought was a German accent. My first thought was about "triangulation"—locating a radio by using three receivers and plotting on a map beams to the transmitter. Afraid that I might get a mortar shell on me, I quickly turned the radio off, and moved to another spot. I later learned that triangulation was not that effective and that mortars were not that accurate. The caller could have been an American with German ancestors, but I took no chances.

Another day, as I was on my knees, digging in, with my entrenching tool raised to strike the ground, a small piece of shrapnel nicked my left thumb, drawing blood. A comrade suggested I go to the medical aid station to have it treated and get a Purple Heart Medal (for combat wounds). I refused, saying that if I did that, I would get hit between the eyes the next day. The "Old City" of BREST was surrounded by a huge ancient wall that was highly fortified by the Germans. We finally got inside, and the enemy soon surrendered. By that time, it was late September.

By then, PARIS had been liberated and the war had moved to the edge of GERMANY. We had a few days of rest, and I was able to visit a small town, LANDERNEAU, where I found a bakery, bought

358

a loaf of warm bread and some butter. It tasted so good I ate it all. Then, about October 1st, we went east—some by train and the rest of us in a motor convoy. We drove through PARIS but did not stop. After four days on the road, on October 4th, we entered GERMANY about 10 miles east of ST. VITH, BELGIUM.

Our front lines, in the Schnee Eifel Mountains, included part of the famous Siegfried Line. Our company area had two "pillboxes." The Command Post occupied one and the other was for supply and our kitchen, where the cooks prepared food for us. A relatively quiet area, we did receive some artillery fire and some enemy patrols, but not much. We were able to re-equip and rest a bit. A few men were given leave each week and visited PARIS or ENGLAND. We remained there just over two months, when we were replaced by my old unit, the 106th Division, newly arrived from the USA.

We moved some 25 miles north and began an attack December 13th on an important crossroads, WAHLERSCHEID, just inside GERMANY. The purpose was to seize the dams on the ROER River before the Germans could breach them and flood large areas downstream. The crossroads was heavily defended with numerous pillboxes. The weather was bitter cold and we suffered many casualties both from enemy action and the brutal weather. The crossroads was captured the night of December 15-16, and the German offensive that became known as the Battle of the Bulge began on the 16th. In danger of being surrounded, the Division commander had us pull back to the vicinity of KRINKELT – ROCHERATH – ELSENBORN, BELGIUM, and halted the German advance there. On the 20th, the commanding general of 1st Army sent a telegram to our Division commander, "WHAT THE 2ND INFANTRY DIVISION HAS DONE IN THE LAST FOUR DAYS WILL LIVE FOREVER IN THE HISTORY OF THE UNITED STATES ARMY."

Our defensive positions were along the ELSENBORN RIDGE and the Germans advanced no further in our area. In late January 1945, the German "bulge" had been erased and we resumed our attack to the east. Then, we were able to see the tremendous damage our artillery and air power had inflicted—many dead bodies, frozen in the snow, that the enemy had not been able to evacuate and the untold number of tanks, other armored vehicles, and trucks that had been destroyed. Each day, we advanced from daylight until after dark, crossing rivers and taking towns and villages, eliminating opposition when we encountered it. On February 11, we were in BRONSFELD and our company commander, Capt. Higgins, was killed by an artillery shell that hit the house he was in. Most of us respected him, highly. A few days later, we moved into another town and expected to be there for a day or so. Our Platoon Sgt. and I went to a small house to determine if it was suitable shelter for some of our men. He directed me to check the cellar while he checked the upstairs rooms. The cellar was dark, but I could see a stocking foot of someone lying just inside a doorway. I shook the foot asking who he was. A reply in German startled me. I took cover and asked if anyone spoke English. One replied in English and I ordered that all come upstairs with hands up. I raced up, told the Sgt. and we went outside. In a few moments seven German soldiers came up and gladly surrendered. They were weary of war and waiting for our arrival. We reached the RHINE River about March 10-11. On March 21, we crossed the river in assault boats a short distance south of the famous Ludendorf Bridge at REMAGEN. A few days later, I was given a week's leave and a choice of several places I could go. I chose the city of NICE, on the FRENCH RIVIERA.

A group of us were flown to NICE in US Air Corps C-47 airplanes, equipped to carry paratroopers. In a first-class hotel overlooking the Mediterranean Sea, we were two men to a room. Clean sheets, a private bathroom, meals in the hotel dining room with white tablecloths and napkins, we were served by the hotel dining room staff. We had not enjoyed such luxury in many months. The week passed much too quickly and we were flown back to the war.

It was early April and meeting very light resistance, our forward progress became easier. So, we mounted tanks and other vehicles of the 9th Armored Division, stopping to deal with any opposition, then resuming our attack. Our 23rd Infantry Regiment went into

LEIPZIG and we continued east to the MULDE River. It had been predetermined that we would halt there and that the Russians would halt at the ELBE River some 20 miles to our east. Two great advancing armies, meeting "head-on" would have been chaos. On April 25, our regiment sent a large motorized patrol forward in an attempt to meet the Russians. I was one of four men from H Co., 9th Inf. in a jeep with a mounted .30 cal. machine gun. We had a light tank, several other vehicles with mounted .50 and .30 cal. MGs and a small observation plane overhead. In mid-afternoon, we encountered small-arms fire coming from a town and returned fire. Bridges over a canal between us and the town had been destroyed, so we could not go further. We returned to our unit back at the MULDE. That same day, a patrol from the 69th Division, just to our north, made contact with the Russians and made history.

May 1st, the V Corps was transferred from 1st Army to the 3rd Army, and we began a 200-mile motor march toward CZECHOSLOVAKIA. On jeeps, trucks, and tanks, we were on the autobahn part of the way, with unseasonable cold weather and some snow. Near the Czech border, we dismounted and began an attack through the SUDATENLAND where the pro-German residents were not glad to see us. May 4th, the 11th Panzer Division surrendered and moved through our columns to the rear. "It was a rare opportunity to see what a full-fledged elite Division looked like in the flower of its full strength and arrogance. Well-shaven, uniforms pressed, the troops moved up in a long line of vehicles and big weapons, still in fairly good condition." (From the Division history book.)

Beyond the SUDATENLAND, the Czech people welcomed us with smiles, cheers, flowers, food, and drink. As the war in Europe came to an end, some of the 2nd Division was in Pilsen, some units in several outlying towns. The 9th Infantry was in ROKYCANY, on the road to PRAGUE. For about a month, the 2nd Division operated Prisoner of War Camps and processed displaced persons. During this time, I received a promotion to Sergeant. Then we departed to return to the States for 30 days leave and regroup to head to the war in the

Pacific. While we were home, on leave, the war there ended, and demobilization began. I was released October 25, 1945, and returned home to resume studies at a college.

According to records provided by our 1st Sgt., H Company had 166 men. As casualties occurred, replacements came to take their place (I was one of the earlier ones). In the 11 months of combat we had 38 killed, 123 wounded, and 107 hospitalized for other reasons. Also, 39 wounded but remained on duty—for a total of 307. The phrase "FREEDOM IS NOT FREE" is certainly true. The Czech people can attest to this. How they endured the 6 years of NAZI occupation and persecution is beyond my imagination. My memory has faded, but I still have fond memories of the hospitality we received in ROKYCANY and PILSEN.

—Glynn G. Raby Jr., MEMPHIS, TN

James Edwards

This photo of Dad was taken at Fort Sam Houston in February 1942 when he was still with Company I, 9th Infantry.

On the back of the photo on the previous page, in my mother's handwriting, is *Corporal James D. Edwards*. Dad's uniform is reminiscent of the era prior to him entering the European theater of operations during World War II and is devoid of ribbon bars yet to be earned. What is plainly visible is the 2nd Infantry Division patch, the French Fourragère, which was awarded to the 9th Infantry during World War I, the 9th Infantry Regimental Crest, infantry collar brass, an Expert Qualification Badge with several attachments for different weapons, and an Expert Pistol Qualification Badge.

The final version of what Dad's uniform should have looked like on September 17, 1945.

In the photo on page 364, the Indianhead, 3rd Army, Meritorious Unit Citation, and Ranger Battle Training patches are all original from the cigar box. Likewise, so is the Expert Qualification Badge, though I added the last two bars to match the one Dad was wearing in 1942. The Three-Year Service Chevron, Overseas Bars, Combat Infantry Badge, Ribbon Bars, Ruptured Duck, rank insignia, Distinguished Unit Citation, Expert Pistol Badge, Bronze Star Medal, and Purple Heart were added by me. The French and Belgian Fourragères were also added. The only decoration I cannot absolutely confirm Dad earned is the Purple Heart. All that I have to go by is George Swearingen's account of Dad being sent to the hospital in France after he was wounded by the land mine. I have been unable to locate a medical record of treatment due to insufficient information. My father passed away on September 24, 1979, at the age of 57.

Army of the United States
HONORABLE DISCHARGE

FILE

DEC 1 1945
R. N. F.

This is to Certify, that James D. Edwards 18 005 119 Private First Class Div.

Company C 512th Military Police Battalion
ARMY OF THE UNITED STATES is hereby Honorably Discharged from the military service of the United States of America. This certificate is awarded as a testimonial of Honest and Faithful Service to this country.

Given at Separation Center Ft. Sam Houston Texas.   Date 17 September 1945

L. L. Stewart Major AGD

ENLISTED RECORD AND REPORT OF SEPARATION
HONORABLE DISCHARGE

1. LAST NAME - FIRST NAME - MIDDLE INITIAL	2. ARMY SERIAL NO.	3. GRADE	4. ARM OR SERVICE	5. COMPONENT
Edwards James D.	18 005 119	Pfc	MP	RA

6. ORGANIZATION	7. DATE OF SEPARATION	8. PLACE OF SEPARATION
Company C 512th Military Police Battalion	17 Sep 45	Separation Center Fort Sam Houston, Texas

9. PERMANENT ADDRESS FOR MAILING PURPOSES	10. DATE OF BIRTH	11. PLACE OF BIRTH
Cleburne Johnson County, 305 E. Anglin St Texas	25 Nov 21	Waynesboro, Tenn

12. ADDRESS FROM WHICH EMPLOYMENT WILL BE SOUGHT	13. COLOR EYES	14. COLOR HAIR	15. HEIGHT	16. WEIGHT	17. NO. DEPEND.
Fort Worth, Tarrant County, Texas	Brown	Brown	5'10"	146 lbs	1

18. RACE				19. MARITAL STATUS			20. U. S. CITIZEN		21. CIVILIAN OCCUPATION AND NO.
WHITE X	NEGRO	OTHER (specify)	SINGLE	MARRIED X	OTHER (specify)	YES X	NO	Soldier 2-68.10

MILITARY HISTORY

22. DATE OF INDUCTION	23. DATE OF ENLISTMENT	24. DATE OF ENTRY INTO ACTIVE SERVICE	25. PLACE OF ENTRY INTO SERVICE
	3 Jul 40	3 Jul 40	Rctg Sta Dallas, Texas

SELECTIVE SERVICE DATA	26. REGISTERED	27. LOCAL S. S. BOARD NO.	28. COUNTY AND STATE
	YES / NO X		Richland Navarro Co Texas

30. MILITARY OCCUPATIONAL SPECIALTY AND NO.	31. MILITARY QUALIFICATION AND DATE (i.e., infantry, aviation and marksmanship badges, etc.)
Military Police 677	Sharpshooter Carbine 21 Jul 43

32. BATTLES AND CAMPAIGNS
Normandy Northern France Rhineland Ardennes Central Europe GO 33 WD 45

33. DECORATIONS AND CITATIONS
EAME Campaign Medal with 5 Bronze Stars; Good Conduct Medal American Defense Service Medal.

34. WOUNDS RECEIVED IN ACTION
None

35. LATEST IMMUNIZATION DATES				36.	37. SERVICE OUTSIDE CONTINENTAL U. S. AND RETURN		
SMALLPOX	TYPHOID	TETANUS	OTHER (specify) Typhus		DATE OF DEPARTURE	DESTINATION	DATE OF ARRIVAL
Feb 44 26	Feb 45 13	Aug 45 27	3 Dec 44		8 Oct 43	EAME	20 Oct 43

38. TOTAL LENGTH OF SERVICE				39. HIGHEST GRADE HELD			
CONTINENTAL SERVICE		FOREIGN SERVICE			Unknown	US	10 Sep 45
YEARS 3	MONTHS 5	DAYS 2	YEARS 1 MONTHS 11 DAYS 3	Cpl			

40. PRIOR SERVICE
None

41. REASON AND AUTHORITY FOR SEPARATION
Convenience of the Government (RR 1-1 Demobilization) AR 615-365 15Dec 44

41. SERVICE SCHOOLS ATTENDED	42. EDUCATION (Years)		
None	GRAMMAR 7	HIGH SCHOOL 0	COLLEGE 0

PAY DATA   Vou 5596

43. LONGEVITY FOR PAY PURPOSES			44. MUSTERING OUT PAY		45. SOLDIER DEPOSITS	46. TRAVEL PAY	47. TOTAL AMOUNT, NAME OF DISBURSING OFFICER
YEARS 5	MONTHS 1	DAYS 14	TOTAL .300	THIS PAYMENT .100	None	.14.70	$ 50.00 Chase Carlos Delins Capt FD 78.33

INSURANCE NOTICE

IMPORTANT IF PREMIUM IS NOT PAID WHEN DUE OR WITHIN THIRTY-ONE DAYS THEREAFTER, INSURANCE WILL LAPSE. MAKE CHECKS OR MONEY ORDERS PAYABLE TO THE TREASURER OF THE U. S. AND FORWARD TO COLLECTIONS SUBDIVISION, VETERANS ADMINISTRATION, WASHINGTON 25, D. C.

48. KIND OF INSURANCE		49. HOW PAID		50. EFFECTIVE DATE OF ALLOTMENT DISCONTINUANCE	51. DAYS OF NEXT PREMIUM DUE	52. PREMIUM DUE EACH MONTH	53. INTENTION OF VETERAN TO
NAT. SERV. X	U. S. GOVT.	NONE	ALLOTMENT X	DIRECT TO V. A.	31 Aug 45	30 Sep 45	6.60	CONTINUE DISCONTINUE X

54. REMARKS (This space for completion of above items or entry of other items specified in W. D. Directives)

Lapel Button Issued
ASR Score (12 May 1945) - 99
Lost 31 days under AW 107.

Print

56. SIGNATURE OF PERSON BEING SEPARATED	57. PERSONNEL OFFICER (Type name, grade and organization - signature)
James D. Edwards	J.F.Schultz 2d Lt CAC Ass't Mil Pers Officer

Recorded this 1st day of October A.D. 19 45, at o'clock P. M.

By Mrs. H.L.Cain Deputy. A.T.Griffin , County Clerk Johnson County, Texas.

ARMY
SEPARATION QUALIFICATION RECORD

LAST NAME	FIRST NAME	MIDDLE INITIAL	ARMY SERIAL NO.	GRADE	DATE OF ENTRY INTO ACTIVE SERVICE	SEX	DATE OF BIRTH
EDWARDS	JAMES	D	18 005 119	PFC	3 Jul 40	M	25 Nov 21

PERMANENT ADDRESS FOR MAILING PURPOSES (STREET AND NUMBER, CITY, COUNTY, STATE)
3055 Anglin St. Cleburne Johnson County, Texas

CIVILIAN EDUCATION

HIGHEST GRADE COMPLETED	LAST YEAR OF ATTENDANCE	HIGHEST DEGREE RECEIVED	MAJOR COURSE OF STUDY	NAME AND ADDRESS OF LAST SCHOOL ATTENDED
7	1936	--	Academic	Richland, Texas

OTHER TRAINING OR SCHOOLING

COURSE	NO. HRS.	COURSE	NO. HRS.	COURSE	NO. HRS.	COURSE	NO. HRS.
--							

SERVICE EDUCATION

SERVICE SCHOOL	COURSE	WKS. OR HRS.	RATING	ARMY SPECIALIZED TRAINING PROGRAM				
				INSTITUTION WHERE ENROLLED	CURRICULUM AND TERM (COURSE OF TRAINING PURSUED)	NO. OF WEEKS	GRADUATED YES	NO
--								

CIVILIAN OCCUPATIONS

MAIN OCCUPATION (TITLE) SOLDIER	SECONDARY OCCUPATION (TITLE)
JOB SUMMARY Was performing the duties of a riflemen in the Infantry in the regular Army.	JOB SUMMARY

NO. OF YEARS	LAST DATE OF EMPLOYMENT	NAME AND ADDRESS OF EMPLOYER	NO. OF YEARS	LAST DATE OF EMPLOYMENT	NAME AND ADDRESS OF EMPLOYER
5/12		U.S. Army			

MILITARY SPECIALTIES
ASSIGNMENTS

YEARS	MONTHS	GRADE	PRINCIPAL DUTY	ARMY CODE NO.	YEARS	MONTHS	GRADE	PRINCIPAL DUTY	ARMY CODE NO.
	1	Pvt	Infantry Basic	521	q2		Pfc	Military Policeman	677
2	2	Pfc	Rifleman	745					
	7	Pfc	Auto Rifleman	746					

SUMMARY OF MILITARY OCCUPATION AND CIVILIAN CONVERSIONS (SHOWN BY TITLE)

MILITARY POLICEMAN: Assisted in the enforcement of military law and control of traffic. Assisted civilian police in England and Ireland and guarded military prisoners.

SUMMARY OF MILITARY OCCUPATION AND CIVILIAN CONVERSIONS (SHOWN BY TITLE)

*THIS INFORMATION BASED ON SOLDIER'S STATEMENT. (INDICATE BY * ANY ITEMS NOT SUPPORTED BY MILITARY RECORD)

DATE OF SEPARATION	SIGNATURE OF SOLDIER	SIGNATURE OF SEPARATION CLASSIFICATION OFFICER
17 Sep '45	James D Edwards	H.B. ALLARD Capt, AGD

WD AGO Form 100 (15 July 1944)

16—43021-1 U. S. GOVERNMENT PRINTING OFFICE

Michael Hitt

Michael Hitt of Roswell, Georgia, honors the MP Platoon by wearing a very close replica uniform similar to the ones worn by Dad and the other MPs during the war. The jeep Michael is pictured with is one that he had remanufactured to resemble MP-6, which is the designation for the jeep that James Earl Hillis drove while the platoon was in the European theater. The original jeep driven by Hillis, also known as "Lula Belle," is pictured throughout this book.

It goes without saying that this tribute to the MPs would not be possible if it weren't for the hundreds of hours spent by my friend Michael, who researched an enormous amount of history related to the MP Platoon prior to our chance meeting. Although I resisted his initial suggestion that I be the one to put into print the story of the MP Platoon, ultimately it was through Michael's repeated encouragement that I accepted the responsibility as the author of this book, being the son of Private First Class James D. Edwards.

However, Michael should be given full credit for locating J. R. Cantrell; George Swearingen; Mark Hillis, the son of James Hillis; and Max North, the son of Major William North. Without the considerable contributions by all of these men, made possible by Michael's investigative skills, this book would be a simple biography of my father. Instead, with the boxes of documents organized in four-inch binders, labeled photographs, personal items of Major North, and the letters and testimonies of J. R. Cantrell and George Swearingen, this book exists to honor the men of the MP Platoon. Michael's desire to honor the 2nd Infantry Division MPs by his contributions to this book cannot be measured in a material sense. Through his passion, hard work, and dedication to preserving the history of the MP Platoon, this book will soon be a reality. To Michael, I am grateful beyond words.

The Friends of US 2nd Infantry Division WWII

Need your help

Posted By: sonofaww2vet   Tue Jan 9, 2007 9:04 pm | Options

My father passed away 28 years ago while I was a teen. Up until that
time dad never spoke of his time in the army. After dad passed away I
found a cigar box (circa 1945) that contained what was left of his
medals (actually) just the ribbons remained. Somewhere along the way
the medals were removed, perhaps by one of us kids. I have been able to
replace the medals using a copy of dads "Honorable Discharge" sent to
me by the NPRC in St. Louis to reconstruct what he might have earned
while in the ETO. My dad served this great nation from 1940-1945 as an
enlisted soldier. He was for a time in the infantry where he recieved
his training at Fort Sam Houston. Sometime, either before, or just
after arriving in Ireland for the preparation for the D-Day invasion,
he was reassigned as an MP with the 2nd Infantry Division. Here's what
I'm not sure about. I know his "Mos" was 677, which by what I can learn
actually does refer to him as an MP. I don't know, other than from his
obituary, that it said his unit was the 115th MP's? He also had a patch
that is blue with a red circle incompassing an "A". What does that mean?

My father's name was James Douglas Edwards, perhaps better known
as "Eddie" to his friends. I have some pictures of dad by his army jeep
in places such as Belgium and Germany. Here's where I need the help of
you pros. I realize after all these years how important this man's
contributions to our country and to me as his son. I am trying to
gather as much information as I can to contruct a family heirloom, a
shadowbox with an original WWII dress jacket and have his original
patches restored and placed on the sleeves, along with his medals and
so fourth. However, I have one piece of family information that
suggests that dad earned other medals, including the "Purple Heart" and
perhaps a meritorius medal for rescuing a wounded soldier. This
information does not appear on his discharge form.

Any information you can provide would of course be greatly appreciated.
I know there are not many of these heros left after all these years. I
do have dads separation orders which has many names on it that perhaps
knew my father.

Thanks for your help,

SonofawwIIvet

370

This is the first post I made on the group site for the Friends of US 2nd Infantry Division WWII. This post represents the beginning of my journey to recreate my father's military service.

My father, James Douglas Edwards, entered the US Army on July 3, 1940, and was separated by honorable discharge on September 17, 1945, serving our country with honor and distinction for five years, two months, and fourteen days. As God's timing has been perfect throughout the creation of this story, my service to honor the men of the MP Platoon by creating this book began on January 9, 2007, and concluded on March 23, 2012. The elapsed time represents exactly five years, two months, and fourteen days.

About the Author

James Daniel Edwards is the third son born to James Douglas and Aleta Edwards in July 1959. James is a twenty-two-year veteran Texas master peace officer, serving as a law enforcement officer in the Dallas metropolitan area. James and his wife, Marsha, have raised five grown children. James believes that success in life can be attributed to a strong relationship with Christ, honor that is exemplified through integrity, courage to overcome adversity, and the commitment to consistently try and do the right things. James believes that his own worth isn't measured by the material things he possesses but by whether or not his children listen to his advice and apply what he's learned to their own lives.